Durham City

David Simpson

The Northern Echo

Business Education Publishers Limited

© David Simpson and *The Northern Echo*

ISBN 1 901888 50 9
ISBN 978 1 901888 50 8

Cover Design Tim Murphy, Bradley O'Mahoney Creative Ltd.

Front cover: Durham Cathedral from Gilesgate. Photograph by David Simpson
Back cover: Durham Cathedral Cloister. Photograph by David Simpson

Published in Great Britain by
Business Education Publishers Limited
The Teleport
Doxford International
Sunderland
Tyne & Wear
SR3 3XD

Tel: 0191 5252410
Fax: 0191 5201815

British Cataloguing-in-Publications Data
A catalogue record for this book is available from the British Library

Printed in Great Britain by The Alden Group, Oxford

For Elise

Acknowledgements

Thanks to Anita Thompson, Jean Garland and all the staff of Durham Clayport local studies library. Thanks should also go to Darlington local studies library. Special thanks to Michael Richardson, June Crosby, George Nairn, John Kitching, Roy Lambeth, Bill Fawcett, David Williams, John Geddes, Barry Wood, Graham Cozens, Dorothy Meade, the late Gordon McKeag, Martin Roberts, John Richardson, Mr Wade, Mike Syers, Graham Robson, Jim Milburn, Dave Shotten, John Bones, Denis Dunlop, David Young, Jo Jones, Mitchells and Butler, Richard Hird, Mary Hawgood, John Lightley, Jean Stirk, Chris Fish, Clive Lawson, Gail Hudson, Jenny Lee and many, many others. In fact thanks to everyone who has phoned, written or taken me on a potted tour of one kind or another.

Thanks should go to Petra Stanton, Chris Moran and Rob Greener for their work on the excellent maps that have accompanied Durham Memories from time to time. They have been skilfully and meticulously recreated from my inky sketches.

Photographs in this and the accompanying book are supplied from a number of sources including Michael Richardson (MR), George Nairn (GN), Gail Hudson (GH), June Crosby, Roy Lambeth (RL) and Hamsteels Hall (HH). Photographs from the archives of The Northern Echo are marked (NE) and photographs by the author are marked (DS).

There are many old history books that have come to my assistance from time to time during my Durham Memories research. Where would I be for example without the nineteenth century histories of Robert Surtees and William Fordyce or the early twentieth century Victoria County History? And then of course there are the modern electronic sources that are such a gift for the historian of today. The invaluable 1881 census of Great Britain published on CD Rom by the Mormon Church is one worthy of mention but also tremendously useful are websites like Tomorrow's History, Keys to the Past and the Durham Mining Museum that have been such a great boon to local history research in our region. Thanks should also go to Peter Barron for inviting me to write the Durham Memories column and many thanks should go to Andrea Murphy, Moira Page and David Taylor at Business Education Publishers. Finally, a very, very special thanks should go to my long suffering wife Abi, who has put up with my obsession and who has been left on more than one occasion, quite literally holding the baby.

Author Biography

David Simpson was born in Durham City in 1967 and is the author of thirteen books on North East history. He has worked for *The Northern Echo* newspaper since January 1994 and has been the author of the Durham Memories column since 2003. David's previous publications include *The Millennium History of North East England* hailed by the Prime Minister Tony Blair and *Northern Roots* which investigates the origins of people in Northern England. He has made many contributions to television and radio with appearances on Tyne Tees Television, Channel Four, BBC Radio 4, BBC Radio Newcastle, Radio Cleveland and other local programmes. He has given hundreds of talks across the North on various aspects of the region's history and in his spare time is an enthusiastic photographer and amateur actor treading the boards with local theatre groups. David lives with his wife, young daughter and two cats in Durham City.

Photograph by John Simpson

Contents

Preface

This book is based on the Durham Memories column that appears in the north edition of *The Northern Echo*. As a Durham lad I was overjoyed when the editor gave me the chance to write this feature focusing on the history of Durham City and the northern half of County Durham.

The Durham Memories column started with a short piece on the history of Neptune's statue back in January 2003 but we have visited many places since then. Indeed there are many aspects of Durham's history that are still waiting to be explored.

I have been writing local history for many years and started publishing books on the North East region in my early 20s before I came to work for the Echo. Like many people in this region I have a huge passion for our history and there is no place I am more passionate about than my hometown and birthplace of Durham City.

Although I was exiled in my childhood, to another part of the region, my family roots have always been in Durham City. My mother was born in Moody's Buildings where Gilesgate roundabout now stands. Her mother, though born in Penshaw grew up in the former pit settlement of Bell's Ville in Gilesgate Moor where members of her family worked in neighbouring mines. In later years my grandma lived for a time in part of a house that is now the University Bookshop in Saddler Street and here, on an upper floor, my aunt was born.

On my Dad's side my grandfather was born and bred in the Elvet area of the city. He grew up in Church Street and Hallgarth Street but moved in later years to Musgrave Gardens in the eastern part of the city. My other grandparents were from the villages of Browney and Esh Winning to the west of the city.

My Dad was born in a house called Nova Lima in a street called Moor Edge at Crossgate Moor on the very edge of the city. It is a spot overlooking the site of the Battle of Neville's Cross, but the house in which he was born took its name from a gold mining settlement in Brazil where his uncle had worked. This little insight into my own family history, demonstrates that many seemingly ordinary houses in and around the city will have their very own stories to tell. Such stories are often known to only a small number of people and I am very grateful to all those readers who have shared their own personal stories and knowledge of Durham City. Your memories are warmly welcomed.

In writing the column and this book I hope to fill a niche and give a slightly broader geographical approach to the history of Durham City. With this aim in mind it has been a most enjoyable task. It is often time-consuming work with tight weekly deadlines that have to fit in with my day-to-day work but it has been tremendous fun ploughing through old maps, photographs and directories. I have enjoyed many a discussion about days gone by with the city's older residents and have even occasionally knocked on the doors of the city's more historic houses to politely ask if I could take a glance at the deeds.

Most people, whether they are experts in their own field or simply locals with an enthusiastic interest, have been keen to help me in my pursuit. I have always been struck by the enthusiasm and pride that people have in their home city.

I have also been constantly amazed about what there is still waiting to be discovered in Durham City. In this respect the Durham Memories column has taught me to open my eyes and investigate. I now see things through a fresh pair of eyes that are always seeking out signs of the past hidden amongst the familiar sights of the present.

At times I have ventured beyond the suburbs of the city out into the surrounding villages, but these villages are covered in the accompanying village book that forms a companion volume to this one. If you have not already purchased a copy I thoroughly recommend you do. It will complete the picture and give a broader perspective of the city in the context of its surrounding lands.

Durham City is of course a very beautiful and historic place and the historic portions of the city, including the cathedral are featured in this book. However at the same time I wanted to investigate some places and features that are perhaps not so frequently explored. The Town Hall and Guildhall spring to mind as examples. They are notable monuments to Durham's civic history and from inside are extremely impressive buildings that contain many historic artefacts and wonderful paintings that tell the story of the city's past.

I also wanted to explore the industrial side of the city's history, of which the most prominent feature was the enormous carpet factory that was once wedged into the riverside area between Walkergate and Freeman's Place. Then of course there was the coal mining that took place as close to the city centre as Elvet, Aykley Heads and Crook Hall. Larger collieries also stood on the edge of the city at Framwellgate Moor and Gilesgate Moor and both of these places owed their initial existence to mining.

We will mention the occasional shop, pub and church in the city and of course visit the colleges of the University of Durham. Here we will head out along the South Road to find nineteenth century mansions and forgotten roadside inns hidden in amongst the modern colleges of today. We will remember the names of some of the influential people that have lived in such places as well as those who resided in equally grand mansions like Western Lodge, Dryburn and Springwell Hall.

We will recall the colourful characters that have lived in and around the city from time to time. Notable are the oversized actor Stephen Kemble, the eccentric former mayor known as Icy Smith and the tiny Polish Count Joseph Boruwlaski, whose remarkable lifetime adventures are remembered here. On a darker side we also recall some of the notorious names that have resided within the walls of Durham Prison. This particular building's history is given some coverage in the book and why should it not be? It is after all just as much a part of the city's history as Durham Cathedral, Castle or University.

In this book we also set out to explore what a guide book might ignore and head out into the city's suburbs. Here we visit Framwellgate Moor and Pity Me, Crossgate Moor and Neville's Cross, Lowe's Barn and Potter's Bank. We also head to Carrville and Gilesgate Moor, Broomside and Belmont, Dryburn and Whitesmocks, North Road and Newton Hall. Some of the more scenic rural areas of the city that have been enclosed by its urban limits are also featured here. We visit the intriguing wooded gorge of Kepier and investigate the tranquil ponds at Brasside as well as the beautiful ruins of Finchale Priory in the north and the lovely valley of the Browney to the west. This particular river on the western outskirts of the city at Crossgate Moor was a home to several paper mills that are surely the forgotten industry of Durham City.

There was once much more rural scenery in Durham than there is today and many suburbs were once separate settlements swallowed up over time by Durham's urban growth. These places have interesting histories in their own right and deserve their place in a book about Durham City. Whether you are a visitor, a local or an exile I do hope that you will enjoy my journey around the history of Durham City and if you have some knowledge to share, I am always glad to hear from you.

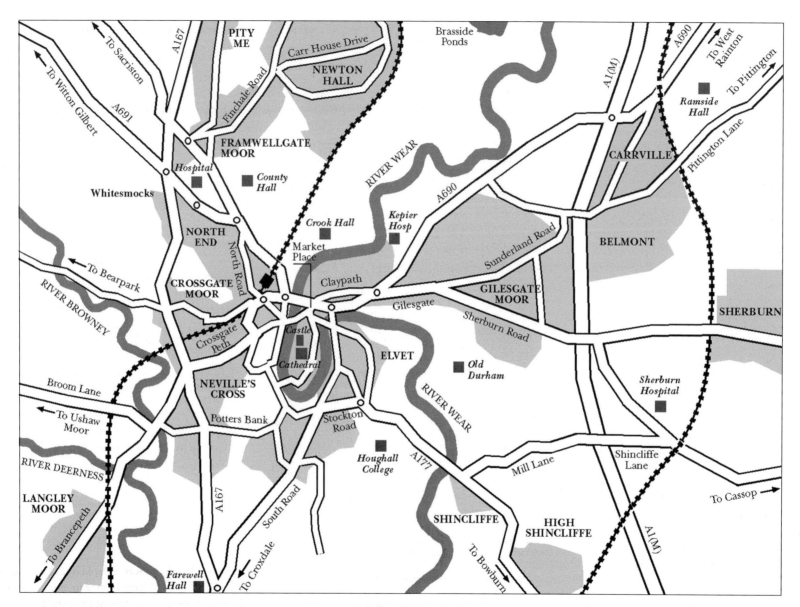

Durham City Map

Introduction

St. Cuthbert's Legacy

St. Cuthbert was a much-loved man, revered throughout the kingdom of Northumbria. He had a reputation for working miracles, a notable affinity to nature and, it is said, a remarkable prowess for athletics.

He lived much of his life as a hermit on the island of Inner Farne just off the Northumberland coast. It was a particularly tough and isolated choice of lifestyle, but like many of the most prominent monks who lived in this Anglo-Saxon period he believed that such a lifestyle would bring him closer to God.

It was on Inner Farne in the year AD 687 that Cuthbert passed away. He was buried on the nearby island of Lindisfarne, a slightly more worldly place, that was joined to the mainland at each low tide. Lindisfarne was the centre for an Anglo-Saxon monastery and about ten years after Cuthbert's death, the monks of this monastery opened Cuthbert's coffin to examine the remains. They found that Cuthbert's corpse had not decayed. It was declared a miracle and Cuthbert was ultimately proclaimed a saint.

Lindisfarne monastery was made wealthy as a result of the pilgrims who flocked to see Cuthbert's shrine, but unfortunately the wealth attracted a party of raiding Vikings in the year AD 793. The raids continued throughout the following century and the monks eventually fled from their coastal retreat. They took with them St Cuthbert's coffin along with relics like the famed Lindisfarne Gospels and the skull of St Oswald, a former King of Northumbria.

The Lindisfarne monks uncover St. Cuthbert's Tomb

For over a century, the monks and their successors carried the coffin and relics around the North, settling for a short time at Norham-on-Tweed. Eventually, after years of wandering, they were granted land at Chester-le-Street, just north of Durham. Here Eardwulf, the last Bishop of Lindisfarne became the first Bishop of Chester-le-Street in AD 882. During the next 113 years there was a succession of nine bishops at Chester-le-Street and the site was so holy that when the notorious Viking ruler, Eric Bloodaxe, visited in AD 952, he came in peace.

Chester-le-Street lay within the ruins of a Roman fort but was not especially well defended and when further raids arose - this time most likely from Scotland - it caused the Bishop and monks to flee once again.

It was in AD 995 that the monks settled at Durham or Dunholm, as it was then known. It is said that St.Cuthbert appeared in a vision and directed them to the site, but in truth it was a deliberate political decision made with good knowledge of local geography. A small church was built from the boughs of trees to house St. Cuthbert's coffin but it was short lived, replaced days later by the Alba Ecclesia, or white church, a whitewashed wooden minster, somewhere within or near the site of the present cathedral.

By this time Northumbria was no longer a kingdom but Uhtred Eadulfson, the Earl of Bamburgh was virtual ruler of that part of Northumbria north of the River Tees. He employed labour from the River Coquet to the River Tees to fortify the site at Durham. The fortification was built under the observation of Uhtred's father-in-law, Aldhun, the last Bishop of Chester-le-Street, who would become the first Bishop of Durham.

Within three years, in September AD 998, the wooden church at Dunholm was replaced by a church of stone called the Ecclesia Major. It was a forerunner of Durham Cathedral and remained in use for 95 years.

In 1006 Scots under King Malcolm attacked the new city and were heavily defeated by Uhtred and his army. The defences of the site proved their worth and after the siege, the heads of the best-looking Scottish soldiers were displayed around the city's walls. Four Durham women washed the faces and combed the hair of the decapitated Scots and were presented with the gift of a cow for their handy work.

Dunholm was magnificently defended, offering superb protection for St. Cuthbert's shrine. Its name aptly described its natural defences. 'Dun' was Anglo-Saxon for 'hill' while 'Holm', was a Scandinavian word for 'island'. Though not a true island, Durham was located on high ground protected on three sides by the steep gorge of the River Wear. It had been cleared of its thick woodland to make way for the church and walled defences were constructed all around.

Dunholm was later called Duresme by the Normans and was known in Latin as Dunelm. Over time it simply became Durham. In the century following the construction of the church, pilgrims flocked to St. Cuthbert's shrine where peaceful visitors included the Viking leader, King Canute the Dane who came in 1027. As a mark of respect, he walked six miles bare-footed from Garmondsway, near Kelloe.

If these were relatively peaceful times for Durham, things changed after October 1066 when King William and his Norman conquerors arrived in England. Just over two years later, on 30 January, 1069, a Norman army of 700 men entered the city under the command of an earl called Robert Comine.

Aegelwine, the Bishop of Durham predicted Comine's defeat but the Normans easily seized control. However, things changed the following morning. A Northumbrian army stormed through the narrow, snow-covered streets of the city, slaughtering the Normans as they went.

St. Cuthbert's Feretory houses the tomb of the saint in Durham Cathedral (NE)

Some Normans, including Comine, fled for safety to the bishop's palace but it was set alight causing a fierce blaze that posed a threat to the western tower of Durham's early church. Locals fell to their knees, 'with eyes filled with tears and elevated hands' and the wind miraculously changed direction diverting the flames away from the tower. Comine and the occupants of the bishop's palace were burnt to death and the streets of the city, filled with the carcasses of dead soldiers, are said to have flowed with Norman blood.

All but one of the Norman occupants lost their lives in the massacre and he fled to warn others of the dangers of Durham.

King William was angered by the event and sent north a second, even greater army to burn and plunder the land between York and Durham. This was known as the 'Harrying of the North' and demonstrated the might of the Norman army to the people of northern England, who were now forced to recognise Norman control. This time Durham was permanently seized and few remained to defend the little city.

King William appointed a Norman called William Walcher as Durham's first Prince Bishop, combining the ecclesiastical role of the Bishop with the political powers of the Earl of Northumbria. The term 'Prince Bishop' came into use many centuries later, but suitably describes the political and ecclesiastical powers of Walcher and succeeding Bishops of Durham. Unfortunately for the King, Walcher's time as a Prince Bishop was characterised by weak leadership that ultimately resulted in the Bishop's murder at Gateshead in 1081.

Walcher was replaced by another bishop, William St. Carileph. It was this bishop who commenced the building of the present Durham Cathedral in the year 1093. His new cathedral occupied the site of the old stone minster built by Uhtred, and was more or less completed to the architect's designs by the year 1133.

Chapter One
Durham Cathedral

An unknown architect employed by Bishop William St. Carileph was largely responsible for building the nave, choir, aisles and transepts that form the heart of Durham Cathedral as we see it today. It is these features, dating from between 1093 and 1133 that form the main body of the cathedral and are the most awe-inspiring parts of the building.

About 300-400 workers were involved in the cathedral's construction and were drawn from the surrounding countryside, within walking distance of the city. The sandstone used in the construction was transported from just across the river in what is now Quarryheads Lane and also from the banks of the Wear at Kepier. Similar stone came from the valley of the River Browney at Baxter Wood near Crossgate Moor.

The oldest parts of the cathedral display many innovative features and we get the impression that the cathedral's architect had experienced a strange and sudden enlightenment.

Standing inside the beautiful nave of the cathedral, we are struck by the massive spiral and zigzag decorated cylindrical columns (called piers) and larger multiple column compound piers that draw the eye upwards, quite naturally, towards the impressive diamond ribbed vaulting of the roof high above.

Ribbed vaulting at Durham was more advanced than vaulting found anywhere else in Britain or the Continent. It showed innovative structural techniques that were the first of their type in the world, enabling much higher vaulting through the use of pointed arches.

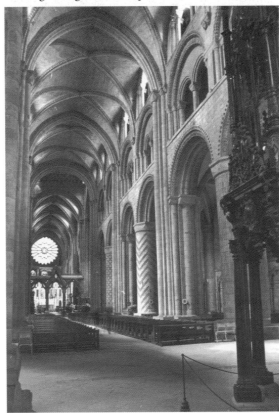

The Nave of Durham Cathedral showing the ribbed vaulting above. Note the rounded and pointed arches (NE)

Forming an intricate mathematical pattern, the gently pointed arches are strategically interspersed between the rounded Romanesque-Norman arches and represent the embryonic stages of a style of architecture that would come to be known as Gothic. From the very beginning the cathedral was constructed with stone-ribbed vaults and they have never been rebuilt. Durham Cathedral is the least altered Romanesque church in Europe.

Also of significance at Durham Cathedral are the Flying Buttresses, an architectural feature seemingly invented by the Durham masons to give extra support to the vaulting. Although these buttresses are the first of their kind in the world, they are high in the roof of the Triforium, an upper level of the cathedral and cannot be seen by visitors.

Architecural experts are best qualified to understand the historic significance of Durham Cathedral, but even these experts have commented that the cathedral has 'special qualities that are not easy to fathom'. In fact laymen, without the slightest architectural knowledge, can easily appreciate these qualities.

Across the country, Durham is perhaps not as well known as cathedrals like Canterbury, Salisbury or St. Paul's in London but it has often found itself voted Britain's best building. The writer Bill Bryson, went further when he said 'I unhesitatingly gave Durham Cathedral my vote for best cathedral on planet earth'. Certainly, recognition of the cathedral's importance is echoed across the world and this was no more exemplified by the announcement in 1986 that the cathedral, along with the neighbouring castle, was to become a UNESCO World Heritage site.

Although it is the internal architecture of 1093-1133 that most significantly contributes to the accolades bestowed upon the cathedral, there were major additions to the building at later dates. Most notable are the Galilee Chapel and Chapel of the Nine Altars. These were built respectively at the western and eastern ends of the cathedral, but are additions that are in no way detrimental to the overall beauty of the building.

An unusual bird's eye view of the Cathedral Nave (NE)

At the western end of the cathedral stands the Galilee Chapel, completed between 1173 and 1189, by an architect employed by Bishop Hugh Pudsey. The chapel is situated right at the top of the gorge formed by the River Wear and from the outside is barely noticeable. Externally it looks like a little annexe that is rather overshadowed by the cathedral's two western towers. The towers were themselves, incidentally, a later addition to the building constructed between 1217 and 1226.

Inside, the Galilee Chapel is home to the tomb of the Venerable Bede (AD 673-735), who was the first historian of England and in his time the most respected scholar in Europe. Bede lived most of his life at Jarrow by the River Tyne but his bones were brought to Durham from the ruins of the abandoned Jarrow monastery in 1020. It is thought that the then Sacrist of Durham, a notorious collector of relics, stole the bones. This is probably true but in reality they were much safer at Durham than they would have been at Jarrow during this particular period of history.

Initially, Bede's remains were buried with those of St. Cuthbert at the eastern end of the cathedral, but they were removed to the western end in 1370. A magnificent shrine was built around Bede's tomb to rival that of Cuthbert, but like Cuthbert's shrine, it was destroyed in 1540, on the orders of Henry VIII.

Bede has remained buried on the same spot in a simple grave at this western end of the cathedral. The shiny black-topped tomb of carboniferous limestone that we see today only dates from 1831. It is inscribed with the words 'Hac sunt in fossa Baedae Venerabilis Ossa', which translated, means 'in this tomb are of Bede the Bones'.

Legend tells us that the use of the word 'Venerable' was inspired into the mind of the writer of this poetic epitaph by an angel who told him how to complete the rhyme. In truth Bede was known as 'the Venerable' from as early as the eleventh century.

A wall above the tomb has the words from one of Bede's prayers inscribed in large gold-coloured letters. In a similar recess at the opposite northern end of the chapel are some rare twelfth century wall paintings depicting Oswald, King of Northumbria and St. Cuthbert as a bishop.

The Cathedral Choir: The Rose Window can be seen in the distance beyond the Neville Screen (NE)

An architect called Christian built the Galilee Chapel for Bishop Pudsey and was also responsible for the construction of the remarkably similar church of St. Lawrence at Pittington, a village, that lies just east of Durham City.

Durham's Galilee Chapel is quite unlike any other part of the cathedral and is accessed through a small door from the cathedral nave. Entering the Galilee Chapel, we get a feeling of separateness. Unlike the awesome nave that dominates the main body of the cathedral, the feeling in the Galilee is of light and intimacy. Its roof and tooth patterned arches of Purbeck marble give the building the appearance of a Moorish palace. It has been compared to the mosque of

Cordoba in Spain and the chapel was certainly inspired by Islamic styles of architecture. However, the chapel is still fundamentally Norman-Romanesque.

The orientation of the Galilee chapel seems quite different to the rest of the cathedral as it is much wider than it is long. Its length is restricted by the closeness of the river gorge. The gorge itself did cause some problems for the chapel and during the early 1400s the building and supporting walls had to be strengthened to stop it slipping towards the river.

For many centuries the Galilee Chapel served partly as a Lady Chapel with a special altar for females. According to the Benedictine rules of the Durham monastery, the Lady Chapel was the only part of the cathedral that could be entered by women. Just outside the chapel doors, a little way inside the nave of the main cathedral building we see a line of black Frosterley marble in the cathedral floor. It marked the point beyond which women could not pass. Nearby is the the cathedral font and a massive font cover of the 1600s.

The Galilee Chapel (NE)

The Tomb of the Venerable Bede in the Galilee Chapel (NE)

So strict was the rule against women entering the cathedral that in 1333 when Queen Philippa, the wife of Edward III crossed the line to find sleeping quarters in the building, she was forced to sleep elsewhere. The Durham monks petitioned the king and insisted she find sleeping accommodation in the castle to avoid upsetting St. Cuthbert.

Normally, Lady Chapels were constructed at the eastern end of cathedrals and not the west, so Durham breaks with a tradition here. However, there was an attempt to build a chapel at the eastern end to facilitate the movement of pilgrims in and around St. Cuthbert's shrine. It was to include a Lady Chapel, but problems arose with crumbling masonry forcing Bishop Pudsey to transfer the chapel to the west.

The construction problems at the east probably arose from unstable ground, but legend attributes damage to St. Cuthbert who is said to have disliked a Lady Chapel so close to his tomb. Strangely, in the following century a new chapel called the Chapel of the Nine Altars was successfully built at the cathedral's eastern end and seems to have had no major structural problems.

Marble maker beyond which women could not pass (NE)

The huge Chapel of the Nine Altars at the eastern end of the cathedral is a much larger structure than the Galilee Chapel and is a natural extension of the nave. However, the floor of this chapel is sunken and sits below the rest of the cathedral. The Nine Altars chapel was begun during the episcopacy of Bishop Richard le Poore (1228-1237) who was also associated with the building of Salisbury Cathedral where he was later a bishop.

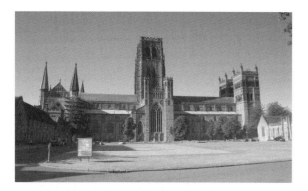

Durham Cathedral from Palace Green (DS)

The Chapel of the Nine Altars was constructed in Early English Gothic style with measurements and structure based on a transept at Fountains Abbey in North Yorkshire. Unfortunately the mason made slight miscalculations with dimensions and a close examination of the chapel roof reveals a mistake in the vaulting.

Before the chapel's construction, the eastern end of the cathedral terminated in the form of three apses close to St. Cuthbert's tomb. The outline of these apses can still be traced nearby in the cathedral floor.

The Chapel of the Nine Altars provided more space for the increasing number of visiting pilgrims who packed the aisles and nave of the cathedral to view the shrine of St. Cuthbert. Here the pilgrims were provided with nine altars at which to worship.

A number of interesting features can be seen in the chapel including some elegant columns of Frosterley marble. This is not a true marble but a decorative black substance originating from the Durham valley of Weardale. The marble is embedded with the white shells of ancient sea creatures.

Another prominent feature of the chapel is a large white statue that was carved in Rome by an architect called John Gibson. Its subject is Bishop William Van Mildert, who died in 1836. Van Mildert was the last Prince Bishop of Durham and the man largely responsible for the foundation of Durham University in 1832. The University is the third oldest in England after Oxford and Cambridge.

Close to Van Mildert's statue is the tomb of one of the most powerful Bishops of Durham called Anthony Bek (1284-1311) who held the title Patriarch of Jerusalem.

Without doubt the most beautiful feature in the Chapel of the Nine Altars is the huge Rose Window that was originally made in the fifteenth century by Richard Pickering of Hemingbrough. The Rose was reconstructed in the eighteenth century by James Wyatt and is 90 feet in circumference with a central core depicting Christ surrounded by the 12 apostles.

The Chapel of the Nine Altars lies just to the east of the elevated Feretory (a chapel for saint's relics) in which we find the tomb of St. Cuthbert in what was once the eastern end of the cathedral.

Durham Cathedral's Chapel of the Nine Altars (DS)

Chapel of the Nine Altars pictured from the Bailey (DS)

In medieval times Durham Cathedral was one of the greatest centres of pilgrimage in England and the chief reason for this pilgrimage was the rich and glorious shrine of St. Cuthbert. Today the simple grey stone tomb inscribed 'Cuthbertus' is all that remains of the shrine but prior to the Dissolution of the Monasteries in the sixteenth century, the whole area around the tomb was an elaborately decorated shrine described as one of the richest monuments in England. It was decorated with an 'ingeniously made structure of costly green marble and gilded with gold'.

The shrine was bestowed with an incredible number of gifts and jewels including contributions from kings, queens, churchmen and wealthy nobles. The gifts were stored in beautifully decorated wainscot lockers situated on the north and south sides of the feretory. The lockers also contained relics associated with St. Cuthbert, and other saints, and were opened for viewing on special occasions like the feast days of the saints.

The magnificent shrine of St. Cuthbert was destroyed in the sixteenth century along with many others throughout the country on the orders of King Henry VIII. The men who opened St. Cuthbert's tomb found a number of precious jewels and a wand of gold that were all confiscated by the crown. Also taken were the beautifully illustrated Lindisfarne Gospels, a rich symbol of Northumbria's culture dating from the eighth century. Today the Lindisfarne Gospels are still separated from their homeland in London's British Museum.

St. Cuthbert's tomb would not be reopened again until 1827 when the tomb revealed a series of coffins of which the last contained a skeleton covered in silk. The oldest, innermost coffin is preserved and can be seen pieced together in the cathedral museum but the bones were returned to their grave.

St. Cuthbert's tomb and feretory are hidden from the choir and nave by the magnificent fourteenth century Neville Screen. This was once decorated with 107 alabaster figures. The figures were removed when the shrine was destroyed and are still said to be hidden somewhere in the cathedral.

The screen itself was donated by John, the fifth Lord Neville (died 1388) and is constructed from Caen limestone originating from a quarry in Normandy. After the stone was shipped from France the massive screen was constructed in London by a mason called Henry Yavele and shipped north to Newcastle. From here it was carried across land by carts to Durham.

Tomb of Bishop Thomas Hatfield (NE)

John Neville's tomb lies in the south aisle of the nave accompanied by that of his wife Matilda. The tomb of John's father, Ralph Neville is also in the cathedral. It was Ralph who successfully helped the English to victory over the Scots at the Battle of Neville's Cross in 1346. As an honour for the victory he became the first layman buried in the cathedral.

The south aisle of the cathedral choir contains the tomb of Bishop Thomas Hatfield (1345-1381) who was bishop at the time of the aforementioned battle. It was Bishop Hatfield who founded Durham College, Oxford, later renamed Trinity College. Hatfield's tomb is covered by his alabaster effigy. It lies tucked away under a decorated arch formed by a short stairway leading to the Bishop's throne or 'Cathedra' directly above. The Bishop's

throne at Durham is the highest in Christendom in keeping with the former mighty status of the Prince Bishops.

To the west of the choir we stand directly beneath the central tower. Viewed from outside, the tower is one of the most imposing features of the cathedral, but was only built in the period 1465-1490. In 1429 lightning destroyed an earlier tower dating from 1233.

The stairway up to the top of the tower is nearby in the south transept near a sixteenth century wooden clock. Known as Prior Castell's clock after a Prior who held the post from 1494-1519 it is remarkable it survives. During the Civil War when 4,000 Scottish prisoners were held in the cathedral after the Battle of Dunbar (1650) prisoners destroyed nearly all the cathedral wood for making fires to keep them warm. The clock was spared, seemingly because it had a carving of the sacred Scottish thistle upon it. Of course the prisoners may have simply wanted to tell the time.

The clock originally only had an hour hand. It was not thought necessary to know anything more precise than the general hour of the day. This explains why the clock is divided into 48 rather than 60 segments. The segments represent quarter hour intervals rather than minutes. The clock was originally erected in 1500, but was remodelled in 1630.

The Cathedral Monastery

To the south of, but adjoining the cathedral, are the buildings of the cloisters clustered around a small square green called the cloister garth. The buildings surrounding the garth were the monastic buildings of the cathedral priory and included the chapter house, monks' dormitory, refectory and great kitchen.

The Cloisters of the Cathedral Priory (DS)

A monastery existed here from around 1083 up until its closure during the reign of Henry VIII around 1540. Some parts of the monastery are actually older than the cathedral and date back to the 1080s. Parts of the south cloister and a former prison in the south east corner of the cloister date from this period, but most of the cloisters date back to a rebuilding of 1828.

Framing the square green are four covered cloister walkways where monks spent considerable periods of time during the heyday of Durham Priory. One of the walkways on the northern side of the cloisters by the main cathedral wall was formerly the monks' scriptorium. It contained a number of reading chambers in which monks could study.

At the western end of this walkway a plaque can be seen informing American tourists and other interested parties that an ancestor of George Washington was once a Prior at Durham Cathedral. The Washingtons were an old County Durham family originating from Washington near Sunderland.

Above the western walkway of the Cloister is the monks' dormitory, the site of the sleeping quarters. It dates from the fourteenth century and has an extremely impressive roof of wooden oak beams. It now houses a library belonging to the Dean and Chapter and has a collection of Anglo-Saxon and Viking crosses from throughout the ancient kingdom of Northumbria.

On the opposite side of the cloisters we find the Chapter House where meetings are held to discuss the day-to-day running of the cathedral. The original medieval chapter house dating from the 1100s was demolished in 1796 and was not rebuilt until 1895 but the floor of the building still contains the tombs of three very important early Bishops of Durham: William St. Carileph, Ranulf Flambard and Hugh du Puiset (or Pudsey). The Chapter House was one of a number of areas in the cathedral that were used in the filming of a Harry Potter movie, but unfortunately it is not open to the public.

Houses and water pump, College Green (DS)

Above the southern walkway of the cloisters was situated the refectory or eating area. This is now a private library belonging to the Dean and Chapter. Behind the refectory is the octagonal shaped building of the kitchen.

A young Tony Blair at Durham Chorister School (MR)

Today most visitors to the cloisters are drawn to the cathedral's restaurant, bookshop and treasury museum which all lie in the south-western corner of the cloisters. The treasury museum is one of the most important museums in the north of England and contains many relics from the 'Golden Age of Northumbria'. The museum's ancient exhibits include the seventh century wooden coffin of St. Cuthbert, which has been carefully pieced together, and St. Cuthbert's pectoral cross. Some very impressive silver plate can also be seen in the museum. It once belonged to the Prince Bishops of Durham.

Immediately south of the cloister area we enter, through a passage, the cathedral's close which is known as College Green or simply 'the College'. Arguably the most beautiful part of Durham City it can be accessed via the cloister or through Prior Castell's gatehouse which links College Green to the North and South Bailey. The gatehouse dates from 1495-1519 and is topped by a former chapel that was dedicated to St. Helen.

Durham Chorister School, College Green (DS)

Entering the gateway from the Bailey, the College has on its south side the appearance of a quiet secluded village. Here picturesque houses cluster around a 'village green' complete with a village pump and water tower. On the north side are the buildings of the cathedral monastery including the Deanery (formerly the Prior's lodgings) and the octagonal kitchen.

The pretty houses on the south side have mostly eighteenth century facades but incorporate medieval masonry of earlier monastic buildings. The houses belong to members of the Dean and Chapter who are responsible for the cathedral's administration and daily affairs. Since the 1540s the Dean and Chapter have been the successors to the priors and monks of Durham.

The College is a beautiful, enclosed, almost traffic free area overlooked by the cathedral with a little passageway

called the Dark Entry leading towards the wooded river banks near Prebends Bridge.

The term 'college' used in connection with College Green is used to describe the cathedral's administrative body and has nothing to do with a college in the sense of a place of education. It is not part of Durham University as is sometimes mistakenly thought.

College Green is however the home to a notable educational institution that can be found in the south west corner. This is Durham Chorister School that has existed in the city for over 600 years having been founded around 1390 as a song school.

In its early days Durham Chorister School was a small institution located at various sites within the cathedral priory buildings and had no more than 24 pupils until about the time of the Second World War. Famous pupils in recent times have included Tony Blair, who went on to become Britain's Prime Minister. Blair was himself born in Edinburgh, but his family originated from Glasgow and after a stint living in Australia moved to Durham where Blair's father became a lecturer at the University.

Blair attended the Chorister School from 1961-1966 and for a time his family actually lived in College Green, before moving later to the nearby Durham village of High Shincliffe. Another famous ex-Chorister School pupil was the actor and comedian Rowan Atkinson, most famous for his role as Mr Bean. He was a pupil at the school from 1964-1968 and his time there overlapped with that of Blair.

Some of the Chorister school buildings were formerly a women's hostel for Durham University. This later became St. Mary's College but was relocated to South Road, Elvet in the 1950s.

Palace Green

Whilst College Green, on the south side of the cathedral has the appearance of a quaint little village, the much larger and more open Palace Green, on the north side, has a more formal appearance. Bordered on its flanks by attractive, but more official looking buildings, this green separates Durham Cathedral from Durham Castle which lies to the north. Once assosicated with the administration of the Prince Bishops, buildings surrounding the green are now largely properties of Durham University.

Palace Green is a site of great beauty and for most visitors provides the first close up view of Durham Cathedral. Until the twelfth century, during the time of Bishop Flambard it was a mass of wooden buildings huddled between the castle and the cathedral. Bishop Flambard cleared them all because of the potential fire threat and possibly moved the residents to Framwellgate. Palace Green thus became the open area that it still is today.

Bishop Cosin's Almshouses, Palace Green (DS)

Most people approach Palace Green from Owengate, a short street linking Palace Green to Saddler Street and the Market Place. The name Owengate, first recorded in the fourteenth century may be a corruption of 'Ovengate' from a possible site of medieval ovens. In the 1400s the Earls of Westmorland (the Nevilles) are known to have owned a house in this street.

Bishop Cosin's Hall, Palace Green (DS)

Known as Queen Street in the nineteenth century, Owengate is said to be haunted by the ghost of a University don who threw himself down the Durham Castle stairs. At the top of Owengate we reach the north east corner of Palace Green with the cathedral directly ahead of us and the castle to our right. Exploring the buildings of Palace Green we should start with those near Owengate that occupy the eastern side of the green.

Nearest to Owengate and overlooking a rather attractive Victorian post box are buildings erected by the architect Salvin in 1841. Next, we find the stately Georgian house called Bishop Cosin's Hall which is the tallest building on this side of the green. It dates from the eighteenth century and was originally the Archdeacon's Inn (a residence of the Archdeacon of Northumberland) but served as a Durham University hall from 1851-1864.

Continuing along the eastern side of the green, the next building is Bishop Cosin's Almshouses that includes an inscribed date of 1666. Unlike Bishop Cosin's Hall the almshouses actually date from Cosin's time. They once looked after the poor and accommodated four men and four women.

Next door, moving closer to the cathedral, is the Victorian looking Pemberton Building (Union Society Lecture Rooms) that actually date from 1931, and were built on the site of a coach house. Finally and slightly set back from the green is the rather plain eighteenth century building called Abbey House.

In 1901 this became a female students' hostel of Durham University and moved here from Claypath. It was relocated a few years later to the Cathedral's College Green but is now St. Mary's College in the city's South Road area. Abbey House is now Durham University's Department of Theology.

A narrow cobbled road called Dun Cow Lane separates Abbey House from the eastern end of the Cathedral and was once the lychgate or corpse gate where bodies were carried to the cathedral's cemetery. A 1915 house at the Bailey end of the lane stands on the site of a pub called the Castle Inn.

Dun Cow Lane is named from its association with a Durham legend that is commemorated in an eighteenth century carving on the exterior of the cathedral. It can be seen nearby if you look up.

It is said the monks carrying St. Cuthbert's coffin to Durham were stopped dead at a place called Warden Law near Houghton-le-Spring when the coffin refused to move. St. Cuthbert then appeared and instructed the monks to go to Durham or Dunholm as it was then known.

On learning the name of their destination the monks found they were now able to move the coffin. Proceeding west they asked a number of local people where they could find Dunholm but unfortunately nobody had heard of such a place.

Luckily by chance in an area later known as Mountjoy a milkmaid was overheard asking another milkmaid if she had seen her Dun Cow - a grey coloured beast that had wandered off on its own. The other maid answered that she had seen the cow roaming about near Dunholm.

When the monks heard mention of Dunholm they were filled with joy and followed the footsteps of the milkmaid as she searched for her cow. By this stroke of luck or divine providence, they found Durham. This legend probably dates from the sixteenth century and is remembered in the eighteenth century carving on the cathedral's north wall that depicts a milkmaid and her cow.

Carving of the Dun Cow on Durham Cathedral (NE)

Walking along the southern edge of Palace Green we are offered some of the closest views of the cathedral alongside the cathedral cemetery. One grave in the cemetery near the cathedral's main entrance (the North Door) is allegedly that of a tightrope walker who fell to his death in 1237 after he was employed by the Prior of Durham to entertain the monks. He fell while walking on a tightrope stretched between the central tower and a western tower. The grave is said to turn gold when rain falls – the gold representing the fee the performer would have received if he had successfully completed his task.

Durham Cathedral's North Door is the entrance into the cathedral from Palace Green and the way in for almost everyone on their first visit. The door itself dates back to 1140 and is most notable for its famous bronze Sanctuary Knocker. The face on the knocker appears to be that of a lion but some attribute its features to some mysterious beings banished by St. Cuthbert from the island of Inner Fame near Lindisfarne.

The knocker we see today is in fact a 1980 replica of the twelfth century original that can be seen in the cathedral's museum. Criminals could seek sanctuary at Durham by loudly knocking upon the door or by alerting the attention of two watchmen who resided in a chamber that existed above the door.

The criminal would be allowed into the cathedral monastery where he would exchange his clothes for a black robe imprinted with the yellow cross of St. Cuthbert on his left shoulder. He would then confess his crime to a coroner and during his time in the cathedral was given food and water. However, the fugitive's sanctuary in the cathedral would last no more than 37 days.

Before or on the 37th day the criminal would decide whether to face trial and possible execution or voluntary exile. If exile was chosen the criminal was escorted by parish constables to an assigned port – usually Hartlepool – and with the cross still upon his shoulder would set sail on the first ship to leave the country.

The Sanctuary Knocker (NE)

Moving on from the cathedral's North Door we return our attention to Palace Green. Here at the south west corner of the green is a former Grammar School that was rebuilt by Bishop Cosin in 1661. It now houses Durham University's music department and is reputedly haunted by a young pupil who suffered a fatal punishment from one of his masters who apparently threw him from a balcony in a fit of anger.

A narrow alley, or vennel runs alongside the building down towards the beautiful river banks. This vennel is known as Windy Gap and stands on the site of a small gateway in the medieval defences of the city called the Windishole Postern.

Windy Gap leads down towards the famous fulling mill that features in the most famous photographic views of Durham Cathedral. Once the property of the Priors of Durham, the Fulling Mill, known historically as Jesus Mill, is now home to the University's Museum of Archaeology.

Returning to Palace Green, Windy Gap divides the music department from the University's Palace Green Library. This partly occupies buildings that were once the Diocesan Registry of 1820. They were on the site of Bishop Cosin's courthouse that existed here from 1664-1811.

Victorian illustration of Durham Cathedral

Chapter Two
The Castle and the Baileys

Durham Castle is the ancient palace of the Prince Bishops of Durham and lies at the northern end of Palace Green directly opposite the cathedral. It is situated on the site of a fortress built to the orders of William the Conqueror on his return from Scotland in 1072.

Waltheof, Earl of Northumbria, who was appointed and later exectuted by William, undertook the building of the castle but over the years a succession of Prince Bishops added important sections to the building.

Durham Castle: The Keep from Palace Green (DS)

The present castle is dominated by the keep which although the most imposing part of the castle is the least historic. In the tradition of the Norman Motte and Bailey castles the keep is situated on a mound and was first erected in the fourteenth century during the episcopacy of Bishop Thomas Hatfield. Over the centuries it fell into a ruinous state but was rebuilt in the 1840s as a sleeping quarters for students when the castle became Durham's University College.

The older and greater part of the castle is situated around a courtyard to the west of the keep. This courtyard is entered from the gatehouse near the site of the castle moat. The moat was crossed by means of a drawbridge just outside the gatehouse.

Primarily the work of Bishop Pudsey (1153-1195), the gatehouse underwent alterations during the episcopacies of Bishop Tunstal (1530-1559) and Bishop Shute Barrington (1791-1826).

Unfortunately, the castle can only be explored by guided tour at assigned times for a fee. Entering the courtyard through the castle gatehouse, the imposing Keep is on the right. On the the left is the thirteenth and fourteenth century Great Hall built by Bishop Anthony Bek (1284-1311) and Bishop Thomas Hatfield (1345-1381).

The nearest part of this building includes a 500 year old kitchen built by Bishop Fox. Fox's coat of arms can be seen in the Tudor style woodwork of the adjacent hatch in the buttery and depicts a pelican piercing its breast to feed its young. Coats of arms associated with various other Prince Bishops of Durham can be seen throughout the castle. The impressive dining hall of Bishop Bek is about 100 feet long and 45 feet high and occupies most of the Great Hall. It serves as the dining hall for University College Durham and is arguably superior to those of Christchurch, Oxford and Trinity College, Cambridge.

Inside, the black staircase of Bishop Cosin adjoins the western and northern wings of the castle. Dating from 1662 it is one of the most impressive staircases of its time in England. The castle's north wing was the site of a hall built by Bishop Pudsey but a number of alterations were made by successive bishops and this part of the castle now includes the Bishop's suite, the Bishop's Dining Room, the Tunstal Gallery and the Senate Room.

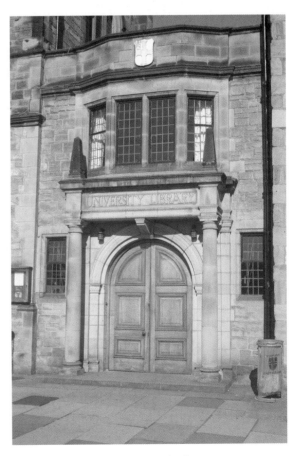

University Library, Palace Green (DS)

Durham Castle Gatehouse (DS)

Durham University

As the resting place of England's first great scholar, the Venerable Bede, it was perhaps only natural that Durham would one day receive a university of its own. Such an institution was first proposed during the religious reforms of Henry VIII and though nothing came of this plan, a similar scheme during the protectorate of Oliver Cromwell gained much ground.

Cromwell, victor of the English Civil War had overthrown the establishment, ousted the monarchy and instigated massive social, political and religious reforms. At Durham, the city fathers thought this was a good opportunity to challenge the educational dominance of Oxford and Cambridge.

In 1650 the Mayor and Aldermen of Durham petitioned Cromwell, suggesting that Durham Cathedral, notably the Chapter House, could be used as a university. Cromwell was persuaded, considering it a matter of 'great importance to promoting learning and piety in these rude and ignorant parts'. By 1657 letters of patent were issued for the university's establishment. It would consist of a Provost, two preachers, four professors, four tutors, four schoolmasters and an initial intake of 24 scholars.

Sadly for Durham, the influential authorities at Oxford and Cambridge raised objections and brought the plan to an abrupt end when Cromwell died in 1658. Cromwell's son and successor, Richard, proved a weak leader and did not wish to offend the older seats of learning. In any case Richard accepted the restoration of the monarchy and with the coronation of Charles II, the old order returned. Durham would have to wait another 174 years for its university.

The objection of Oxford, England's oldest university was something of an irony considering the part Durham men had played in the foundation of Oxford's university colleges. William of Durham, a theologian and one time Rector of Wearmouth in Sunderland had founded Oxford's oldest college (University College) in 1249.

Oxford's Balliol and Trinity College also had Durham links. John Balliol of Barnard Castle, son of the Bernard from whom the Teesdale town is named, founded the Oxford college that bears his name. Balliol insulted Walter Kirkham, Bishop of Durham in a land dispute and as

penance agreed to finance students. His grant, confirmed by his widow in 1263 marked the foundation of Balliol College.

Durham Castle Courtyard (DS)

In the early days the nearest thing Durham had to a university of its own was also at Oxford. This was Durham Hall, later Durham College, established in 1286 by the Bishop of Durham Thomas Hatfield to educate

Benedictine monks from Durham Cathedral Priory. Unfortunately, because of its monastic connections the college was surrendered to Henry VIII in the Dissolution. Its links to Durham were severed and it was reformed as Trinity College, Oxford in 1554.

It was not until the 1830s, that Durham, England's third oldest university, came into being. Once again, its foundation was linked to religious and political reforms. These were associated with the Northumbrian born Prime Minister, Earl Grey who stripped away privileges held by the establishment including the Church. Enormous church revenues and countless privileges had made senior figures like bishops wealthy and this was very apparent in the case of William Van Mildert, the Bishop of Durham.

Van Mildert, who actually opposed the reforms, held privileges dating back to the time of the medieval Prince Bishops.

Though reluctant to see the break up of the Palatinate (the Prince Bishops' territory) Van Mildert wanted to see that the funds freed up by the termination were used for establishing an educational institution. Towards this purpose the bishop's castle at Durham was donated.

The University officially came into being following the Cathedral Chapter Act of 1831 and the Durham University Bill of 1832. It was initially an ecclesiastical foundation controlled by the Cathedral's Dean and Chapter and concentrated on theological training for Anglican priests.

Apart from Durham Castle, which became University College, early university buildings included the old Red Lion Inn in South Bailey. It became Hatfield Hall College in 1846, while the eighteenth century Archdeacon's Inn on Palace Green became a hall of residence called Bishop Cosin's Hall.

Non-collegiate students were admitted from 1871 and in 1888 they established St.Cuthbert's Society, located in the South Bailey from 1951.

At Gilesgate, Church of England teacher training colleges called St. Bede (for men) and St. Hild (for women) were respectively established in 1839 and 1845. These colleges were completely independent of Durham University but developed a close association with the University in the 1890s. They eventually became a constituent part of University in 1979. This was three years after the two colleges had amalgamated to form the College of St. Hild and St. Bede.

The University Dining Hall, Durham Castle about 1911

Around 1901 the eighteenth century building called Abbey House on Palace Green became a women's hostel for the University and subsequently became St. Mary's College in 1919. It moved to South Road near Elvet Hill in 1952.

In the early days of the University, attempts were made to pursue science and engineering degrees, but these were not a success. However, rival colleges specialising in these particular fields at Newcastle upon Tyne were very well attended, so, in 1852, the Newcastle Medical School was

incorporated into Durham University. In 1871 Newcastle's College of Science (later Armstrong College) followed suit.

From 1937 the whole Newcastle campus of Durham University was collectively known as King's College, but following a separation from Durham in 1963 it officially became the University of Newcastle upon Tyne.

In the early 1900s the Durham City part of the University still focused on theology and was concentrated in the Baileys where St. Chad's College (1904), St. John's College (1909), St. Cuthbert's Society and Hatfield College are still located today.

In 1908 the governance of the University transferred from the cathedral's Dean and Chapter to a new federal system. This and the establishment of a University science block at Elvet in 1924 showed the University was branching away from its religious roots.

Since the Second World World War, several University Colleges have sprung up in the South Road area of Elvet where most of the Durham University colleges are located today. Away from the city the main exceptions to this are Durham University's Queen's Campus site at Stockton-on-Tees that opened in 1992. Also a few miles to the west of Durham City, is the magnificent Ushaw College, a licensed hall of residence for the University since 1968. Ushaw College is featured in the accompanying book.

North and South Bailey

The Baileys are widely regarded as the best streets in Durham and are divided into two parts, called North Bailey and South Bailey. The two streets meet near the College Green gate but are not easy to separate and along with Saddler Street, form a more or less continuous street.

Until 1820, the Great North Gate, a massive fortified gateway separated Saddler Street from the Baileys. This gate was only one section of the extensive medieval defences that encircled Durham City.

Defensive walls surrounded the peninsula area of the city and a supplementary set of walls encircled the Market Place as far as the foot of Claypath. Towers were also situated on bridges but it was the walls encircling the peninsula that were most significant. They protected the cathedral but were in many respects an extension of Durham Castle. The castle protected the peninsula neck so that the cathedral lay within the defensive walls of the castle. In fact, the entire 58 acres of the peninsula was referred to as 'The Castle' in medieval times. This situation gave rise to the name of the Durham Baileys.

Fine Georgian Houses dominate the Bailey (DS)

Bailey usually refers to the outer wall of a castle or a courtyard enclosed by such a wall. Durham's Bailey now takes the form of two streets. In the earliest times, Bailey residents would have been military tenants employed by the powerful Prince Bishops of Durham to defend the city from attack. However, as the threat from Scottish invaders subsided after the 1600s, the Baileys gradually became some of the most sought-after streets in the city.

Most houses were rebuilt and refaced in Georgian style in the eighteenth century and the Baileys came to be home to some of the most famous and wealthy members of Durham society. Bailey residents included the Earls of Strathmore, (the Bowes family) who were ancestors of the present royal family. Also resident here were the coal-owning Liddell family. They included the great grandmother of Alice Liddell, a little girl who inspired the Alice in Wonderland story.

At number 24 lived Captain Boulby, who fought at Waterloo, and at number 5, Ignatius Bonomi, the Durham architect. Another famous Bailey resident was Sir

Robert Ker Porter, an artist to the Tsar of Russia, who married a Russian princess. The 3ft 3in Polish Count, Joseph Boruwlaski, also lived in the Bailey with the Ebdon family before moving to a house near Prebends Bridge down by the river.

A notable memorial to the Count can be seen in St. Mary the Less Church, in the South Bailey. This was once the parish church for the South Bailey. The larger St. Mary-le-Bow Church, so called because of its former proximity to a prominent bowed gateway, served the North Bailey. The arch collapsed in 1635 and destroyed part of the church tower which was rebuilt in 1702.

Perhaps the most remarkable resident of the Bailey was John Gully, a one-time champion boxer of all England. Gully learned to fight during a period of imprisonment for debt at Bristol, where he caught the attention of a group of wealthy businessmen with a penchant for pugilism. They paid off Gully's debts and secured his release on the proviso that he agreed to fight the then-champion boxer of England, Henry 'The Game Chicken' Pearce.

Of course this was the age of bare-knuckle fighting, but Gully believed he had the talent and, in any case, it seemed a small price to pay for the secure of his release and payment of his debts. In the event, 'The Game Chicken' was the victor, but not before Gully had pushed him to a staggering 59 rounds on 8 October 1805. It is hard to imagine the physical state of these two men after the bout. In fact, it may have proved too much for 'The Game Chicken', who retired shortly afterwards, leaving Gully to successfully challenge and defeat a new champion called the Lancashire Giant.

Gully clearly wished to avoid the debts of his earlier life and invested his winnings wisely and carefully. For a time, he served as MP for Pontefract and took a keen interest in racehorse ownership, winning the Derby on two occasions.

Coal mine ownership was another form of business in which Gully invested, and it was this that brought him to County Durham, where he owned mines at Trimdon, Hetton, Thornley and Ludworth. His wealth was exemplified by his choice of residence in Durham's best street.

It was at number 7 North Bailey that Gully died at the age of 80. He left behind a remarkable legacy of 24 children, from two successive marriages. His two wives were clearly a match for him in stamina and endurance! Unfortunately Gully's house no longer stands, but a plaque recalls the site of his home.

Most properties in the Bailey today belong to Durham University and several are occupied by some of the university's older colleges.

Left: John Gully a champion boxer who resided in Durham's North Bailey

Right: 'The Lancashire Giant' who John Gully defeated despite his superior weight

The oldest college in the Bailey is Hatfield College named from a fourteenth century Bishop of Durham. It was founded in 1846 and occupies what was previously a coaching inn called The Red Lion. It is an attractive building set back slightly from the North Bailey between Bow Lane and Kingsgate Bridge. Also in the North Bailey is St. Chad's College, established in 1904 on the site of a house occupied by the afforementioned Porter family.

Bow Lane links the Bailey to New Elvet across the river via the Kingsgate footridge which opened in 1963. The bridge, built by Ove Arup is used mainly by students and tourists. In the 1400s Bow Lane was known as 'Le Chare' but in earlier days was seemingly called 'Kingsgate'. The lane crossed the river by means of a ford. King William Rufus is said to have fled on horseback along this route. He was struck with fear after visiting St. Cuthbert's shrine with the intention of removing the saint's remains from the tomb. Kingsgate was alledgedly named after William.

The South Bailey is home to St. John's College of 1909 and the associated Cranmer Hall. Part of St. John's College (the former Bowes House) is said to be haunted by the ghost of some children and a crooked man.

Two small schools existed in the street during the nineteenth century and Cranmer Hall served as a voluntary aid hospital during the First World War. At number 12 South Bailey is the non-collegiate University institution called St. Cuthbert's Society. It was founded in 1888 and has been situated in the South Bailey since 1951. All of the colleges in the Bailey including St. Cuthbert's Society occupy attractive Georgian houses.

Over time the Baileys have become an enclave for students and wandering tourists. The Baileys have an air of quiet separateness compared to the adjoining, more worldly, Saddler Street. However, one advantage of the university's presence is that it has prevented the Baileys from becoming overwhelmed by commercial concerns, so that it is still possible to imagine the Durham of a more genteel age with a stroll along the Baileys.

The Little Polish Count

Joseph Boruwlaski, a one time Bailey resident, was one of the most remarkable men ever associated with the City of Durham. His memoirs, running to hundreds of pages, read like a travel companion to late eighteenth century Europe. They recall the many people, places and strange events he encountered during his 97 year life. His travels took him to many places including France, Italy, Germany, Croatia, Turkey and the Syrian Desert. He journeyed across Ireland, visited every Scandinavian country and even crossed the inhospitable stretches of Siberia as far as the Bering Sea, visiting small towns and cities where he could make friends and entertain.

In cities like Paris, Vienna, Strasbourg, Brussels and Munich, Boruwlaski achieved great heights of fame, drawing people from miles around to see him in person. He was received at the court of several European rulers and made friends with kings, queens, princes and princesses. All were charmed and delighted by his presence.

It was a great compliment to Durham that a man so widely travelled should choose the little city as the place of his retirement. He admired the situation of the city and, in his own words, was 'much struck with the River Wear, which runs round it in the shape of a horseshoe'.

He acknowledged that the city was small but praised its cathedral, recognising that the city 'contains not many buildings of fine architecture'. This disadvantage, he declared, was 'abundantly compensated by the hospitality and kindness of its amiable inhabitants and occasionally by their brilliant assemblies, which give us so favourable an opportunity to admire the elegant and beautiful features of the ladies'. Lady friends were never far from Boruwlaski's thoughts and the admiration was often mutual. It was in a letter to one such friend that Boruwlaski included a poem explaining his love for Durham with the memorable words 'Poland was my cradle, England is my nest; Durham is my quiet place. Where my weary bones shall rest'.

Boruwlaski's endearing qualities are not difficult to understand. He was a man with a great wit and intelligence that often surprised the aristocratic personalities he entertained. He was a talented dancer and a master of the violin, but his most remarkable feature was undoubtedly his height. Boruwlaski, or Count Joseph Boruwlaski, as he was perhaps erroneously known, was a dwarf, and throughout his life never grew more than 3 foot and 3 inches tall.

Born in Chaliez, the capital of Pokucia, in Poland in 1739, Boruwlaski was 8 inches long at birth, growing a further 3 inches in his first year. His origins seem to have been relatively humble for a man who described himself as a count. His father held land near their hometown, but the estate was lost through some misfortune that Boruwlaski does not relate.

Joseph had few, if any, memories of his father, as he was only nine when his father died. His mother was left to look after six children, Joseph being the third oldest with two older brothers. The second brother was, according to Joseph, more than 6ft tall, but the eldest was also a dwarf.

The other children were of normal height, except for the youngest, Anastasia, the only girl. She measured 21 inches at the age of six and only lived to the age of 20.

Lifesize statue of Boruwlaski in Durham Town Hall where his clothes and possessions are displayed (DS)

Boruwlaski's mother struggled to bring up the children, and with a mixture of regret and relief she allowed her friend, the Lady of Caorlix, to adopt Joseph and help with his education. Unfortunately, when this woman subsequently married the Count of Tarnow and fell pregnant, Joseph found himself out of favour. It was left to a friend of the Tarnows, the Countess of Humiecka, to take Joseph under her wing.

She would have a profound influence on his life. He was now 15 years old, and as a travelling companion to the countess on her many European journeys, Boruwlaski's lifetime adventures had truly begun. The Countess called him Jou-Jou, a pet name for a 'plaything', and he was universally known by this name to the many women he encountered during his life.

On one of his early foreign visits accompanying the countess, Boruwlaski travelled to Vienna where he remained for six months. Here he was presented to the Empress Maria Theresa. He sat on her lap and delighted her with his charm and wit. It was a situation that would be repeated again and again with high society ladies across the length and breadth of Europe.

However, this was a particularly memorable occasion. As he kissed the hand of the empress, he remarked upon her beautiful ring. She was so charmed that she offered to present it to him as a gift. Unfortunately, it was too large for Boruwlaski's little fingers, so the Empress called upon one of the young princesses, who presented her ring instead.

This princess was the six-year-old Marie Antoinette, the future queen of France, who would ultimately lose her head at the guillotine for betraying French secrets to Austria. All of these events would happen later, but during Boruwlaski's lifetime, and his encounter with the princess was no doubt a tale he would recall as he walked through Durham in the later years of his life.

This portrait of Count Joseph Boruwlaski can be seen in Durham Town Hall where some of his clothes and possessions are also displayed (DS)

The Countess Humiecka was instrumental in encouraging the musical talents of Joseph Boruwlaski. As his benefactress, she ensured that he was taught by the best. The ballet master of Vienna taught him to dance, and violin lessons at Paris came from none other than Gavinies, a leading musician of the age. These talents would prove useful to Boruwlaski as time went by and ultimately provided him with a means to a living.

It was love that forced Boruwlaski to seek independence from Humiecka. On his return to Warsaw from his travels with the Countess, Boruwlaski found a new young lady-in-waiting employed by the Humiecka household. Her name was Isalina Borboutin, a woman of French parentage and normal height. He fell in love at once.

After some time it became apparent that Isalina shared these feelings, but their clandestine meetings came to the attention of the furious countess. She ordered the dwarf to end the romance and Isalina was returned to her parents. Boruwlaski was locked in his room for a fortnight and the countess employed a footman to watch over him and prevent future encounters.

Fortunately the footman sympathised with Boruwlaski and allowed love letters to be sent to Isalina. In one letter Boruwlaski, signing his name Jou-Jou, declared to Isalina that if he were to lose her, 'he would renounce life itself'. The countess, perhaps jealous of losing her influence seems to have thought Boruwlaski could not survive without her financial support. She demanded that he renounced his love for Isalina or quit the house. The strength of his feelings for Isalina left him with no choice.

Boruwlaski now had to sustain a living without the countess. Fortunately he acquired some financial support from the Polish King who gave him a pension of 100 ducats. It is said that the King made Boruwlaski a Count at this stage, but sources disagree on the authenticity of Boruwlaski's title. With the King's blessing, Boruwlaski and Isalina were married but the dwarf realised his pension would not be enough to support a wife. Friends suggested he could make a living through concert performances. So, Borruwlaski began his extensive travels across the continent, to the far-flung corners of Europe.

It was at Vienna that Boruwlaski first met Sir Robert Keith Murray, a British ambassador who encouraged him to visit Britain. Boruwlaski eventually arrived in Britain in 1782 where he continued his travels. He became a friend of the lords and ladies of the land and even of King George IV himself. Boruwlaski's journeys included a two year tour of Ireland and a performing tour of Scotland that took in Orkney and Shetland. It is said that the Scots often struggled with the pronunciation of his name and called him 'Barrel of Whisky'.

Clothing and items belonging to Boruwlaski in Durham Town Hall (DS)

Boruwlaski portrayed during his time in Durham

During a visit to Newcastle the Count was encouraged to visit Durham and instantly fell in love with the place. He was most impressed with the intelligent company of the Ebdon family who lived in the Bailey. Mr Ebdon was a composer and the family held property close to where the so-called 'Count's House' (a former summerhouse) stands today. Boruwlaski initially stayed with the family in a house that is now part of St. Cuthbert's Society.

Boruwlaski was full of praise for the Dean and Chapter and their maintenance of the Durham peninsula and riverbanks and set up a home there in a cottage, now demolished, near Prebends Bridge.

When Boruwlaski retired to Durham in 1791 he was long since separated from his wife and was not sorry to hear of her eventual death. The Count claimed she had humiliated him on numerous occasions and he recalled with great bitterness to friends in Northumberland that she often sat him on the mantle piece and treated him like a child.

Throughout his life Boruwlaski was at pains to demonstrate that despite his size he was like any other man and should be treated accordingly. As he reached old age he was well used to those who saw him merely as a curiosity. In Durham it is said that local miners followed him about the city calling him the 'canny aad man'. Interestingly one of his Durham friends was the enormous, oversized actor Stephen Kemble. Together they must have seemed a rather comical pair.

Boruwlaski's time in Durham was the quietest and least eventful time of his life, although his memoirs lavishly praise Mr Ebdon and the situation of Durham. In his own words Durham was 'most happily adopted to his wishes for a retired life; not only from its romantic situation but from its being the abode of a friend whose manners were so congenial with my own and whose society afforded me such heartfelt delight'.

This riverside summerhouse is mistakenly known as the Count's House. Boruwlaski's home stood close by (MR)

Writing the closing sentences of his travel memoirs at Durham, Boruwlaski stated that he had 'now quitted the busy theatre of the world and its noisy promiscuous intercourse'. He would reside in Durham for 47 years of his life and finally passed away on 5 September, 1837 aged 97, a record breaking age for a dwarf.

He was remembered with great affection by the people of the city and given the high honour of burial inside the cathedral. His grave can still be seen not far from the cathedral's main door, marked by a little stone slab 15 inches square simply inscribed with the letters JB.

Boruwlaski lived in a cottage (now demolished) near Prebends Bridge

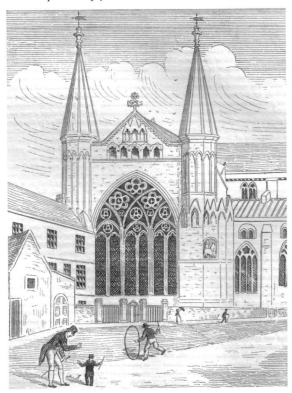

Boruwlaski on Palace Green

Victorian illustration of a garden party at Durham Castle

Chapter Three
The Market Place

Durham is known to have been the site of a 'Market Place' since at least 1040 and very probably much earlier. Palace Green has been suggested as the site of a market place but it is known that Bishop Flambard cleared the buildings on what became 'Palace Green'.

A pre-1857 photo of the original St. Nicholas Church

In truth it is more probable that the market place was always located on its present site. Medieval towns nearly always focused their road networks on market places to ensure that tolls and taxes could be collected on traded produce and the present market place site is as good as any in this respect.

Today's market place has certainly been in use since medieval times but none of the present buildings are medieval. Most are Georgian, Victorian or twentieth century in origin. In fact in the early nineteenth century, the only obvious medieval feature was the market place church.

Tracing its origin to Norman times, the church was dedicated to St. Nicholas, the patron saint of merchants but this was not the same church that stands today. The present St. Nicholas was constructed in the mid-nineteenth century and vaguely resembles the earlier structure. The most pronounced difference is that the present church has a spire rather than a tower.

The earlier church of St. Nicholas was repaired extensively over the centuries and in 1841, its eastern end was shortened to allow for the widening of Claypath. However, in 1857, the church was demolished altogether. If its loss was lamented it was not for long. The new church built in 1857 by J. B. Pritchett of Darlington was described in the *Illustrated London News* as 'the most beautiful specimen of church architecture in the North of England'.

The southern face of the original church looked out onto the Market Place, and just in front there was a walled

Historic view of Durham Market Place pictured here on an old postcard. Notice the ornate pant or fountain upon which stands the statue of King Neptune (MR)

graveyard. The graveyard aroused concerns over health and was later covered over with flag stones.

Drawing circa 1830 showing the piazza near St. Nicholas Church. New Place can be seen just to the left of the church and Neptune can be seen in the foreground

The area in front of the church was also once the site of a piazza – a kind of covered market of nine arches built in 1780. The piazza was built partly with material from an earlier arched market cross and stones from a tollbooth that had stood in the Market Place near Saddler Street.

The north wall of St. Nicholas' church faced out towards Claypath bank and was described as a wall of great strength and height and this is a feature emulated in the present church. The wall was in effect part of the city wall and continued across Claypath in the form of an archway called Clayport Gate where Claypath joined the Market Place. Unfortunately the gate was an obstruction to traffic and was removed along with shops and neighbouring houses in 1791.

At the other end of the church, on the west side of the Market Place, stood a massive stone house built for the powerful Neville family in the early 1500s. Known as New

Place, or Bull's Head, from the Neville crest, it stood alongside the Guildhall of 1535 that was rebuilt in 1665.

New Place was confiscated from the Nevilles following their part in a Catholic rising in 1569 and in subsequent centuries, large parts of the building were occupied by Durham's carpet and weaving business. During the 1700s and early 1800s other parts were occupied by the Blue Coat School and the St. Nicholas parochial workhouse.

Parts of New Place were still standing in the mid-nineteenth century when a regular butchers' market was held in the courtyard of the house.

In the 1850s, it was decided that the old church, market piazza and Guildhall were no longer suitable to the needs of the city and that they should, along with New Place, be demolished. In their place were built a new Town Hall, indoor markets and the Market Tavern. These were constructed by Philip Charles Hardwick between 1849 and 1851 and were followed by Pritchett's new church in 1857.

Durham Town Hall is one of the most historic and least visited buildings in Durham City and consists of three rooms. These are the historic Guildhall, the beautiful adjoining room called the Mayor's Chamber and the more familiar, but equally impressive Main Hall to the rear.

Durham's Guildhall is the part of the town hall with the balcony outside and is the oldest part of the whole building. It has medieval roots, and was first built in 1356 during the reign of Edward III. Largely rebuilt by Bishop Tunstall in 1535 it was damaged during a Scottish occupation of the city about 1640. In 1665 the hall was rebuilt by Bishop Cosin.

Further refacing and rebuilding took place in the 1750s but there is no doubting the Guildhall's antiquity. Durham's trade guilds, of which there were once 16, met

at the Guildhall long before the city appointed its first mayor in 1602. Records of the weavers guild, (officially the oldest known guild in the city, but now defunct) stretch back to 1450. It is thought that some guilds were at least a century older.

The Guildhall Balcony (DS)

Guild members called 'freemen' earned their rank through patrimony and seven years of servitude. Sons inherited the privilege from fathers, while apprentices earned their rights through years of hard work and dedication to their appointed trade.

Inside the Guildhall (DS)

Guilds in Durham ultimately owed their powers to charters confirmed by various Bishops of Durham. The guild members endeavoured to maintain high standards and strived to protect themselves from competition through a strict preservation of their monopoly. One of the harshest rules was that no Scot could be employed by the guilds. It was a vestige of the Border troubles that long ravaged Northumberland and Durham.

The members had certain ceremonial duties enforced by the Bishop with fines. Most notable was the participation in the feast of Corpus Christi. On this day (the Thursday after Trinity Sunday) guild members paraded in a procession from St. Nicholas Church to Palace Green with their banners held high. The spectacle, which moved after 1660 to Oak Apple Day (29 May) probably had a striking resemblance to the miners' gala of more recent times.

Brass measures in the Guildhall (DS)

At Palace Green, guild members were greeted by the Prior and monks of Durham and were expected to perform a religious play. Each guild had its own particular play but unfortunately none of the Durham plays survive. Similar plays performed by guilds at York are known. They were religious in theme, but often incorporate comic or bawdy elements.

Durham received its city charters in 1179, 1565, 1602 and 1685, and it was the third of these charters that introduced the office of mayor. Guild members called aldermen played an important role in the mayor's election. Their political influence was further enhanced when Durham received its first elected Members of Parliament in 1672. The Freemen were the only electors.

Legislation like the Reform Act of 1832 and Municipal Corporations Act of 1835 gradually reduced the political and trading privileges of guilds in Durham and other cities but eight guilds with a ceremonial role still exist in the city today. Durham's surviving guilds are the Barbers, Butchers, Cordwainers, Curriers, Drapers, Joiners, Masons and Plumbers.

The freemen of the guilds retain privileges like the right of herbage on the Sands, a right to hold meetings in the Guildhall and a right to erect a stall in the market free of charge. It is worth noting that since 1885 Durham has also introduced honorary freemen who are appointed by the Mayor and Council. Famous holders of this honour have included Archbishop Desmond Tutu and General Montgomery.

Inside, the Guildhall does not have the same grandeur as the mayor's chamber or main hall but it has an impressive oak roof and displays historic items associated with the city's civic history.

Corpus Christi procession depicted in Town Hall window (DS)

The Mayor's Chamber (DS)

The crests of various guilds are displayed around the walls and near the balcony window is a large wooden sea chest of the 1600s that is said to have belonged to Nathaniel Crewe, a Bishop of Durham. Around the room, items displayed in cases include a copy of the city's charter of 1179 and a confirmation from the pope. A glass case includes a set of brass measures that set the standard by which merchants in the market measured their produce. These include old corn measures like a bushel, half bushel, a peck, a gill and a half gill.

Another glass case displays various items of silver, mostly from the 1700s, much of which was associated with the trade guilds. This particular case occupies a doorway that was once linked to a prison cell below. It was useful for bringing offenders swiftly into the Guildhall as the building served as a magistrates court until December 1964 when the present court opened in Elvet. The prison cell dating to 1848 was associated with the city's police station that was once located here.

The most impressive displays in the Guildhall are undoubtedly the various ceremonial items hanging on the wall that are associated with the mayor and his band

of bodyguards. Durham has the only English mayor outside London with an appointed band of bodyguards. Items inside the Guildhall associated with the mayor and his bodyguard include the city's ceremonial sword and mace as well as several rather lethal looking pikes.

The walls of the mayor's chamber, tucked behind the Guildhall are surrounded by oak pannelling upon which hang the portraits of former mayors and dignitaries. Dating from the 1500s the chamber was once a stone walled room, but the pannelling was added in 1752 by George Bowes who raised the room's height by three feet.

Bowes became mayor the following year but had also been mayor back in 1738. He belonged to the well known County Durham family whose recent members have included the late Queen Mother.

A painted relief of the Bowes coat of arms can be seen incorporated in pannelling at one end of the room near the fireplace. It is easily identified by three red longbows symbolising the family name.

The Mayor's Chamber is a fairly intimate part of the Town Hall and holds up to 50 people mostly for council committee meetings presided over by the chairman.

There are several portraits of mayors in the chamber including Robert Wharton (1690-1752) who was Mayor in 1736. He lived at Old Park near Spennymoor but his family purchased Dryburn Park near Framwellgate Moor in 1760. The Whartons built the city's Dryburn Hall in the 1850s and another family member gave part of the land to the city of Durham as a park. We know it today as Wharton Park.

Another portrait of interest is that of the Seventh Marquess of Londonderry, a descendant of the Third Marquess whose statue stands on horseback outside the

Town Hall. It was the Seventh Marquess who invited the leading Nazi, Joachim Ribbentrop to his inauguration ceremony at Durham Cathedral when the marquess was appointed mayor in 1936. This led to a rather embarrassing incident for the new mayor. The German national anthem was played on the cathedral organ as a form of greeting to Ribbentrop who stood to give the Nazi salute. He was swiftly discouraged by Londonderry.

Apart from portraits, the other major feature of interest in the chamber is the wonderful wooden fireplace of the early 1600s. It formerly stood within the coaching inn and mail stop called the Red Lion that stood in the Durham Bailey. Later called Hatfield Hall, this building was sold by its owner Walter Scruton, a Deputy Clerk of the Peace, to the University of Durham in 1846 and is now Hatfield College.

Detail of fireplace in Mayor's Chamber (DS)

Scruton sold the fireplace separately, to the City of Durham Corporation. Three intricate wooden figures, seemingly of a king, a knight and a man with a scroll are carved into the fireplace and in between them are portraits of King Charles I and his Queen, Henrietta Maria.

The portraits were allegedly painted by Van Dyck so Scruton kept them as family heirlooms which they remained until they were bought by the city in 1865 after Scruton's death. Although the paintings date from the 1600s they are actually copies of the originals found in America and London.

Other interesting paintings of note in the chamber include a portrait of Lord Crewe who was a Bishop of Durham from 1674-1721. His coat of arms can be seen above the door.

A portrait of King William of Orange hangs nearby and experts believe the king's head was painted by a different artist to the rest of the body. The reason for this, though possibly political, is unknown.

Alongside the meeting table half way along the room hangs a large bell and a coat of arms with the emblem of a foot. The bell looks like it is there to keep order at heated council meetings but is in fact from the destroyer HMS Witherington, a ship adopted by the City of Durham during the war in 1942. When the ship was broken up, its bell and arms were recovered and displayed here in the chamber.

Before 1849 the Guildhall and chamber served as Durham Town Hall, but the Mayor, William Henderson, wanted something bigger and better. In the nineteenth century towns across Britain were building enormous town halls as striking symbols of their emerging civic pride and Durham did not want to be left behind. At the suggestion of Henderson, the citizens of Durham

subscribed to the erection of a brand new building alongside the existing Guildhall.

Inside the main hall of Durham Town Hall (DS)

Thankfully, Durham's Town Hall, although impressive in its own way, was not built in the ostentatious scale of a typical Victorian town hall. The result was something far more subtle, 'for a Victorian civic building, nicely humble', wrote the architectural historian Nikolaus Pevsner.

It was William Henderson, Mayor of Durham and owner of the city's carpet factory that set in motion the building of the new Town Hall adjoining the Guildhall. He employed the influential London architect Philip Charles Hardwick who constructed the new building along with the markets and tavern between 1849 and 1851.

We can reach the interior of the main hall through an entrance foyer and corridor. It is here that we find the portrait, statue and artefacts of the 3ft 3inch Polish Count, Joseph Boruwlaski (1739-1837).

At the end of the corridor we get our first glimpse of the 72 feet long main hall with its impressive pannelling and stained glass windows. Upon entering the hall we can see just to our left a huge portrait of a young man examining some plans. This is William Henderson and the plans are those for the Town Hall.

However, the first thing we should admire in the hall is the solid wooden roof approximately 56 feet above the floor. It appears remarkably medieval but it is quite dark up there so we should give our eyes time to adjust to the sight of 12 magnificent carved angels hovering at the end of the hammerbeams.

The hall's walls are adorned with extensive wooden pannelling upon which are mounted seemingly hundreds of wooden plaques. They give the names and years for each individual mayor dating back well over a hundred years. Other panels commemorate honorary freemen of the city and there are several coats of arms representing notable families, including dukes and earls from throughout the County of Durham.

As well as Henderson's portrait, paintings in the hall include a portrait of Sir Robert Peel. There is also a portrait of the actor Stephen Kemble (1758-1822) playing Hamlet. Kemble was manager of a theatre in

Saddler Street and this painting clearly depicts Kemble in his younger, slimmer days.

Window in Town Hall depicting Edward III at Durham (DS)

Close to Kemble's painting is a portrait of Robbie Burns, the Scottish poet, who has no obvious connection with Durham. It was donated to the City of Durham by Durham's Caledonian Society in 1859 to commemorate Burns' centenary.

A window in the hall dating from 1951 commemorates the Durham Light Infantry but it is the Great West Window of 1853 that is possibly the most striking feature of the hall. Its centrepiece depicts the city's guilds on their corpus christi procession along with another scene depicting King Edward III in the Market Place. He appears on horseback throwing coins to the city's populace as thanks for the recovery of a baggage train lost during his campaign against the Scots. A coin throwing

ceremony performed by new mayors of Durham from the Guildhall balcony may be an emulation of this. Around the four corners of the window are depicted the four bishops who gave the city its charters.

Mayors, aldermen, bailiffs and bishops have all played their part in the development of Durham City's government. In early times the bishop held sway, but power was gradually vested in an elected body headed initially by an alderman and later by a mayor.

Durham city government can be traced through a series of charters back to 1179 when the first known charter came into force. It was introduced by Bishop Pudsey but probably confirmed rights and privileges dating back to the city's foundation.

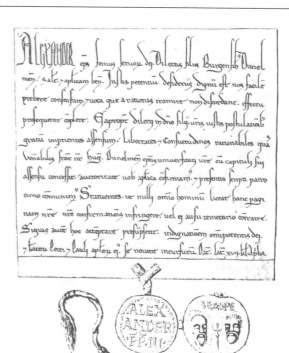

Left: Bishop Pudsey's City Charter of 1179. This is the first known charter of Durham City and shows the attached seal of the Bishop. The document is preserved in Durham County Record Office. Above: is the papal bull that confirmed Pudsey's Charter. It includes the seal of pope Alexander III. City charters would follow in 1565, 1602 and 1685

Pudsey's charter applied to the Bishop's Borough in and around the Market Place and the separate Borough of Framwellgate across the river. It was concerned with trade and granted the citizens freedom from certain tolls and taxes.

Pudsey's charter survives in Durham County Records Office and is one of the oldest city charters in the country. It is more remarkable for receiving a papal bull, in which Pope

Alexander III confirmed the charter and its privileges. Beverley is the only other place in England known to have received a papal confirmation of its charter.

In those days the Bishop of Durham governed the city and appointed a bailiff and marshall to undertake his work. These men enforced payment of duties and tolls, guarded against fraud and raised money for the repair and maintenance of the city's walls.

The dominance of the bishops in the city changed only slightly when Durham received its next charter in 1565, from James Pilkington, Durham's first Protestant bishop. This charter united the Boroughs of Durham and Framwellgate and established a governing body or corporation that was arguably the first step towards the council of today.

The body consisted of 12 senior merchants headed by an alderman, with the first being Christopher Surtees. The 12 merchants elected a further 12 members and each year the whole 24 elected an alderman as leader.

Members were granted the right to establish certain laws, permission to hold a weekly market and three annual fairs. Pilkington's charter aimed to improve commercial development but made it clear that the bishop could veto any appointments or decisions if he wished to do so.

The charter of Bishop Toby Matthew in 1602 was less restrictive and introduced the office of mayor. A body of 36 corporation members elected each mayor from one of 12 lifetime aldermen who numbered amongst their members. The remaining 24 men were common councillors from the ranks of the trade guilds and were appointed by the aldermen.

Durham's first mayor was Hugh Wright, whose name appears as mayor in 1614, 1623 and 1632. Because these early mayors were appointed from such a select

band certain family names like Walton, Wright, Hall, Wanless, Hutchinson, Pattinson and Heighington regularly appear in the list of mayors.

The Durham City Seal of 1606

The issuing of borough charters in the County Palatine of Durham was a key privilege of the Prince Bishops, but for some reason, King James I decided to issue a royal confirmation of Bishop Matthew's charter in 1606. A new Bishop of Durham called William James was appointed in that year and it is probable that the city's government had persuaded the King to issue the confirmation.

It was seen as a significant event and Matthew Pattinson, (the son or brother of a Durham aldermen) issued a new city seal to mark the occasion almost as if it marked the rebirth of the city. The king's involvement was effectively an insult to the Bishop and the Durham historian

William Hutchinson writing in the late eighteenth century described it as 'a scab on the constitution of the privileges of the palatinate'.

Bishop James was determined to retain his powers and came into conflict with the corporation over the collection of tolls. Toll collecting was centred upon a tollbooth in the market place near Saddler Street. It was a building that included shop stalls at ground floor and a borough court upstairs where fines were enforced. Bishop James believed his bailiff should preside over this court, but the charter of 1602 said it was the Mayor's job.

Things reached a head in 1609 when a new mayor, Edward Wanless was appointed. Edward Hutton, the Bishop's bailiff and his steward John Richardson took up seats in the courtroom and attempted to open the court in the bishop's name. Six of the aldermen promptly dragged them from the court into the market place where boisterous locals called for them to be placed in the stocks or ducked in the fountain. The two men managed to get away and escape further indignity.

The angry Bishop began a suit against the aldermen in regard to his authority over the court and a hearing in London in 1610 found in the Bishop's favour. It was a remarkable outcome because the charter seemed to give the aldermen a very solid case.

The London hearing virtually denied the customs and privileges of the 1602 charter and tensions naturally continued to boil between the bishop and the city. Resolution came, quite dramatically, from King James himself when he visited the city in April 1617.

At Elvet Bridge the King was greeted on horseback by the Mayor, George Walton who read a carefully worded statement asserting the rights of the city as confirmed by the King. In the Market Place a young apprentice also recited a hastily written verse in a further plea for recognition of the city's privileges.

The King made no comment but continued towards Palace Green where he spent a number of days in the company of the Bishop. Here the King severely reprimanded the prelate. For the Bishop the toll dispute had finally 'taken its toll'. So shaken was he by the King's strong words, that he fell ill and died three weeks later. There were riots in the city on the night of the Bishop's burial, but for Durham's democracy, there were many changes yet to come.

The Prince Bishops continued to control the government of Durham City up until the early decades of the nineteenth century. It was true that city charters in 1565 and 1602 gave significant powers to the guildsmen but it was the bishops who issued the charters and they set the rules.

When the monarchy was overthrown by Oliver Cromwell in the 1640s things changed for a while. The Bishop lost control of the city's affairs and the Mayor and corporation could exercise their privileges independently. It was during this brief period, that the corporation petitioned Cromwell for the establishment of a university in the city. The plan came to nothing despite Cromwell's support.

The Bishop regained control of the city's affairs in 1660 and Durham was once again administered under the terms of the 1602 charter. A new charter issued in 1684 by Bishop Crewe was abandoned owing to a legal technicality concerning the surrender of the previous charter.

We have noted that Durham's government was drawn exclusively from the freemen of the trade guilds who were elected through patrimony and apprenticeship. Over time it became obvious that some corporation members gained election through illicit practices that did not obey the rules.

In 1728, a by-law was passed to prevent such abuses but on 2 November, 1761 the corporation repealed the law in line with their own interests. The members wanted to influence the outcome of a parliamentary election in the city following the death of the city's MP, Henry Lambton.

The city freemen had exclusive voting rights for electing the MP and the corporation immediately swore in 264 new freemen to influence the vote. Some 215 were eligible and they secured the election of the corporation's favoured candidate, Major Ralph Gowland.

The Civic Sword (DS)

Gowland was elected with 775 votes including 215 from the new freemen. Gowland's opponent, Major John Lambton received 752 votes and was quite naturally, furious. He petitioned the House of Commons and in 1762 they found in Lambton's favour. Lambton was duly elected in Gowland's place.

In the 1760s, irregularities, deaths, resignations and refusals of duty, threw the council into turmoil. Technically there weren't enough members to elect a mayor under the terms of the charter, and it raised doubts about the corporation's legality.

A new charter was requested from Bishop Trevor in 1780 but he died that year and the task was taken up by Bishop Egerton who produced the city's very last charter. It was issued in an official ceremony at Durham Castle on 2 October, 1780.

There were no further charters but the Municipal Corporations Act of 1835 brought the next major change to Durham city's government. It took away the bishop's powers once and for all, and removed the dominating influence of the trade guilds. Everyday citizens of the city could now be elected as common councillors.

Durham was divided into wards and elected representatives from each ward governed the city under the leadership of a mayor.

Today Durham still has a mayor, but since 1974, the old city boundaries have ceased to exist and the mayors no longer lead the council as they did in the past.

Durham's mayors still have an important civic status and the Right Worshipful Mayor, though not a Lord Mayor claims a precedence fifth in rank behind the Mayors of London, York, Belfast and Cardiff.

Though Durham's modern mayors are elected councillors, the activities associated with the office of mayor are largely ceremonial, with a strong charitable emphasis.

Most of the ceremonial features associated with the mayor, though rooted in the distant past, often only date to the nineteenth century. It is notable that portraits of old mayors suggest that the mayors did not wear a chain of office before the 1850s. Similarly the city's beautiful civic sword, dating from 1913 superseded an earlier sword that only dated to 1895.

The city's sword plays a role in civic processions involving the mayor. Such processions are headed by a billet master, sword bearer and mace bearer followed by the mayor himself. The city mace can be seen along with the two swords in Durham Guildhall. It includes four silver bands representing the charters of the city.

The collection of rather lethal looking pikes displayed in the Guildhall are also utilised in civic processions and are held by members of one of the more unusual institutions associated with the Mayor of Durham.

Here I refer to the band of 13 men who are officially the Mayor's Bodyguard. In fact Durham is the only mayor in England outside London to have his or her own bodyguard. One member of the bodyguard serves as captain in the civic processions, but the mace bearer, sword bearer and billet master are not part of the bodyguard.

The institution of Bodyguard dates back to the thirteenth century when a band of men were employed to ensure that the civic work of the Bishop in the city was carried out without hindrance and that the city was protected from marauders.

After the charter of 1602 the bodyguard became attached to the office of Mayor. Their fearsome reputation has depleted since the nineteenth century as it was at that time that they began to wear the long black Tudor style cloaks with the city crest on their breast and the beefeater hats.

Market Place Statues

The two most prominent features of Durham Market Place undoubtedly are the statues that stand near its centre. One is of a man on a horse and the other is of King Neptune. Despite its modern plinth, the statue of Neptune has the longest history and it is worth recording its interesting adventures.

Suffering from a broken spine, damaged limbs and a missing right leg below the knee, Neptune had endured many years of neglect when he was finally transported to Telford, in Shropshire, for emergency repairs in March 1984. He had been the gift of George Bowes MP, who presented the statue to the City of Durham way back in 1729. For 194 years he stood proudly on a succession of ornate pedestals in Durham Market Place.

A fountain beneath the statue provided water to the people of Durham and it was pumped across from a well at Crook Hall on the other side of the river. However Neptune symbolised more ambitious plans than the supply of drinking water.

In 1720 it was proposed that Durham could be made into a sea port by digging a canal north to join the River Team, a tributary of the River Tyne near Gateshead. Nothing came of this plan, but Neptune was a constant reminder of Durham's maritime possibilities. The thought of ships docking at the Sands or Millburngate remained fresh in the minds of Durham businessmen.

In 1759, a new proposal hoped to make the Wear navigable from Durham to Sunderland by altering the river's course, but the increasing size of ships made this impractical. Neptune is all that remains of Durham's dockside dream, but it is only due to the foresight and determination of conservationists that he survives at all.

Durham Market Place showing the Guildhall and the two statues (DS)

Neptune as he appeared in 1869

Neptune stood in the Market Place from 1729 until 1923, and by that time had increasingly become a hazard to traffic. To ease the flow, he was reluctantly removed to Wharton Park and within a few years his old Market Place home came to be the site of a traffic control box.

For decades Neptune was largely neglected and forgotten and fell into disrepair. A victim of vandalism, he had to be supported on metal crutches and became a very sorry sight indeed. Neptune's predicament was discussed in the 1970s, but the final crunch came, quite literally, in 1979, when he was struck by lightning and suffered severe damage. He was stored temporarily in a garage at Brandon while funds were raised for his repair. Only his leg and an adjoining dolphin ventured out to attend a fundraising event at Brancepeth Castle in 1983.

After full restoration in Shropshire, Neptune returned to Durham in October 1986, lodging for a short while in the town hall foyer, before removal to a shop window in Claypath. Discussions ensued about where Neptune should be located, with at least 10 sites suggested.

For a time the Magdalene Steps, in Saddler Street, were the favoured location, but in May 1991 Neptune returned to his rightful home in Durham Market Place, only yards from where he had first been sited 262 years earlier. The total cost for his restoration was £10,000, with an additional £15,000 paid towards a large sandstone plinth.

It is surprising that when Neptune's statue was removed from Durham Market Place in 1923 that the statue of the Marquess of Londonderry wasn't taken with him. This statue, 'the man on the horse', though not as old as Neptune, arrived in 1861 and became an equally imposing feature of the Market Place.

'Who is that guy?' ask visiting Americans, believing the horseman to be some kind of city father. The man on the horse is however a symbol of County rather than City. He is Charles, William Vane Stewart (1778-1854), the third Marquess of Londonderry, a man with ancestral links to the old monarchs of Scotland.

The sculptor was an English-based Italian artist from Milan, called Raphael Monti (1818-1881) who utilised a remarkable new technique in his monument to the Marquess. The Galvano-Plastic or electroplating process involved embedding an electroplated copper covering on to a plaster base. The corroded copper gives the statue its green appearance.

According to legend, Monti boasted that he would reward anyone who could find fault with his masterpiece. Many rose to the challenge, but no fault was found,

until, it is said, a visiting blind man was granted permission to inspect the statue. Hoisted up to the head of the horse, the man inspected it carefully with his hands before announcing to the astonished crowd that he had found a fault. The horse, apparently, had no tongue. It is said that the sculptor was so devastated that he committed suicide. However, this well-known legend does not seem to be true and the horse does appear to have a tongue.

Like many historic figures commemorated in stone, the third Marquess was a military hero. Born in Dublin in 1778 and educated at Eton, he was a Major by the age of 17. A great cavalryman, in 1808, he led the Hussar Brigade and was Adjutant General to the Duke of Wellington. He fought in successful campaigns in Belgium, Holland, Portugal and Spain and was active as a diplomat in an age when Napoleon was a constant threat to European peace.

Statue of the Third Marquess of Londonderry (DS)

The Marquess inherited his title after the suicide of his famous older half-brother, Robert Stewart, Viscount Castlereagh (1769-1822), who was the second Marquess of Londonderry. Castlereagh was British Foreign Secretary and Leader of the House of Commons and like his younger brother, a successful soldier. Castlereagh had no direct link with Durham and the connection between the third Marquess and Durham only arose from his marriage in 1819 to Frances Anne-Vane Tempest, an heiress to estates in Durham and Ireland. The Marquess took his wife's name, Vane, as part of his own.

The Vane estates in Durham included Long Newton village (where the Marquess is buried), and Wynyard Hall, both near the outskirts of Stockton-on-Tees.

However, it is the town of Seaham Harbour with which the Marquess is principally associated. After his retirement from military matters, he invested much time and money in the development of coal mines and railways in eastern Durham. In Sunderland he entered into negotiations with the River Wear Commissioners to obtain certain exclusive rights to the river for exporting coal. He was refused and rather angrily proclaimed he would 'see grass grow in the streets of Sunderland'.

By 1828, he built a substantial port of his own called Seaham Harbour, to rival Sunderland, and although this did not bring an end to Sunderland's economic prosperity it proved a successful venture.

Unfortunately, his activities as a coal owner did not endear him to the miners. Very much the aristocratic businessman of his time, the Marquess opposed all reform, banned inspections of his mines, opposed trade unions, broke Durham coal strikes with imported Irishmen or Cornish tin miners and objected to the raising of the school leaving age to 12, since many young boys were employed in his mines.

One of the staunchest Tories of his age, the Marquess had friends among the gentry. When he died in 1854 his widow set up a subscription committee for the building of a statue to commemorate his life. A total of £2,000 was raised and it was decided that a double life-size equestrian statue should be built. A number of County Durham towns were considered for its location, including Seaham Harbour and Sunderland but Durham was eventually chosen. However, when the council in the city realised how big the statue was going to be, it panicked and unsuccessfully attempted to persuade the university to erect it on Palace Green instead.

Five local tradesman also objected and filed a lawsuit against the siting of the statue, believing that it would restrict free passage into the Market Place. They failed in their suit, but the statue almost did not arrive at all. The sculptor, Monti went bankrupt and his creditors seized the statue, forcing the widow of the Marquess to pay a further £1,000 for its release. It was eventually unveiled on 2 December, 1861 hailed by the rifle volunteers of Sunderland, Seaham and Durham City. It has remained in the Market Place ever since, but had to undergo major repairs 90 years later, in 1951. It was absent from the city centre throughout that year.

When the statue returned home in 1952, a plaque was added to the plinth, unveiled by the eighth Marquess. The 'Man on the Horse' would have to wait a further 39 years before his old colleague, King Neptune returned to keep him company on the other side of the Market Place.

The statues do not cause traffic difficulties today because the flow of cars into the Market Place is very small compared with what is once was. The reduction in traffic is largely due to the building of new through roads in the 1960s and 1970s and the Market Place is now bypassed by traffic on Millburngate and New Elvet Bridge. In more recent times

the introduction of a toll gate at the entrance to the Market Place has further reduced the chaos.

Traffic in the City

Durham's narrow, medieval streets were not built for modern traffic. The city was chosen as the site for a cathedral and castle precisely because it was so naturally well-defended and difficult to access.

Only the narrow neck of Durham's river peninsula could be entered without crossing the steep gorge of the river. It is here, on the peninsula neck, that the long, descending street of Claypath enters the city's Market Place. As the threat of Scottish invasion subsided, improving traffic access became increasingly important and over time alterations were made that were sometimes detrimental to the city's appearance.

One of the first significant steps took place way back in 1820 with the removal of a huge and wonderful medieval structure called the Great North Gate. Its removal was designed to ease the movement of carriages along Saddler Street but a century later it was not enough to ease the flow of motor traffic.

The second market place police box (MR)

For most of the twentieth century, as car ownership increased, Durham thronged with traffic. The ancient bridges of Elvet and Framwellgate along with Saddler Street, Silver Street and the Market Place were choked with lorries, buses and cars. So, in 1932, the police box appeared for the first time. It was initially a small, domed, cylindrical, windowed structure, located on the western side of the Market Place close to where the statue of Neptune had once stood.

The police box was designed to house a traffic policeman responsible for controlling traffic in and out of Durham's city centre. He assessed the volume of traffic approaching the Market Place from three directions. He could clearly see traffic in Claypath to the east, but could only guess the volume of traffic on the medieval bridges to the north and south. Here signals were under his control, but out of his sight.

A new rectangular police box with a sloping roof was erected in December 1957 and special cameras attached to poles were erected near the bridges. They were linked to TV monitors in the new box where the traffic policeman sat. This pioneering system proved successful and remained in use until November 1975. By that time, two new concrete traffic bridges called New Elvet Bridge (1975) and Millburngate Bridge (1967) had been built. These new bridges bypassed the Market Place and relieved the older bridges and medieval streets of their chaotic traffic.

When the new bridges and associated roads were proposed back in 1960, it was hoped they would create new sites for shops, car parks and office buildings. Developments included a new shopping centre on the Millburngate side of the river, but the contract for this was not awarded until 1971. Unfortunately, the traffic scheme initially resulted in more demolition than development as new roads and roundabouts were built to serve the bridges.

The new roads included the A690 dual carriageway which bypassed Claypath and Gilesgate. The eastern section of this road follows a former railway line and the western part called Leazes Road was built in what was mostly undeveloped riverside land. The two sections of the A690 were joined at a new roundabout that sliced the ancient street of Gilesgate into two parts near the College of St. Hild and St. Bede. Many properties in the street were demolished.

The Great North Gate between Saddler Street and the North Bailey was a major obstruction to traffic

Back in the heart of the city centre the volume of traffic in the Market Place was considerably reduced but the appearance of the Market Place underwent a major change. Just outside the Market Place an underpass road was built beneath the adjoining street of Claypath. It required the destruction of several Claypath shops and houses. This particular demolition destroyed the enclosed nature of the Market Place on its eastern side leaving it hanging on the edge of a busy through road. The little nearby street called Walkergate leading down to the river between St. Nicholas church and Claypath was totally obliterated.

Just across the river on the northern side of the new Millburngate Bridge, another roundabout was built along with another new road that followed the course of the ancient streets of Framwellgate and Framwellgate Peth near St. Godric's Church. A pedestrian bridge had to be built across part of this busy road to reach the city's railway station. Throughout the city, the road developments of the 1960s and 70s affected about 150 houses, 19 businesses and 21 public buildings. Many well-known Durham landmarks were demolished including the Tanners Arms and Blagdon's Leather Works in Framwellgate and the Palace Theatre in Walkergate.

Of course Durham Market Place, Silver Street, Saddler Street and the area around the cathedral in the historic core of the city experienced the benefits of the new road system and became much safer places to walk and explore.

Elvet and Framwellgate Bridges are no longer open to traffic except for deliveries and the Market Place and adjoining streets have become increasingly pedestrianised. In October 2002, a toll was introduced to Durham Market Place to reduce the number of vehicles entering the peninsula towards the cathedral. Although controversial, this scheme was almost as innovative as the traffic box of 1957 and is the latest in a long-running series of attempts to solve the city's age-old traffic problem.

Silver Street and Saddler Street

Durham Market Place is joined on its western side by Silver Street and on the south side by Saddler Street. They are two of three medieval streets in the city called 'streets' rather than 'gates'. The other is South Street just outside the peninsula area. The name Silver Street is sometimes said to be a reference to some kind of mint that existed here but this is unlikely and it is most likely connected with trade. There has been a street here since medieval times and one building (number 11) has timber framing dating back to the fifteenth century. Interestingly the lower part of the street that joins Framwellgate Bridge was once called Smithgate and is reputedly where the city's medieval blacksmiths resided.

In times gone by Silver Street was the main route in and out of the city to the north and this narrow street thronged with carts and horses and people. There were a number of coaching inns in the street catering for travellers including one large inn called the Rose and Crown where Woolworths now stands.

On the north side of Silver Street is the Post Office, at number 33 that moved here from Claypath. It is on the site of a Victorian Primitive Methodist Chapel that stood here from 1825-1862. Nearby number 39 was once the home (demolished in the 1960s) of a famous Durham character called John Duck, known as Durham's Dick Whittington. Duck was born at Kilton on the Cleveland coast and came to Durham in 1655 with the intention of becoming a Butcher's apprentice.

Every Durham butcher, except one refused to employ Duck because he couldn't prove his birthplace. There was a suspicion that he might be a Scot and the employment of such was forbidden by the Butcher's Guild. It was a butcher called Hislop who defied the rule and took on Duck as his apprentice. Duck went on to marry the

butcher's daughter but eventually the guild forced Hislop to dismiss his son-in-law. As Duck wandered the river banks pondering his predicament, a raven dropped a coin of gold at his feet. It was in the words of the Durham historian, Surtees 'the mother of a dozen more' as with this gold coin John Duck went on to make his fortune.

A Victorian illustration showing a narrow and very busy Silver Street

Exactly how Duck acquired wealth is not clear and it is uncertain whether the story of the raven is true. It is possible that Duck may have been crooked in some way

but there is no evidence to prove this except that on one occasion he bought cattle from a livestock thief. Duck eventually set up his own butcher's business and gradually became a man of great wealth and influence in the city. Remarkably, in 1680 he became Mayor of Durham and ultimately became a baronet as Sir John Duck of Haswell on the Hill where he owned an estate to the east of the city. Duck retired to a mansion he built at West Rainton and died in 1691 aged 59.

Saddler Street which joins the south side of the Market Place was historically called Saddlergate. In its upper sections where the Great North Gate once stood it becomes the South Bailey but not before a short street called Owengate leads off towards Palace Green and the Cathedral. Archaeological excavations in Saddler Street have revealed that there were wooden houses here as far back as about AD 1000 and show that there were shoemakers, cobblers, wooden bowl turners, butchers and fishmongers in the street. These would have been some of the earliest tradesman to occupy the city.

The lower part of Saddler Street near the Market Place was originally called Fleshergate or Flesh-Hewer-Rawe. Here the Butchers' shambles were situated in times gone by and animals were once slaughtered in the street much to the disapproval of visitors to the city.

Saddler Street began further up where Fleshergate splits into two at the Magdalen Steps. Saddler Street is the street on the right while the street on the left leading down towards Elvet Bridge was Souter Peth – the 'shoemakers' street'. In the eighteenth century Saddler Street was famed for its theatre, covered elsewhere in this book, and in the nineteenth century was home to the city's two Victorian newspapers. One was the liberal-conservative *Durham Advertiser* established by Francis Humble in 1814 and situated at 47 Saddler Street (later 64). The other was the more liberal, *Durham Chronicle* established by John Ambrose Williams in 1820 with the encouragement of John Lambton, the Earl of Durham. The *Durham Chronicle* was later published by John Harding Veitch.

Today Saddler Street is primarily noted for its shops. One of the most notable is a clothes shop distinguished by a teapot hanging from its wall. This well-travelled emblem has been situated on previous occasions in Claypath, the Market Place and Gilesgate.

The Saddler Street shop with the teapot was once The House of Andrews, bookshop and stationery business. It was founded in 1808 at a nearby site by George Andrews, the son of a Durham draper. Early customers included William Van Mildert, the last Prince Bishop of Durham. The shop had an important place as a cultural institution in the city. In 1816 it published Robert Surtees' famous four-volume *History of Durham*, a publication that is still regarded as the classic history of the county.

Mr Andrews owned the business until his death in 1832 and his son, who was also called George, succeeded him in the year that Durham University was founded. Andrews soon became the university's official bookseller. George Andrews junior died in 1861 but the business remained under the proprietorship of the family until 1895. In that year, Warneford Smart acquired the business and moved premises.

Andrews' business moved from 64 Saddler Street to number 74 that was formerly the premises of Ainsley the printer and mustard maker. Mr Smart, the new proprietor of Andrews' business was an old acquaintance of the Sherlock Holmes author Sir Arthur Conan Doyle. He remained proprietor of the Andrews shop until retirement in 1963. Two years later he died at the age of one hundred.

Changes were made to the shop in 1963 when four young businessmen bought the outlet. Calling it the 'House of Andrews', they sold records, paperbacks, sheet music and stationery and even added a restaurant. Sadly, the House of Andrews ceased trading in 1980 and has housed a number of different retail outlets since that time.

Durham Mustard

According to an old saying Durham City was famed for seven things: 'wood, water and pleasant walks, law, gospel, old maids and mustard'. This saying probably originated in the eighteenth century when Durham's mustard achieved great fame. Both Saddler Street and Silver Street were associated with its manufacture.

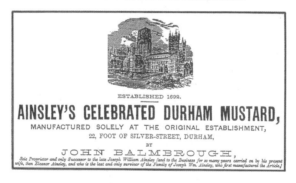

ESTABLISHED 1692.

AINSLEY'S CELEBRATED DURHAM MUSTARD,

MANUFACTURED SOLELY AT THE ORIGINAL ESTABLISHMENT, 22, FOOT OF SILVER-STREET, DURHAM,

BY

JOHN BALMBROUGH,

Sole Proprietor and only Successor to the late Joseph William Ainsley (and to the Business for so many years carried on by his present wife, then Eleanor Ainsley, and who is the last and only survivor of the Family of Joseph Wm. Ainsley, who first manufactured the Article.)

An advertisement for Balmborough's Ainsley's Mustard

Mustard was introduced into England in the twelfth century. In early times seeds were coarsely ground using a mortar and it was consumed in this rough state at the table. It was known in the North East by at least 1486 when monks on the Farne Islands (a monastic cell tied to Durham Cathedral) are known to have used quern stones in the grinding of 'mwstert'.

In those early days mustard was used primarily to disguise the flavour of rotten meat and it wasn't until the late

1600s that it came to be recommended in its own right. At that time, the town of Tewkesbury was primarily noted for mustard making, but in those days it was a much weaker substance and it was not until 1720 that a luxury English style of mustard resembling that which we know today really came into being.

English style mustard was born largely due to the vision and energy of a Durham City woman by the name of Mrs Clements, whose forename has, despite her remarkable achievements eluded all historians that have strived to tell her tale.

In the year 1720 Mrs Clements invented a new method for extracting the full flavour from mustard seed. Her methods were secretly guarded but involved grinding seeds in a mill and passing them through several processes used in the making of flour from wheat.

This resourceful woman soon recognised the potential of her new invention and travelled the country collecting orders for the substance. She regularly visited London where her product soon tickled the palate of none other than King George I. The King's liking for the mustard brought Mrs Clements numerous orders from those who wished to share in the tastes of the royal.

It is said that Mrs Clement's mustard mill was situated to the rear of a property in Saddler Street (the shop with the teapot outside) but this is not certain. Mustard seeds were certainly grown for Mrs Clements by local farms in the early days including Houghall Farm near Shincliffe. It must have been a lucrative trade because mustard crops worth up to £100 an acre were occasionally known. Mustard manufacture also stimulated other industries and it is known that a Gateshead pottery came to specialise in supplying pots for Durham's mustard export.

Durham Cathedral and Castle from Leazes Road (DS)

Durham Castle pictured from Gilesgate (DS)

Durham Castle Gateway (DS)

Durham Cathedral and Castle from the railway station (DS)

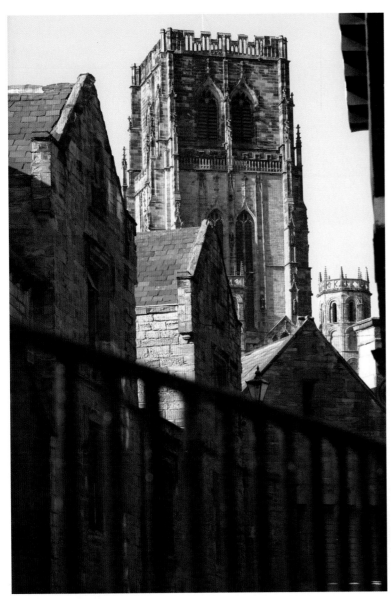

Durham Cathedral central tower pictured from Owengate (DS)

Close up of the Cathedral's central tower (DS)

Exterior view of the Rose Window (DS)

Framwellgate waterside (DS)

Framwellgate Bridge (DS)

Castle and Cathedral above the Market Place (DS)

Elvet Bridge (DS)

The Keep, Durham Castle (DS)

Durham Cathedral from Hild and Bede College (DS)

Durham Market Place (DS)

Statue of the Marquess of Londonderry, Durham Market Place (DS)

Durham Market Place viewed from St. Nicholas' Church (DS)

Statue of Neptune in Durham Market Place (DS)

Durham Cathedral from Frankland Lane (DS)

South End on the South Road (DS)

St. Mary's College, Durham University (DS)

In the eighteenth century the name of Durham became synonymous with mustard and in local slang Durham people were known as 'knock-kneed Durham men' from the alleged grinding of mustard between their knees.

Later in the century, rival mustard firms sprung up around the country including London where Messrs Keen and Sons manufactured the product from 1742, supplying it to taverns and chophouses. Though later acquired by Colmans of Norwich (who made mustard from 1814) the London firm is still remembered in the saying 'Keen as Mustard'. By 1810 the *London Journal* recorded that the once frowned upon condiment of 'mustard seed is now used and esteemed by most of the quality and gentry'. However by this time Durham had lost its mustard monopoly.

The Teapot, Saddler Street (DS)

Meanwhile, Mrs Clement's daughter who was heir to the family business married a local man called Joseph William Ainsley. The Ainsley family had been involved in Durham flour making since 1692.

The Ainsleys became the big name in Durham mustard making and their business was situated at the foot of

Silver Street at number 22. Perhaps this location was the original site of Durham's mustard manufactory. The Ainsley family history is not altogether clear but at the beginning of the nineteenth century the business passed into the hands of a son or grandson, also called Joseph William Ainsley, while another family member, possibly a brother, called John, worked at a flour mill at Crook Hall. This mill seems to have been involved in making mustard for the Silver Street premises.

Following Joseph Ainsley's death around 1830, his widow Eleanor carried on the business but later married John Balmborough who became the proprietor in the 1840s or 1850s. At around this time a new mustard business also opened in the city, this time in Saddler Street and was operated by William Ainsley who was I believe the son of the Crook Hall John.

Balmborough was clearly threatened by this rival firm and his advertisements were at great pains to emphasize that he was the true heir to the Ainsley name. William Ainsley, however was a successful entrepreneur noted for his printing and stationery business at number 1 Saddler Street.

After branching out into mustard William Ainsley moved to larger premises at number 74 that were later occupied by the relocated House of Andrews. A William Ainsley advertisement of 1865 only lists mustard as a footnote to a whole host of enterprises that included gunpowder making, but Ainsley's business must have affected Balmborough's trade.

By the early 1870s Saddler Street was too small for William Ainsley's business and he uprooted to Waddington Street in the northern part of the city. In 1874 he passed away and was succeeded by his sons William and John Ainsley who traded as William Ainsley and Brother.

Balmborough had also passed away during this period and his Silver Street business ceased to trade. A new Durham mustard business came into being in 1888 operated by John Simpson and James Willan initially in Providence Row and then later in Gilesgate's Station Lane but it barely lasted a decade.

Saddler Street (DS)

Simpson who died in 1908 concluded his years as a timekeeper at the city's gas company. William Ainsley passed away in 1896 and the Ainsley firm lasted only two or three years into the following century. Durham's mustard making concerns fell into the hands of Colmans, the Norwich firm most closely associated with mustard making today.

Silver Street (DS)

Chapter Four
Theatres and Cinemas

The eighteenth and nineteenth century was the peak period for theatre in Durham but the twentieth century witnessed the rise and fall of cinema. With the growth of tourism, the importance of cinema and theatre in Durham has increasingly been recognised, but Durham has often struggled to sustain the two enterprises.

During the last 40 years there were constant campaigns in Durham for a purpose-built theatre and this often coincided with similar campaigns for the preservation of cinema. It was not until 2000 that Durham finally received the purpose built professional theatre it had longed for with the opening of the Gala Theatre.

Sadly, in January 2003, the city's last cinema closed, bringing an end to one form of entertainment in the city just as another was re-emerging. Fortunately, the Gala Theatre incorporates a cinema meaning that the theatre is now the sole provider of the cinematic experience in the city.

The Gala was by no means the first theatre in Durham to also serve as a cinema. The Palace Theatre in Walkergate, the Palace of Varieties in Court Lane and the Assembly Rooms in the Bailey all once served this dual purpose.

Entrance to Drury Lane (DS)

Dramatic performances have taken place in Durham for many centuries and it is known, for example, that medieval mystery plays with a religious content were performed in the city in early times by the city's trade guilds.

No doubt travelling performers and showman visited the city from time to time, but the first mention of a purpose built theatre does not appear until the year 1722. In that year the *Newcastle Courant* mentioned 'a very handsome playhouse built for the reception of quality and gentry' in Durham City. Companies from cities like York, Newcastle and Edinburgh would come to perform at the theatre, booking the venue for specific performances in the years to come. In 1742, for example, it is known that a Newcastle theatre company performed the Beggars Opera in the Durham Theatre.

The theatre of 1722 was situated off Saddler Street, in Drury Lane. This is an alleyway or 'vennel' named in honour of London's theatreland. Durham's Drury Lane is clearly marked on a map of Durham published in 1754. It shows a long building trailing along the course of the lane down towards the river and this was almost certainly the city's first theatre.

Durham had a very small population for a city and it may have struggled to support a theatre even during the heyday of Georgian drama. Performing companies were keen to book the theatre in periods when they could be assured of a captive audience. Assize week or race meeting week in the city were especially popular choices. Horse racing, held on the former racecourse at Elvet could attract crowds of up to 80,000 people and it is known for example that during the race meeting of 1743, a company from Edinburgh booked the theatre for performances.

By 1746 the future of the Drury Lane theatre hung in the balance when it was merely mentioned in part of the sale of a dwelling house that belonged to a certain John Smith, a joiner who leased the property. Smith died in that year and the property came up for sale. It was simply described as a 'dwelling house with shop and stables, a cock-pit and playhouse with conveniences belonging thereto'. The history of the Durham theatre after this period is not certain until 1754 when a man called John Richardson acquired the old property and continued to operate it as a theatre.

In 1760, a new theatre opened in the city, in addition to that in Drury Lane. A theatrical company from Edinburgh established this new venue, which opened in Hallgarth Street in Elvet, but little else is known about this theatre or how long it operated. Whatever its fate, it certainly did not bring an end to Saddler Street's role as Durham's 'Theatreland'.

During the 1760s the Drury Lane Theatre experienced a boom period under the influence of a company of actors managed by a Mr Bates. In the third quarter of the eighteenth century Bates opened theatres across the region at Scarborough, Whitby, Stockton, Darlington, Sunderland and North Shields and with Durham they formed a circuit for performing plays.

Durham's Drury Lane theatre did not actually belong to Bates. The theatre's lease had been in the hands of John Richardson since 1754 and in 1771 Richardson closed it down to build a brand new theatre in the lane.

The new theatre opened with a production of a play called 'The West Indian', along with other entertainment in front of a genteel audience who 'expressed the greatest satisfaction at the elegance of the house and of the performance in general'. Contemporary plans suggest the theatre stood behind the shop now occupied by Oxfam adjacent to the lane.

The stage was situated down the bank at the river end of the lane with the dressing room located below the stage. The raked (inclined) auditorium followed the slope of the lane.

In 1782 a young relative of Bates called James Cawdell became a partner in Bates' company and took full control after Bates' retirement in 1787. The Durham Theatre remained part of Cawdell's circuit but it was in Richardson's possession until his death in 1785.

Unfortunately, after 1785 the new owner, Richardson's daughter Sarah, refused to renew the theatre lease. The

loss of the Durham Theatre was a great blow for Cawdell and a bitter dispute with Sarah ensued, but it was to no avail. All was not lost for Cawdell however, as he took great comfort from the popular support for a theatre that existed in the city at the time. With public support he set about building a new theatre all of his own.

The actor, Stephen Kemble in the role of Falstaff

Cawdell's theatre opened in March 1792 and was located on the opposite side of Saddler Street, behind the Lord Nelson Inn, a little to the south of the earlier venue. The Lord Nelson was later renamed the Shakespeare Tavern because of its theatrical connections and the pub still exists today.

As with the Drury Lane venue, access to the new theatre was along a narrow alley, this one called Playhouse Passage, but the new theatre was a much bigger building. It would become Durham's Theatre Royal and its opening productions included a comedy called 'The Wild Oats' and a farce called 'The Spoiled Child'. Comedies were always popular with the Durham audiences. Cawdell was so impressed by Durham's charms that he came to live in the city, residing in the South Bailey until his death in 1800.

During the nineteenth century Durham's new theatre experienced increasing popularity under the influence of a new manager called Stephen Kemble. He was almost literally a 'larger than life' actor famous for performing the part of Falstaff without padding. Kemble had regularly appeared at London's Drury Lane Theatre and was a member of a famous acting and theatre-owning family.

Kemble had become manager of a theatre in Newcastle in the 1790s and when Cawdell died in 1800, he took the opportunity to purchase the Durham theatre. Kemble brought actors of a higher calibre to the region and a number of esteemed London performers appeared on the Durham stage.

Kemble, like Cawdell, came to live in the city, and became a popular member of Durham society. He was a close friend of another famous Durham resident, the three foot, three inch high Polish dwarf called Joseph Boruwlaski.

When these two little and large friends strolled along the wooded paths of the city they must have provided great comic entertainment for the local people.

In later life Kemble concentrated on theatre management, making only occasional appearances on the stage.

Kemble's last performance at Durham was in May 1822, a fortnight before his death. He was fondly remembered by the natives of Durham, and was honoured with a burial in the cathedral. The heyday of Durham theatre came to an end with Kemble's death, but Kemble's theatre continued to operate until 1869 when it was almost completely destroyed by a disastrous fire.

Later Theatres

Unlike the 1780s, when a new theatre was built with strong public support, enthusiasm for a new venue did not materialise after the fire of 1869 and for many years Durham was without a proper theatre. Some slight rebuilding of the burnt out theatre was undertaken, but it fell into decline. It had already lost its popularity with the Durham gentry who kept clear of its dingy alley and even before 1869 it had become a struggling music hall venue.

Over time the theatre came to serve as a soup kitchen, bible warehouse, exhibition hall, art school, piano sale shop and auctioneers. The last surviving remnant of the theatre was part of its dressing room, demolished in 1974 to make way for student accommodation. Today the only reminder of the theatre is in the name of The Shakespeare Tavern, recalling one of the most popular playwrights performed at the venue.

Following the theatre fire of 1869, Durham's next theatre would not open for a further 15 years when a new theatre was built a little out of the city centre in the ancient street of Framwellgate.

Framwellgate was one of the main routes through the city, but was a run-down and a generally less appealing setting for a theatre than Saddler Street had been. The new venue opened in 1884 near the Framwellgate Gas Works and its proprietor was John Holliday who lived nearby and owned a grocery shop in the street.

Holliday's theatre was a plain brick building but could hold up to one thousand people. It was named the 'Albany Theatre' in honour of the Duke and Duchess of Albany who visited the city that year. It was a short-lived concern, and after only five years of entertaining the local populace the theatre lost its licence in 1889 when its heating was declared unsafe.

Shakespeare Tavern, Saddler Street (DS)

However, theatre would regain its foothold in the more genteel part of the city. Thomas Rushworth, a Saddler Street resident with fond memories of the theatre that had once operated on his doorstep saw the potential of the Assembly Rooms, just along the street from the old theatre in the adjoining Bailey.

The Assembly Rooms had been built in the eighteenth century and had long been used by members of Durham society for entertainment and performances of song and dance. Rushworth undertook work to have the building restyled and redeveloped for theatrical performances.

In 1891 the Assembly Rooms reopened as a theatre with a performance of *Il Travatore*. The Assembly Rooms are still used as a theatre today by the students of Durham University.

Only two years after the Assembly Rooms reopened, a brand new venue for entertainment was opened in the city. This was Tudor's Circus, a wooden building constructed in Court Lane behind the Court Inn between Old and New Elvet. A large wooden stage was added to the building in 1894 and it became the 'Peoples Palace of Varieties'.

The Court Lane theatre played host to all kinds of more popular entertainment with an emphasis on music hall, but it does not appear to have been a focal point for drama.

Like the Albany, the People's Palace of Varieties proved to be a short lived concern lasting only four years. Described 'as a rotten old building' its suitability as a theatre was personally examined by the County Court Bench before they retired to the neighbouring court to close it down.

In 1902 there was talk of building a theatre in Claypath on the corner of Providence Row. It was to be a 1,500 seat venue called the Coronation Theatre and despite opposition from the neighbouring Congregational Church, permission was given for its construction. In the end it turned out that there was insufficient interest and the capital failed to materialise.

Historic view of Saddler Street looking towards the Market Place

Theatre, with short, but popular footage featuring a Spanish coastal cave, part of a football match and the Newcastle fire brigade. They were displayed using an instrument called a Thatograph with shows before 9pm so that people could watch the film before catching the last train at Elvet Station.

Court Lane in Elvet was once the site of a theatre (MR)

Durham's next theatre was called The Palace and would not open until 1909. It was situated in Walkergate near St Nicholas Church, just off the market place and occupied a redundant dye house that once belonged to Henderson's Carpet Factory.

The Age of Cinema

The Palace Theatre in Walkergate had been opened by T.C. Rawes and was used for music hall rather than the production of plays, but significantly it was also occasionally used for the showing of films.

By 1909 cinematic shows were already well established in the city. The Assembly Rooms and Palace of Varieties in Court Lane both displayed moving images in the 1890s and even the Gilesgate Drill Hall was used as an occasional venue for cinema shows by 1902.

The first showing of cinematic images in Durham seems to have occurred in November 1896 at the Court Lane

The following month a travelling minstrel show was demonstrating similar films at the Assembly Rooms using a Vitagraphe. In 1897 Durham Camera Club also displayed a moving picture show at the Shakespeare Hall, a community venue in North Road. Other shows were demonstrated in temporary booths at outdoor events like the Sands Easter fair or the Durham Miners' Gala. However, more permanent cinemas did not come until the early 1900s.

The short films were always of secondary importance to dramatic performances or music hall acts in the early days. The fledgling movies were still a novelty for audiences and they had yet to reach their full dramatic potential, being just one of a number of types of peculiar entertainment that included comedians, ventriloquists and dancers.

When the Palace Theatre opened in Walkergate in 1909 it operated primarily as a venue for live performances rather than cinema. Variety and music hall was still quite popular at the turn of that century and it is said that Charlie Chaplin once performed at the Palace in his pre-cinema days. Records show differently however and Chaplin himself later denied that he had ever performed in Durham.

The demolished Palace Theatre in Walkergate was once a carpet factory dyehouse (MR)

Despite its early days as a music hall, the Palace is most fondly remembered by Durham people as a cinema and was known to many residents as the 'Flea Pit'. In fact films did not permanently replace live performances at the Palace until quite late on.

The transition from live performances to cinema was not always clearly defined. Even when cinema became firmly established in Durham as an entertainment in its own right, live turns were still a common supplementary feature at early movie shows. At the very least, a live pianist was considered an essential aspect of a film in the silent movie era.

The Assembly Rooms in the North Bailey were one of the most important early venues for moving pictures in Durham. In 1903 they hosted a showing of a dramatic film called 'The Great Train Robbery'. This was probably the first movie drama of its kind to be shown in Durham, since the earlier films in the city, as elsewhere, showed factual subjects like Edward VIII's coronation or Queen Victoria's funeral procession.

It was in 1912 that film shows virtually replaced live drama at the Durham Assembly Rooms. Film had become increasingly popular at this particular theatre in the early 1900s and it was recognised that films were the most important source of revenue. The Assembly Rooms, with a history stretching back to the eighteenth century can thus effectively claim to be the city's first cinema.

Unfortunately, the Assembly Rooms had been the main centre for performing plays, (as opposed to music hall) in Durham. This meant that there was now a gap in Durham's entertainment market waiting to be filled.

The Palace Theatre music hall venue in Walkergate was quick to exploit the opportunity left by the Assembly Room's transition from drama to cinema. In 1913 the

Palace successfully applied for a licence for the performance of dramatic plays. Over time plays replaced the variety acts and the Palace filled the void. Comic plays, melodramas, revues and pantomimes were now shown at the Palace with productions from both professional and amateur performers.

The tower of the Essoldo Cinema, North Road (MR)

Of course it was only a matter of time before the Palace also recognised the ever-increasing potential of cinema and in 1921 films completely replaced live performances at Walkergate. In fact this was the general trend with theatres across the length and breadth of Britain.

Over time the Assembly Rooms became increasingly unsuited to cinematic needs. In 1930 after the death of its owner Thomas Rushworth, the building was purchased by the University of Durham but was used for a time as a drill hall. It would not be restored for dramatic purposes until the early 1950s and has often been used by students and amateur performers since that time.

Today older Durham people remember the Palace as the cinema and the Assembly Rooms as the theatrical venue. It is interesting to see that this was not always the case. However, both were really theatres that had been adapted as picture houses. The first purpose built cinema was yet to open.

Durham's first purpose built cinema arrived in May 1913. Called the Globe Cinema it stood at the northern railway station end of North Road, where a Chinese restaurant stands alongside a roundabout. It should not be confused with the later cinema that occupied the Old Miners' Hall Building on the opposite side of the road near the bus station. The Globe Cinema ran parallel to the street and had been converted from a former timber house. It was noted for the twice a night performances at 7pm and 9pm. At around the time of the First World War a glass canopy was added to its facade confirming the show times.

The Globe continued operating until the 1950s by which time several cinemas had opened in the City of Durham including the other cinema in North Road. During this period several cinemas opened in the mining villages surrounding Durham City and two opened on the outskirts of the city at Gilesgate Moor. The first of these was the Crescent Cinema (later the Rex) on Sunderland Road which opened in 1927 and the second was the Majestic on Sherburn Road which opened in 1938.

The former Palladium Cinema in Claypath (DS)

After the opening of the Globe, the next cinema to open in the actual city centre area was the Palladium in Claypath. It opened on 18 March, 1929 with Rex Ingram's 'Garden of Allah' and was much larger than the Globe. Its Proprietors were Messrs Holliday, Thompson, Gibson and Drummond who would later open the Majestic. Mr Holliday, the chairman of the directors was a Durham City Alderman and a nephew of John Holliday who had opened the drama theatre at Framwellgate back in 1884.

It is interesting that the live theatrical possibilities of the Palladium were not entirely overlooked since the cinema officially opened for both 'film and theatrical purposes'. However, in practice it operated exclusively as a cinema.

The Palladium closed in 1976 and served for a time as a Bingo Hall. In 1986 a number of its seats were purchased at just over £1 a time and installed in the City Theatre, a new little theatre in Back Silver Street behind the Market Place. The tiny theatre is the home of Durham Dramatic Society.

In 1934, only five years after the opening of the Palladium, a new cinema appeared in North Road. This occupied the site of the Old Miners' Hall vacated in 1915. With its distinctive tower and green copper dome, the former miners' hall was the most imposing building in the street.

The new cinema was opened by the Mayor, James Fowler on the 27 March, 1934 and called the Regal. It was notable for its inclusion of a Ballroom. It operated as a cinema for almost 60 years, changing ownership on several occasions, each time with a different name. From 1947 it was The Essoldo, changing to The Classic in 1972 and then the Cannon in 1979. The Cannon closed in 1990, but reopened the following year as the Robins Cinema. It remained the Robins until the cinema's final closure in 2003, despite a passionate campaign to save the cinema.

Chapter Five
Claypath and Walkergate

Claypath, anciently called Clayport or Claypeth has medieval origins. It includes Georgian houses, a timber-framed building and, as late as the nineteenth century, even included a farm. It was one of Durham's busiest shopping streets until New Elvet and Millburngate Bridges were built nearby. In the 1960s and 1970s an underpass road linking the two bridges cut through Claypath. It took some of the life out of the street and in the 1980s ambitious plans to rectify this by building shops above the underpass came to nothing.

Fortunately in recent years new developments in Claypath have revitalised the street. They include some new shops near the underpass and more significantly the city's Gala Theatre and Clayport Library. These very modern buildings opened on the north side of Claypath in early 2002 and face each other on opposing sides of a brand new square called Millennium Square.

Historically Claypath has always been the only medieval street to enter Durham's peninsula without crossing the River Wear. It was the main entry into the city from the east. The street may have been called Clay Peth, as peth is an old North East term for a climbing road. Peth occurs in other Durham street-names like Framwellgate Peth and Crossgate Peth, which like Claypath climb steeply away from the city centre.

The first part of the name Claypath may come from the Clayport Gate, an ancient gateway that separated Claypath from the Market Place. Its name may have derived from cleur-port or cleaverport, meaning gate with a sluice.

One theory is that Claypath's narrow neck of land was defended by two sluice gates connected to the city walls that could be lowered into the river to the north and south of the street.

In medieval times most of Durham's river peninsula was enclosed and protected by walled fortifications but the peninsula's narrow neck was particularly vulnerable. The neck was defended by Durham Castle with adjoining walls encircling the peninsula around the cathedral, crossing Saddler Street at the Great North Gate. Clayport Gate was however associated with a supplementary set of walls that enclosed the Market Place area.

Clayport was thus of secondary importance to the Great North Gate. This might explain why Clayport Gate was a relatively weak arch of stone and rubble, while the Great North Gate (demolished in 1820) was a more solid and imposing structure. At the bottom of Claypath bank Clayport Gate marked the western end of Claypath until it was removed in 1791.

Up the bank the eastern end of the street terminated at a structure called the 'Leaden Cross'. This stood at the top of Claypath near Tinkler's Lane, but has long since gone. It was here that Claypath became Gilesgate. The cross also marked the boundary between St. Nicholas parish and St. Giles parish.

According to Robert Surtees, a nineteenth century historian of Durham, the Leaden Cross marked the site of a cattle market that was later held on the Sands.

Today the eastern or top end of Claypath is very easy to miss because it is almost indistinguishable from the lower part of Gilesgate. To add to the confusion, the demolitions in the street of Gilesgate that made way for a roundabout in the 1960s split Gilesgate into two parts so that the lower part of Gilesgate effectively became part of Claypath.

Tinkler's Lane on the south side of Claypath is the only clear dividing line to mark the real boundary between Claypath and Gilesgate. This lane along with Bakehouse Lane on the north side were the historic boundaries of St. Nicholas and St. Giles.

Tinkler's Lane is a rapidly descending, narrow, cobbled alleyway or 'vennel' that is hemmed in by high walls on two sides. It now ends rather abruptly at the Leazes Road dual carriageway but once descended towards the river near Baths Bridge.

Claypath in the 1960s looking towards St. Nicholas Church in the Market Place. Fowler's Store can be seen on the left with the Co-op on the right. All of the buildings in this part of Claypath were demolished to make way for the Leazes Road underpass (RL)

Bakehouse Lane was named from a Gilesgate manorial bakehouse of which the location is uncertain. Today the lane is a road leading to a tiny estate of modern houses on the north side of Lower Gilesgate. Near the modern houses some little nineteenth century terraces like Kepier Terrace, Renny Street and Ellis Leazes can be found, all within walking distance of the Gilesgate roundabout.

Nearby, Mayorswell Close refers to the site of an ancient well that was either dedicated to St. Mary or named from its former possession by Robert and Grace Maire who held land hereabouts.

Grace was the daughter of an influential Durham mine-owner called Henry Smith who set up a charity for the city in the 1500s. This was the Henry Smith Charity to which he diverted funds originally intended for his daughter. She apparently upset her father by converting to Roman Catholicism and Henry never forgave her. Her conversion had taken place after she had witnessed the execution of some Catholic martyrs at Dryburn in the north of the city.

If Mayor's Well was in fact Mary's rather than Maire's Well it may have been associated with the medieval chapel of St. Mary Magdalene, a structure that lies in ruins a little to the east beyond the Gilesgate roundabout.

The chapel of St. Mary Magdalene was the chapel for a hospital (not Kepier Hospital) which cared for the local poor. The master of St. Mary's was the master of the Cathdersal's Almonry School which was situated in the South Bailey just outside the gates of College Green.

St. Mary Magdalene was one of two medieval chapels in the Claypath-Gilesgate area. The other, dedicated to St. Thomas the Martyr was first mentioned in the thirteenth century and could be reached by a lane from Claypath. Its burial ground was used as late as 1597 when plague victims were laid to rest in the cemetery. The site of the chapel was approximately half way between Bakehouse Lane and Providence Row somewhere close to what is now Hillcrest Mews. Nothing can be seen of the St. Thomas chapel today as it was demolished centuries ago.

Kepier House was once a penitentiary prison (DS)

A prominent but rather stark Victorian building called Kepier House stands close to Mayorswell Close and was the Durham County Penitentiary of 1853. It was built with the support of an MP called Roland Burdon along with George Waddington, the Dean of Durham Cathedral, and a Durham Prison Chaplain called George Hans Harrison.

The Penitentiary provided a half-way house for carefully chosen prisoners who seemed willing to make a break from a life of crime. It attempted to rehabilitate the inmates and help them find work. In 1881 there were 26 inmates from all over the country with a significant number hailing from large local towns like Sunderland and Newcastle.

Later in the twentieth century, the building served as an old people's home called St. Mary's House, but became a residential block for Durham University students in the 1960s. Since 1981 it has been part of Durham University's Graduate Society that is now Ustinov College. As an accommodation block Kepier House is likely to be superseded by the University sites at Howlands Farm and Dryburn.

Bakehouse Lane and Tinklers Lane are only two of several old lanes, yards and streets that joined Claypath in times gone by. Amongst the many, often overcrowded yards that joined the street were Oswald Yard, Gray's Yard, Pyle's Yard, Burdon's Yard, Houst's Yard, Heron's Yard, Chamber's Yard and Maltman Yard. Only a few of the old yards remain but their names are largely forgotten.

The three most notable lanes adjoining Claypath were Walkergate and Wanlass Lane on the north side of Claypath and Paradise Lane on the south.

Wanlass (or Wanless) Lane was and still is the main route from Claypath to the Sands down by the riverside but some time during the mid nineteenth century the lane changed its name to Providence Row. The earlier name was used from around 1600 and recalled a wealthy dyer called Edward Wanless.

Edward owned a mansion in the lane that he built on land acquired from the city's weavers. Before Edward's time the lane was called Woodman's Chair, possibly because it formed a riverside route to Kepier and Frankland Wood. A chair or chare was a steep turning alley or a sudden drop. The lane was narrower than the present Providence Row.

Edward Wanless is still recalled in a little Victorian street called Wanless Terrace that adjoins Providence Row on the eastern side. There are presently two different street signs for this terrace featuring two different spellings of the Wanless or Wanlass name. A brickworks stood in this area during the early nineteenth century.

In more recent times one of the houses in Providence Row was home to a family called Blair whose son, perhaps through providence, went on to become the Prime Minister of Great Britain.

At the foot of Providence Row just before we enter the riverside area called the Sands we find a small mortuary chapel and cemetery. It belongs to St. Nicholas Church in the Market Place and there are reports that it is haunted.

The graveyard of St. Nicholas Church was originally situated in the Market Place alongside the church but was considered a health hazard and covered over with paving and later cobbles. St. Nicholas graveyard was relocated to the Sands in the mid nineteenth century.

On the opposite side of Providence Row from the chapel is Durham Sixth Form Centre which has long been a part of Gilesgate Comprehensive School. It was formerly a Girls' Grammar School and dates from 1913. A house called Ebenezer Cottage once stood just to the south of the school and was itself a small nineteenth century girls' school under the governorship of a Mrs Annie Chambers. The cottage was demolished in the 1960s or 70s.

A Georgian Chapel of 1751 lies hidden behind Claypath's Victorian United Reformed Church of 1885 (DS)

Providence Row climbs steeply from the Sands and upon reaching the top at its junction with Claypath we find *The Northern Echo's* Durham office on the eastern side of the street. The office was relocated here from another site a little down Claypath where there is now a restaurant. Just opposite the new office on the west side of Providence Row are some new apartments called Claypath Court occupying the site of the city's former Post Office at 33 Claypath.

A plaque on the wall of 33 Claypath helpfully informs us that in 1899 Durham University founded a hostel for women on this site. It was relocated to Abbey House on Palace Green in 1910 and developed later, on a separate site into St. Mary's College. It wasn't the only educational institution founded at 33 Claypath. In 1884 Durham High School (for Girls) was founded in the same house but had vacated the premises by 1886. With such a strong tradition of girls education hereabouts it was perhaps only fitting that the Girls' Grammar School of 1913 was built nearby.

Alongside the old Post Office is the United Reformed Church with its prominent but rather grim Victorian spire. It was built by the Durham architect H. T. Gradon in 1885 as a Presbyterian church but was later united with the Congregationalists.

Presbyterians had worshipped in this area since 1672 when a Thomas Dixon, formerly of Kelloe set up his house here as a place of worship. It became a legal meeting house for prayers and worship in 1688 but was superseded in 1751 by a new purpose built Georgian chapel.

The Georgian chapel can still be seen hidden behind the United Reformed Church and is a rather charming building, that is arguably one of the most attractive non-conformist chapels in the Durham City area. With the United Reformed Church at its front, it provides a rather interesting contrast between Georgian and Victorian styles of church architecture. When the Victorian church was built in 1885 the Georgian chapel came to be used as a Sunday School.

Leazes Place and Leazes Road

Other than Providence Row the only other street of note to join Claypath is the tiny but exceedingly quaint Leazes Place. This little street joins Claypath on the south side at the Gilesgate end of town. It was built in Regency style around 1836 and consists of a terrace of rather attractive brick cottages. From around 1846 Number 4 Leazes Place became the home of a little boarding school that was later extended to number 5. The school moved to nearby Ravensworth Terrace in the 1880s but has long since departed.

Tucked away behind Leazes Place are some flats for student accommodation in what appears to be a converted stable block, possibly associated with the nearby mansion called Leazes House.

Leazes House hidden behind Claypath (DS)

Leazes House was built by the Henderson carpet manufacturing family in 1848 on the west side of Tinkler's Lane and its architecture has been described as being of the Newcastle type. From 1910 until 1968 it was home to Durham High School for girls. As we have already noted, this school was originally founded in 1884 at 33 Claypath but moved to a property in the South Bailey two years later before relocating to Leazes House in 1910.

After 58 years at Leazes House Durham High School for girls moved in 1968 to its present location at Money Slack near Mount Oswald on the southern outskirts of the city.

Leazes House subsequently passed into the hands of Durham University but in recent times has once again reverted to the status of a private house and is currently home to an estate agent. A neighbouring house called

Belle Vue situated to the west, was the nineteenth century home of a Borough Magistrate and Alderman called Robert Robson.

Much of the area below these houses on the south side of Claypath and leading down towards the river was occupied in the nineteenth and early twentieth century by Paradise Gardens. These gardens belonged to the Henderson family of Leazes House and could be reached by Rashell's Lane, better known in its later days as Paradise Lane near the foot of Claypath.

Paradise Lane led off from Claypath near the Market Place towards the riverside and skirted the western edge of the gardens. Part of the old garden site is now occupied by the Leazes Bowl roundabout just outside the Prince Bishops Shopping Centre car park. This roundabout is often log-jammed with traffic seeking parking spaces and seems far removed from Paradise today.

In truth Paradise Gardens and Paradise Lane were far from idyllic. The lane was noted for open gutters, ash pits and illegal gambling, while the neighbouring gardens were notorious for a prominent dunghill. So much for paradise lost!

The word Leazes associated with the whole area around Claypath is recalled in local names like Pelaw Leazes, Ellis Leazes and Leazes bowl and seems to be a reference to the 'leas' or river meadows of the area but it could also be a medieval word meaning freehold of land.

Today the name Leazes in Durham is primarily associated with the section of the A690 dual carriageway called Leazes Road that dominates the former riverside lands to the south of Claypath. Leazes Road completely changed the scenery here and many houses were demolished to make way for its course.

Demolitions included part of the Victorian street called Ravensworth Terrace which joins the lower part of Gilesgate. This steeply rising street at the Gilesgate end of Leazes Road dates from 1881 and its nineteenth century residents included the architect, civil engineer and County Surveyor called William Crozier who lived at number 7.

Before the Leazes Road dual carriageway was constructed, the main routeway through this whole riverside area was Pelaw Leazes Lane, otherwise known as Bede Bank, a steeply rising street near Bede College that is now found on the south side of Leazes Road. A 'Model school' was once situated alongside the lane and was used by trainee teachers at the college for teaching young children, but closed in 1933. A similar school was attached to the neighbouring St. Hild's College. Pelaw Leazes Lane terminated on the banks of the river near Baths Bridge.

Claypath:
Shops, Schools and Pubs

The street of Claypath has long been a centre of leisure, education and worship and was home to dozens of shops and pubs. It was the site of the city's post office, as well as a cinema, a working-men's club and the Blue Coat School. The school was established in 1708 by the Mayor and Alderman of Durham City using funds from the Henry Smith Charity but was initially located behind the Market Place in part of the vacated mansion called New Place. In 1812, after 104 years at New Place it moved to a new building that was specially built in Claypath. The new building was erected with funds provided by Shute Barrington; the Bishop of Durham.

For 153 years the school was situated on the south side of Claypath in the area now called Blue Coat Buildings and it overlooked the Paradise Gardens. Modern houses now occupying the site of the school lie just within the entrance to the yard. It is notable that remnants of a small timber framed building can be seen nearby on the west side of the yard.

In 1965 the Blue Coat School needed to acquire larger, more suitable premises and was relocated once again. This time it moved to the Newton Hall housing estate on the northern outskirts of Durham City where it is still located today. It educates children of primary school age.

When the Blue Coat School was situated in Claypath it had stood very close to a Quaker meeting house. This was located in a vennel just to the east of the Blue Coat School and was built in 1693. Quakers had been associated with Claypath since 1657 when the house of a John Heighington had been used as a meeting place for members of the society. A Quaker burial ground stood nearby and was possibly swallowed up at a later date by part of Paradise Gardens. There were not many Quakers in Durham City and the meetings discontinued in 1859. The building, long since gone, was sold off in 1873.

Regency style houses in Leazes Place off Claypath (DS)

Tinkler's Lane (DS)

Paradise Lane

Shopping has long been an important aspect of Claypath's life but many shops at the market place end of the street were demolished during the 1960s for the building of the underpass road.

The unfortunate shops that were demolished included the former Richardson's Travel Agency, a business established in 1947 by Norman Richardson on the south side of Claypath, just outside the Market Place. Richardson was a former Durham Johnston pupil and ex-RAF pilot who became Durham's first travel agent. He made Claypath Durham's gateway to the world but was also keen to bring the world to Durham.

In 1963, Richardson was elected mayor of the city and was one of the first mayors to recognise Durham's important tourist potential. He campaigned successfully for the establishment of a dedicated tourism committee and brought about the opening of the first Tourist Information Bureau in the city. Part of the town clerk's office in Claypath was converted for the purpose, although the mayor would have preferred a more central location in the Market Place.

Richardson was not the first Claypath businessman to become mayor. In the late nineteenth century, a Claypath grocer called James Fowler was elected mayor on a number of occasions. James Fowler and his son, Matthew, had established a grocery store at 99 Claypath in 1853.

Fowler's store was widely used and became especially popular with the Durham miners after Fowler supported them during a lengthy mid-nineteenth century strike. He helped the miners with provisions during this difficult period and many miners returned the favour, becoming loyal customers once the strike was over.

Fowler's shop stood on the south side of Claypath and in its later years proudly displayed the famous Durham teapot. This was symbolic of a grocery store and had previously hung outside a grocery in the market place and then a post office in Gilesgate. After the Gilesgate demolitions of the 1960s the teapot was moved to Saddler Street where it still hangs today.

The Claypath Co-operative Store

In competition with Fowler's, Claypath's biggest and best-known store was undoubtedly the Durham Equitable and Industrial Co-operative Society's store, or

Co-op for short. It stood opposite Fowler's and occupied a number of buildings that were eventually demolished to make way for the Claypath underpass road. The Co-op was divided into several departments covering food, furnishings, insurance, holidays and funerals.

One Claypath outlet of sorts that still exists today is the Army recruitment office, which has been located in the street since the Second World War. It is interesting to note that a neighbouring outlet that is now a newsagent was once home to a recruitment office of a quite different kind. In the 1930s, this was home to the Durham branch of the British Union of Fascists. However, they were not there for long and support dwindled very rapidly with the onset of the Second World War. Later, the premises became the home of Ben Clark's cycle shop, selling bicycles, toys and fancy goods.

Claypath was once home to many pubs and inns, but there are only a few in the street today. The Big Jug Hotel, now just called the Jug is a successful survivor, with its prominent jug emblem hanging from the facade. Like the teapot, the jug is a reminder of days when people were often illiterate and identified outlets through symbols rather than words.

In 1899, Durham was a much smaller place in terms of population than it is today so it is remarkable that the little street of Claypath played host to 15 pubs. In fact many Durham streets were similarly crammed with places to drink. The nearest Claypath pub to the Market Place was the Wheatsheaf on the north side of the street at number 3, two properties up from St. Nicholas Church. Other pubs on this side of the street included the Golden Eagle at number 9, the Grapes at 16 and Wearmouth Bridge at 17. The last of these was also called the Nottingham House (from the home town of a proprietor) but officially changed to the Wearmouth Bridge in the 1850s.

Further up the street on the north side of Claypath stood the Maltman Inn, with the Palladium Cinema next door from 1929. The Maltman is now a cycle shop but the old Palladium building can still be seen.

On the southern side of the street, opposite the Wheatsheaf, stood the Angel Inn, Kings Arms and the Claypath Gates Inn. They were located at 107, 105 and 104 Claypath, but like the former Wheatsheaf all the properties were demolished for the underpass road.

Other Claypath pubs in 1899 included the Cellars at number 18, the Princess Mary at 20, the Masons Arms (52), the General Gordon (63), Seven Stars (90) and the Travellers Rest.

The last of these pubs, a little up the street from the Jug is now called The Age Bar and according to a rather modern legend is named after Agnes Granger Edwards who is said to haunt the place. It is claimed that Agnes married an otherwise unrecorded son of Count Joseph Boruwlaski called Francis Isaac Boruwlaski. He was supposedly murdered by the gypsy piper, Jimmy Allen. Unfortunately the elements of the story are best summed up in the initials of the Count's supposed son.

Walkergate: Cloths and Carpet Making

In historic times, the weaving industry, once Durham's City's busiest industrial activity was focused around the north side of the Market Place and western end of Claypath. Here leading off from the Market Place near St. Nicholas Church, is Walkergate, a street otherwise known as Back Lane.

In the nineteenth century many of the houses and tenements of lower Claypath, Providence Row, Walkergate and New Place were houses and former carpet

factory buildings occupied by weavers and carpet makers who worked for a trade that was once Durham City's biggest employer.

Houses and former carpet factory buildings in Walkergate prior to demolition (RL)

Most of Walkergate was demolished in the late 1960s to make way for the Claypath underpass but the street sign Walkergate, still appears on a wall near St. Nicholas' Church. In medieval times, a Walker was a cloth worker so Walkergate was the cloth worker's street.

Weaving was first mentioned in the city in 1243 and there was a guild of weavers from 1450. Items like sack cloth, hair cloth and linen were manufactured in the early days, as well as woven tapestry for bed covers and blankets.

The first mention of weaving on a significant scale in Walkergate did not come until the late 1600s and in subsequent centuries, the industry was crammed into buildings stretching along Walkergate down to the river and along the nearby road of Freeman's Place that leads to the Sands. Freeman's Place is the road in between the former ice rink and new Gala Theatre.

The cloth industry of the 1600s was stimulated by a charitable donation from Henry Smith, a coal owner and staunch Durham protestant, who donated the contents of his will so that 'some good trade may be devised for the setting of youth and other idle persons to work … whereby some profits may rise to the benefit of this city and relief of those that are past work and have lived honestly upon their trade'.

Smith, who died in 1598, had originally intended that the main benefactor of his will would be his daughter Grace. Unfortunately Grace became a Catholic sympathiser after witnessing the execution of some Catholic activists at Dryburn in 1591. The disappointed Henry decided that his 'grace-less Grace' – as he now called her – should be removed from the will.

The executors of Smith's will included an influential dyer called Edward Wanless who resided in what is now Providence Row and a draper called William Hall. It is not surprising that a draper and dyer wanted to encourage the cloth trade. They hoped to use Smith's money to establish the industry in the house of New Place that bordered the Market Place and Walkergate. New Place was the large town house, occasionally described as a palace, that had belonged to the Neville family but was confiscated from that family after they organised a Catholic rising against Queen Elizabeth I in 1569.

In 1614, cloth workers Henry Doughty and William Bastoe were based at New Place and utilised some of the funds from the Smith charity. Land at Brasside Moor in the north of the city was enclosed for the purpose of the works, presumably with plenty of sheep, but the New Place venture was not successful. Doughty and Bastoe had ceased trading by 1616.

Another cloth making enterprise that followed in the same premises had also failed by 1619 and although other attempts at establishing the business continued throughout the century, they all failed.

Despite these numerous failed attempts, most of the money in Smith's bequest remained idle and was eventually mixed with another major donation – a bequest from George Baker, of Crook Hall, in 1699.

By 1718, part of New Place came to be occupied by the city's Blue Coat School and another part became the workhouse of St. Nicholas parish, but attempts to establish weaving industries continued in the 1720s and 1740s.

In 1745, William Archer, a schoolmaster, and Richard Wharton, a draper, set up a weaving business in part of the workhouse but this ceased manufacturing in 1755.

Following on from this failure the charity once again advertised a loan to anyone willing to establish a woollen industry in this part of the city. The awarded applicant was a weaver and manufacturer called John Startforth, who became the first man to successfully establish the business at New Place and Walkergate.

It was in 1780, the year in which John was joined by his brother, Gilbert, that the firm began the production of carpets at Durham. Startforth's carpet and weaving business became one of the largest in the country with about 69 looms, employing 800 people in the 1790s.

Meanwhile in 1796, a Mr Salvin had built a cotton spinning mill in Church Street, at Elvet but this burnt down in 1804 and was never rebuilt.

Further disaster hit the city's linen trade the following year when the French Wars and subsequent calling in of loans caused Startforth's business to fall bankrupt. About 10% of the city's population worked at the factory at the time and the resulting unemployment caused a drop in the city's population from 7,530 in 1801 to 6,763 by the time of the 1811 census.

A succession of weavers – William Cooper, James Bell, Mr Waddington and Mr Wood all tried in vain to re-establish the business but the Napoleonic Wars had a disastrous effect on the economy and by 1811, all failed. In 1814, the year of Waterloo, a fifth concern owned by Mark Oliver, operating 18 looms, also ceased trading.

Fortunately, funds were still available and during 1814 the recently launched *Durham Advertiser* carried notice of a loan for anyone willing to establish a woollen manufactory in the Back Lane (Walkergate) area. Gilbert Henderson, a weaver from Kirk Merrington near Bishop Auckland soon rose to the challenge.

Henderson had a talent for mathematics and a passion for learning that existed from an early age. He was the son of a Middlestone farmer and as a boy pursued an education against the wishes of his father who wanted him to follow the family trade.

With his mother's assistance, the young Gilbert had regularly climbed down from his bedroom window to make a two-mile walk across the countryside to receive lessons from a local teacher. Young Gilbert eventually became a clerk in Startforth's factory and although he was one of many to lose his job following its closure, Gilbert played a very efficient role winding up the factory's financial affairs.

Gilbert found new work as a cloth company agent in the west of England but unfortunately, at the age of 26 was caught in a storm near Whitby and struck down with a terrible illness. It left him crippled for some time and he had to be wheeled around the village of Merrington with the aid of a donkey.

As his health improved, Henderson took a keen interest in Merrington's cottage-based weaving industry. He mixed with workers to learn more about the practicalities of weaving and by 1810 made enough of a recovery to establish a manufactory in the village with 14 looms. By 1813 he employed 60 weavers, about 30 of whom were taken to Durham.

Henderson uprooted home and business to Durham and for a house purchased a ramshackle farmhouse called Shacklock Hall on the eastern side of Freeman's Place.

Employment at the Durham factory was a far cry from the 800 people employed by Startforth, but Henderson was a shrewd man and the factory grew steadily. One major turning point came in 1820 with the installation of Brussels type carpet looms from Kidderminster. These were somehow smuggled into Durham from that town after a secret business deal.

Kidderminster had possessed a virtual monopoly on Brussels-type looms in England and until this point successfully prevented other towns acquiring their looms. The new looms meant Durham could now manufacture high quality carpets and by the early 1820s, Henderson was selling carpets as far away as Manchester.

In 1824, Henderson's firm suffered two major setbacks.

Firstly, a major fire almost stopped carpet production and secondly Gilbert Henderson passed away at the age of 42.

Gilbert's son, John, aged 17, had only just entered the business and was to be groomed for the role. However,

the intention had been for young John to learn the trade progressively from the workshop upwards.

Fortunately the charity trustees stuck with the plan and temporarily took over the running of the firm. In reality, however, it was Gilbert's more-than-capable widow Ann, who effectively managed the business during this period. Ann was dedicated to the firm and, according to legend, during the early days of her husband's business used to single-handedly clean the whole factory every day before taking a bath in a factory vat.

This illustration of Shacklock Hall depicts an incident involving the Henderson family cat. The Hall stood near Freeman's Place (MR)

Within a few years of learning the trade John Henderson came of age and was appointed head of the business. In 1835, his younger brother William joined him as partner in the firm. The Hendersons employed about 150 people by this time but many employees probably worked in their own homes.

In the 1850s and 1860s huge, purpose-built factory buildings were erected in the Bishop's Mill and neighbouring Freeman's Place area where a total of about 500 workers were employed. The factory underwent

constant technical improvements during this period and in 1851 a boost to trade came with a display at the Great Exhibition in London. It stimulated the first signs of overseas trade.

By this time, the city factory had almost single-handedly made County Durham the third largest carpet making area in the country after Yorkshire and Worcestershire. By 1863, Hendersons were the country's largest producers of Venetian style carpets.

The now wealthy Hendersons had demolished their family home of Shacklock Hall to make way for a factory extension and after residing for a time in Church Street, Elvet they moved in the 1850s to the purpose-built villa called Leazes House on the south side of Claypath.

The two increasingly influential brothers had interests other than carpet making and took an active part in politics. John, a Liberal became a councillor and later, an MP. He pursued other industrial interests and was for ten years chairman of the directors of the Consett Iron Company.

William was a Conservative and became Durham's mayor in 1849. During the 1850s he had a strong involvement in building Durham's Town Hall and the city's covered markets.

In 1872, William Henderson resigned from the carpet factory and two years later his brother passed away. New family members took on the role, but waiting in the wings was a young factory employee by the name of Hugh Mackay whose time was yet to come.

Although the business was taken over by John Henderson's eldest son (another John), John junior passed away during 1874 and the firm fell into the hands of a younger son, Arthur. The later Hendersons do not seem to have had the same passion for the business as William and John and, in 1903, they sold the family firm in Freemans Place and Walkergate to a well-known carpet maker called Crossleys, of Halifax. It came as a great shock to the 300 plus workers at the Durham factory when they read the report of the firm's closure in the *Durham Advertiser*.

Negotiations were made with Crossley's regarding the takeover, but Crossley's were only interested in Henderson's trademarks, designs and foreign clients. Most of the staff found themselves out of work in what can only be described as a takeover and strip policy. In fact, Crossley's wiped out their major competitor in a manner

that must have made John Startforth and Gilbert Henderson turn in their graves.

Amongst those made unemployed by the Crossley takeover, was the 54 year-old Hugh Mackay, of Western Hill, a Henderson works manager employed by the

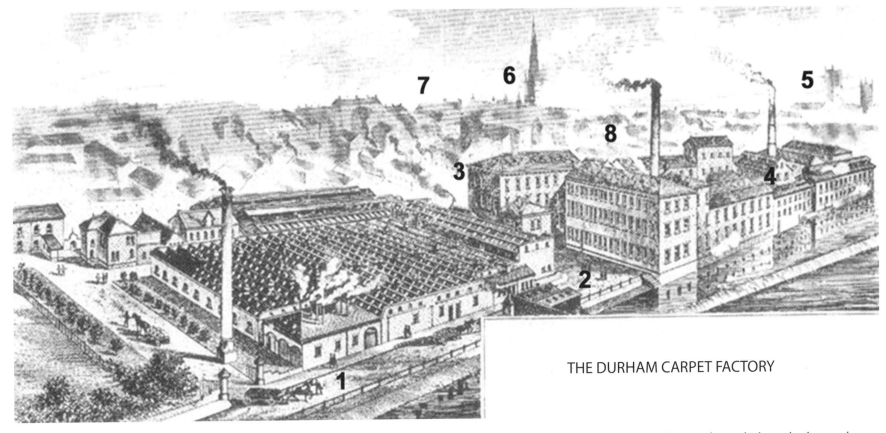

THE DURHAM CARPET FACTORY

Henderson's carpet factory in the 1880s alongside the River Wear in Freemans Place (1). Nearby is the riverside entrance to Walkergate (2) and the carpet factory dye house that became the Palace Theatre Cinema (3) in the early twentieth century. The factory buildings extended behind the market place towards Back Silver Street (4). Nearby we can see Durham Cathedral (5). St. Nicholas Church (6) and Claypath (7). The former palace or sixteenth century house of the Neville family called New Place was approximately situated at (8). The old Bishop's Mill and Mill race was situated just off the bottom left of this picture

company since the age of 12. Mackay was shrewd enough to realise that the takeover was not necessarily the end of carpet-making in Durham and in 1903, he leased some of the old buildings and machinery from Arthur Henderson.

Carpet maker William Henderson pictured in later days. He was a keen angler and a one time Mayor of Durham (MR)

With restricted funds, Mackay, could only employ about 30 former Henderson workers for the time being, and acquired only a few sections of the factory.

Some of the other buildings were acquired by different proprietors and in 1909, a former carpet factory dyehouse in Walkergate became the Palace Theatre Music Hall. Later a cinema, it was one of the buildings demolished in the 1960s to make way for the Millburngate Bridge throughroad.

Mackay's lease was initially for five years but the Hendersons retained a clause allowing them to give Mackay six months notice to vacate the premises should it be required.

Mackay, assisted by his sons Hurbert, Godfrey and Laurence, was determined to make the venture a success and the firm owned 25 looms by the start of the First World War. The 1920s saw much expansion at Mackays and the families of former Henderson workers were often given jobs as Mackay purchased more of the factory buildings.

By 1921, the Mackay works officially became the private firm of Hugh Mackay and Company Ltd. but, sadly, Hugh Mackay died three years later, in 1924.

Hugh's son, Laurence, succeeded him as the head of the firm and the business went from strength to strength, making a big impression at Newcastle's North East Exhibition in 1929. The Prince of Wales (later Edward VIII) operated a Mackay loom at this exhibition and the rug he worked on was later auctioned to raise funds for some restoration at Durham Castle.

By this time, Mackay's factory employed around 150 people and in 1930 the firm bought the remaining Henderson buildings outright. The firm was hit hard by the depression in the 1930s, but it was during this

decade that it bought new German-style looms that enabled it to increase its production in subsequent years.

Hugh Mackay

During the Second World War, carpet production ceased at Durham, as sections of the factory were used for the war effort, making blankets, camouflage nets and small parts for bombs.

In a temporary compromise that might have infuriated workers with longer memories, the Government allowed Crossleys of Halifax to weave Hugh Mackay's quota of production during the war. Laurence's son, John Mackay, became a director of the company in 1947 and from 1950 to 1970, the firm experienced significant expansion employing around 550 people by the mid-1960s.

In 1969, disaster struck when a severe fire, started by a former employee, destroyed most of the factory in Freemans Place. Fortunately, by this time the Mackays owned additional factory units at Dragonville, in Gilesgate Moor, where they had owned land since 1957. These factory buildings were intended for storage, but were quickly adapted to carpet production. By 1980, the whole factory was moved to Dragonville and the old riverside site was sold.

Mackays had received a Royal warrant back in 1972, and in subsequent years they had become noted for an impressive list of high profile clients. In the 1990s, these included EuroDisney in Paris, London's Dorchester Hotel, Buckingham Palace and the Cardiff Millennium Stadium.

However, despite these lucrative orders, the firm had been suffering significant losses since the late 1980s. Despite a management buyout in 1999, and a £4m investment in a move to a new site at Meadowfield the following year, the firm went into administration in April 2005 bringing an end to more than 200 years of carpet making in Durham.

The former factory site at Dragonville is now a Tesco superstore, but in truth the spiritual home of carpet-making in Durham will always be at Walkergate and Freeman's Place down by the river.

After a stint as a rather rubble-ridden car park, the land at Freeman's Place is currently being developed for flats, bars, shops, restaurants and a 500-space multi-storey car park. It is a prime riverside site close to the city's Gala Theatre and is now unrecognisable as the former factory site of Henderson and Mackay.

Skating in the City

From Walkergate and the Market Place, Freemans Place leads east towards the unspoilt but rather flat riverside land

called the Sands. From the fifteenth century this meadow was common pasture belonging to the freemen of Durham City. The Sands provides important breathing space for the city and is at the apex of a great wedge of open countryside that stretches out east towards Kepier.

At the city end of the Sands is Providence Row that climbs up towards Claypath and Freemans Place which continues along the flat river bank towards the city centre.

In Freemans Place we find a large car park and a brand new footbridge called Pennyferry Bridge which links Freemans Place to Framwellgate Waterside and Crook

Hall on the opposite bank of the river. The bridge officially opened in April 2002 and commemorates an old ferry service that was still operating here in the early decades of the twentieth century.

This area was obviously an important river crossing as a ford existed only a few yards east of the present bridge. A massive shed with an iron roof currently overlooks the modern developments that are taking place here. This is the city's former ice rink but the building's future is uncertain. Its most recent role has been as a ten pin bowling alley and it stands across the road from the old carpet factory site.

Ice skaters near Prebends Bridge around 1895 (MR)

The great shed stands on the bank of the river occupying the site of what was once the Bishop's Corn Mill. Here in times gone by, the Freemen of the city were allowed to grind their corn.

Remnants of the old mill can still be seen at the western end of the building. A mill race – a deep channel constructed to power the mill – ran from this point along the western flank of Freemans Place as far as the Sands. The stream was filled in by the 1930s or 40s but once effectively formed a large man-made island in the river that could be reached by seven tiny footbridges. The island existed from at least 1754 when it was shown on a map and is now largely occupied by the former ice rink and car park near the Pennyferry Bridge.

Durham ice rink is a fondly remembered part of Durham's history and was home to one of England's most successful sporting teams. The rink, the team and Icy Smith, the man who created them, have a remarkable story to tell.

In truth Durham people were no strangers to ice skating before the days of the ice rink. In times gone by, people took advantage of ice on ponds and rivers, during periods of cold weather. Out came the boots, and huge gatherings of people paraded across the ice at high speed in their skates for sheer pleasure. Old photos of Durham confirm the popularity of skating. An image of 1929 shows schoolboys skating on the Wear near Framwellgate Bridge and Victorian photographs show skating families gathered on the river near Prebends Bridge.

But the story of Durham's riverside rink begins about a hundred years ago, 20 miles to the south-west of Durham City in the Teesdale village of Lartington. Here lived the Smiths, a family of 14 children whose father was a Smith by name and smith by trade. Indeed, for four centuries the family was dedicated to the working of iron.

It was the 13th of the 14 children who came to be the founder of ice skating in Durham. His name was John Frederick James Smith, and he was destined to become Alderman Smith, the Mayor of Darlington and later the Mayor of Durham City. However, almost everyone who recalls his name, remembers him affectionately as Icy Smith.

Former ice rink and mill buildings pictured in 2006 (DS)

As a boy Icy and his brothers had spent the coldest winter days skating on the frozen fishponds at Lartington. It was a pastime that gave them much joy, but also brought disappointment each time the sun appeared to spoil their fun. Icy had an inquiring mind and was determined to find a solution to the problem. He recognised that by the time he was old enough to join the family business there would be too much competition from his siblings. So, when he reached his mid-20s, in 1907, he was already in pursuit of his dream,

Icy's early efforts proved disappointing, and he soon discovered that the costs of sustaining a whole field of ice were astronomical. This was an age when the mechanics of refrigeration were very much in their infancy. Nevertheless, Icy recognised that the production of ice on

a smaller scale for commercial and household purposes was a far more practical pursuit.

Despite the scepticism of others, Icy recognised the business potential of ice and established a factory for ice production in an old mill at Barnard Castle. Initially, it produced about a ton of ice every 24 hours, but demand was increasingly high and the factory was extended. He followed it with another factory at Darlington and then one at Durham. The Durham factory was situated on the Framwellgate waterside area only a short distance across the River Wear from where the ice rink was eventually built.

Throughout the 1930s, the development of small, practical household refrigeration techniques began to improve and this posed a major threat to Icy's ice making business. Icy increasingly turned his attention to his original dream and purchased a row of terraced houses near the river in Freemans Place. They stood near the site of the ancient corn mill that once belonged to the Prince Bishops of Durham. Here there was a noisy weir across the River Wear that had in times past been used to generate power for the mill. Icy wanted to utilise this same water power in new ways.

Rubble from demolished houses was dropped into the river, raising the water level, and this facilitated the use of the river for generating hydro-electrical power. It would help to considerably reduce the running costs of the rink. Icy's riverside rink required the setting of seven miles of twisting pipes that would lie beneath the great pad of ice to keep it cool. The pipes were in place by 1939, but when the rink finally opened on 6 March, 1940, it was somewhat exposed to the elements.

There was, initially, no roof of any kind, but an enormous marquee, allegedly the largest in the world, was brought in to cover the rink. The marquee was erected in the style of a Big Top circus with the support of two poles. The poles were frozen into the ice and provided a novelty obstacle for skaters to navigate around.

Unfortunately, the marquee was very much at the mercy of the elements and blew into the river on more than one occasion. In 1944, a severe gale destroyed the marquee altogether, and a new ice rink with a permanent roof was required. However, despite the problems with the weather, ice-skating – including ice hockey – was a well-established leisure activity in the city by the end of the Second World War.

Keeping the ice rink running during the early 1940s proved to be a major task for Icy Smith as he often had to rely on enthusiastic skaters to help with the rink's maintenance. Men were in short supply during these war years and one challenge was finding volunteers to protect the rink's marquee from the wind and snow. Nevertheless, the rink proved to be a huge success. It was a place where Durham folk could skate for enjoyment, or sit back and watch the ice shows or ice hockey and temporarily escape the worries of the war.

Ice hockey was established as a regular aspect of the ice rink's attractions in 1942, and there was a ready supply of individuals with enough talent and experience to ensure its popularity. They came in the form of Canadian airmen, stationed at air bases like Middleton St. George near Darlington.

Ice hockey was hugely popular among the Canadians, as it still is today, and the Royal Canadian Air Force encouraged competition between the airmen as it was considered good for morale. Many Canadian professionals came to play at Durham during these war years. They included talented players such as Milt Schmidt, Woody Dumart and Bobby Bauer, all players with the world-beating Boston Bruins, a United States team that employed the cream of Canadian talent.

Ice hockey played at Durham was of a particularly unique brand in its early days. The two poles that supported the marquee formed a major obstacle for the players, but they became an integral part of the Durham game.

Crowds flocked to the ice rink to see the games, even though Icy Smith was not allowed to advertise because it was wartime and the Home Office would not allow the movements of military personnel to be known.

In the event, it was a severe gale and not military action that destroyed the ice rink's marquee in 1944. A new rink, with a permanent roof, was now required.

In 1945, the war was over and many Canadians returned home. Some, however, remained, as did Durham's enthusiasm for ice hockey. It was now down to Smith, by then in his sixties, to build the ice rink that the city's skaters desired. So the new rink, complete with a permanent roof, opened on the site of the original one at a cost of £64,000.

Icy Smith

One big problem had been finding wood for constructing the stands that would house the expected crowds. Wood was in short supply at the end of the war, but Smith saw there was a great surplus of wooden coffins, and bought many for use in the rink's construction.

When the final nails went into the former coffins, it would signal the beginning, rather than the end, of a successful era for the rink. Fundamental to this success was the ice hockey team. The Durham Wasps began their life in 1946 and were established by Mike Davey of Ottawa, along with three other Canadians who had made Durham their home. In the 1950s, Smith was so inspired by the success of ice hockey that he also established an ice hockey team at Whitley Bay. The Durham Wasps team was split into two to help create the Whitley Bay team, known initially as The Bees, then The Braves, and finally as The Warriors.

This created a healthy local rivalry, but also meant that Smith could organise games so that well-established teams from Scotland could play both of the North East teams in a weekend. Ice hockey maintained a degree of popularity throughout the 1960s and 1970s, but it was the period from 1982 to 1992 that was the real heyday for the Durham Wasps. The team dominated British ice hockey during these ten years, winning the Heineken Championship four times, the British National League six times, and the Norwich Union cup on three occasions. Two of the most influential players of this period were the team captain Paul Smith, a great grandson of Icy and the Canadian player-coach Mike O'Connor.

Sadly, ice hockey in Durham ultimately became a victim of its own successes and ambitions. The last days of The Wasps came within only a few years of their greatest era. In 1995, Sir John Hall purchased the team as part of the Newcastle United Sporting Club, with the intention of moving the club to a rink that was to be built near St. James' Park, in Newcastle.

However, the expected planning permission in Newcastle was never granted and the Durham Wasps first season under new ownership was played at Sunderland's Crowtree Leisure Centre. When they moved to Newcastle Arena the following season, they were renamed The Newcastle Cobras.

Durham Ice Rink pictured in its heyday (MR)

Historic view of skating near Durham Cathedral (MR)

In the next four years, ownership of the team changed hands twice, with subsequent name changes, first to Newcastle Riverkings and then Newcastle Jesters. It was no joke for the fans of the Durham Wasps. The links with Durham had been lost forever.

Unfortunately, the departure of The Wasps brought financial difficulties to the Durham rink. It closed on 8 July, 1996, reopening a year later as a 20-lane bowling alley. Like the ice rink, the bowling alley proved to be a popular leisure attraction for the people of Durham and although its eventual role in the current riverside developments seems uncertain the days of ice skating in Durham City would appear to be over.

Historic view of skating on the river. St. Oswald's Church can be seen in the distance (MR)

Chapter Six

The Elvets

Elvet is the south-eastern suburb of Durham City and four bridges link the area with the very centre of the city. First there is Kingsgate footbridge, which we have already mentioned in connection with the Bailey then there is Baths Bridge. Largest of the four is New Elvet Bridge with its busy traffic and finally we have the historic Elvet Bridge.

Baths Bridge is a footbridge and links the Leazes Road side of the river beneath Claypath with the public swimming baths (scheduled for relocation) on Elvet Riverside. Baths Bridge was first built as a wooden structure in 1855 but was replaced by an iron footbridge in 1898 and then by a new bridge in 1962.

An eighteenth century riverside house called Woodbine Cottage stood near Baths Bridge at the foot of Pelaw Leazes Lane. It belonged in the nineteenth century to George Swinburne who was the owner, along with John Swinburne of a watchmaking business at number 1 Market Place. Another member of the family called Thomas owned a similar business on Elvet Bridge.

In later days part of Woodbine Cottage was a sweet shop but unfortunately the whole building was demolished in the 1960s when construction of the new Leazes Road caused it to subside.

Standing between Baths Bridge and Elvet Bridge is Brown's boathouse near the site of another cottage called Ivy Cottage that was demolished in the 1960s. The busy Prince Bishops Shopping Centre stands close to this point and the massive New Elvet Bridge carries busy traffic above our heads to feed the Leazes Bowl roundabout at the top of the bank. It is rather remarkable we have such a pleasant riverside walk here.

Woodbine Cottage was home to a watchmaking family

The riverside hereabouts (on the Leazes Road side) was formerly the site of Paradise Cottage, that was once the home to a family of boatbuilders called Ebdy in the mid-nineteenth century. Later in the 1880s it was the residence of a cabinet maker-publican-turned boatbuilder called Thomas Colpitts.

The cottage dating from the eighteenth century was acquired by Joseph Brown, a pleasure boat proprietor and boat builder sometime in the 1890s. Since then it has been known as Brown's Boat House, a building of great character that leans ever so slightly over the riverside footpath. In 2004 Brown's Boathouse became the Chase riverside bar.

The Boathouse was on the edge of Paradise Gardens (DS)

It was at the boathouse that a walled vennel or alleyway called Paradise Lane once terminated near the river bank. The lane once passed through Paradise Gardens that were situated between Claypath and Elvet Bridge but the gardens have long since gone. Today the quickest route from Elvet Bridge to Claypath is through a concrete pedestrian subway that passes underneath Leazes Road. It emerges near a large grass verge at the rear of Claypath which is just about the only hint we have that gardens once stood here.

During the nineteenth century an iron foundry operated at the foot of Paradise Lane in the vicinity of Elvet Bridge. It was operated by a family called Chisman who were variously described as whitesmiths, bellhangers, iron founders, and hot water engineers. At the time of Robert Surtees' History of Durham City (1840) the business was owned by a Mrs Chisman.

New Elvet Bridge was completed in 1976 as part of a through road that bypasses the Market Place but by far the oldest and most beautiful bridge in the Elvet area is Elvet Bridge itself.

Elvet Bridge was constructed on the orders of the powerful Prince Bishop, Hugh Du Puiset, better known as Bishop Pudsey who was arguably the most prince-like of Durham's bishops. A nephew of King Stephen, Pudsey became Bishop in 1154 but had previously been treasurer of the Archbishopric of York where he was also an Archdeacon.

As a Prince Bishop Pudsey held a number of political powers, but he seemed hungry for yet more influence. The importance of his role in the North was recognised by the King and, in time, he became Earl of Northumberland, Chief Justiciar of England and Regent of the North.

By 1189 his possessions included Newcastle, Durham, Bamburgh and Windsor Castle. He was the virtual ruler of Northern England during the King's absence. Such absences were frequent because the King, Richard the Lionheart, was often away fighting in the Crusades.

Pudsey instigated much building work in northern England. He was responsible for Norham Castle on the River Tweed, St. Cuthbert's

church in Darlington and the Galilee Chapel at Durham Cathedral.

However, Elvet Bridge is perhaps the most striking reminder of Pudsey's time. The bridge was begun around 1160, and was spurred on by urban development in what was called Elvet borough.

Most of Elvet belonged to the Priory of Durham Cathedral and could be reached from the Cathedral by a ford across the river where Kingsgate Bridge now stands or by the long route over Framwellgate Bridge via Quarryheads Lane and South Street.

Seal of Bishop Pudsey

Around 1160 Bishop Pudsey seized the northern parts of Elvet from the priory and made it into 'bishops land'. The part of Elvet he seized was called Elvet Haugh and came to be known as the Borough of Elvet. Here he built about 40 merchants' houses in a new street which we know today as Old Elvet. Ironically, it seems that the street now called New Elvet was already in existence and was thus the older street.

The Bishops Borough of Elvet was separated from the remainder of Elvet to the south. The southern part of Elvet continued to be owned by the priory and was known as the Barony of Elvet. It was separated from the Borough by a lane or street called Ratten Rawe (Rotten Row). Ratten Rawe is known today as Court Lane.

A lane leading down to the Kingsgate ford also formed part of the boundary as did the eastern continuation of Court Lane called Green Lane. Green Lane runs along the southern edge of Durham 'Racecourse'.

The erection of the merchants' houses in Elvet was tied in with the opening of Elvet Bridge. This bridge was fortified with a turret at the city end and became a focus for trade and commerce. In 1195 Pudsey repented from his underhanded land seizure and handed Elvet Borough back to the cathedral priory. Over time Pudsey's settlement at Elvet merged with that of the priory in and around their farm and settlement in what is now Hallgarth Street and New Elvet. By 1347 several shops and stalls were built across Elvet Bridge and these establishments yielded their rent to the priory.

A chapel stood at either end of Elvet Bridge. Chapels were a common feature on medieval bridges and were often associated with raising money for the upkeep of the bridge. The receipt of alms from travellers for the maintenance of a bridge was called 'pontage'.

At the eastern, Elvet end of the bridge stood the Chapel of St. Andrew. William, son of Absalon, established this chapel during the time of Bishop Robert De Insula (1274-1283). At the city end of the bridge stood the other chapel dedicated to St. James. It also had medieval origins and was built by a Durham burgess called Lewin. A building still stands on the eastern end of the bridge today and is easily identified by its Dutch gabled exterior.

This building may incorporate part of the ancient chapel of St. Andrew, and the lower parts of the building display medieval masonry that seem to be contemporary with the bridge itself. The presence of such a historic house on a medieval bridge is a rarity in Britain.

Elvet Bridge

Many merchants and other residents lived in houses on Elvet Bridge but the instability caused by the constant force of the river was a threat to the bridge's residents. In 1760 several overcrowded houses were removed from the north pillar of the bridge after they were declared unsafe. Those that survived demolition were seemingly not much safer.

Eight years later in 1768, a blacksmith watched as the floor of his shop on the bridge fell into the river as he opened the door to his workplace. All his tools were washed away and the fabric of the building soon followed.

The blacksmith had a lucky escape, as did the bridge's residents in the great flood of 1771, when the River Wear rose 18 inches higher than it had ever done before. The flood destroyed three or perhaps four of the central arches of the bridge, carrying away a number of houses.

Despite the destruction, some buildings survived. As late as the mid-nineteenth century the bridge was still home to about 100 residents, most of whom lived on the approach road to the bridge on the city side. This road leads down to the bridge from Saddler Street and the Magdalene Steps and was known in historic times as Souter Peth meaning 'the shoemakers steep street'.

Although Pudsey was responsible for building Elvet Bridge, parts were completely reconstructed in 1500. It is probable that the original arches were rounded and replaced with the present slightly pointed arches in the later medieval period.

There is some dispute over how many arches exist. The sixteenth century antiquarian John Leland said the bridge had 14 arches, but this has never been proven. The river flows through four full arches and the remaining arches are dry or semi-dry. Ten arches have been identified but others may be concealed beneath the street on the Elvet side or beneath Souter Peth. One rounded arch on the Elvet side survives and is still visible beneath the gabled building on the Elvet side of the river. It may be Pudsey's original.

A Victorian illustration of Elvet Bridge

On the Durham (Souter Peth) side of Elvet Bridge, is a dry archway beneath the bridge that is now occupied by a pub. This archway served as a debtor's prison in the nineteenth century. It was linked to a house of correction on the city end of the bridge.

In 1632, this institution appears to have replaced or come to occupy part of a chapel dedicated to St. James that stood on the bridge at this point. The prison cells beneath the bridge were linked with others in the Great North Gate, a massive defensive gate that straddled nearby Saddler Street.

The Great North Gate served for many years as a prison, and a prison reformer who visited the cells and prison in the eighteenth century was appalled by the conditions, finding many of the prisoners, (who were mostly awaiting transportation), living in dreadful conditions where they were plagued with sickness.

The Great North Gate built by Bishop Langley dated from 1417 and apart from being a horrific place of imprisonment was also an annoying obstruction to traffic. It was finally removed in 1820 when prisoners were moved to a new jail at Elvet. The new jail was started in 1809 and is the Durham prison we know today.

In November 1821 one of the last and most famous inmates of the Elvet Bridge prison passed away. His name was Jimmy Allan (or occasionally Allen), a gipsy piper who was one of the most notorious characters in our region's history. He was known across the length and breadth of Britain, but there is a great deal of uncertainty about his life, as many legends surround his name.

It is believed that Jimmy was born near Rothbury, in Northumberland, about 1733, and at some time during his early years was adopted by the Faa family. Also known as the Faws, they were a well-known gipsy clan in the

Border region and lived at Kirk Yetholm, in Teviotdale, just across the Scottish border.

Jimmy Allan

Kirk Yetholm was the headquarters for the Border gypsies, and the Faws were one of the most important clans. Wull, or Will Faa, who adopted Jimmy, was regarded as the King of Border gypsies, and may have taught Jimmy to play the Northumbrian pipes. Jimmy was playing the pipes from about the age of 14.

Skilled pipers gained great acclaim in the Borders, where there were three classes of piper. Lowest in the social scale were the wandering or gipsy pipers, while higher up were town pipers, and higher still the appointed pipers who served particular dukes or noblemen. Jimmy was a particularly talented piper and would ultimately achieve the status of official piper to the Countess of Northumberland.

Unfortunately at heart, Jimmy was always a wandering gipsy, and a notorious one at that. He seems to have lived the life of a loveable rogue. He had many lady friends, and often charmed them out of purse. He may have left a number broken-hearted, and on at least one occasion, he committed bigamy.

Jimmy's other vices included drinking and gambling, and he often indulged in cattle and horse thieving to raise money for his deviant ways. Regularly enlisting and then deserting from various armies was another way in which Jimmy found himself in trouble, and he was on the run for most of his life. He is said to have travelled widely in Europe, where he entertained audiences with pipes, and may have ventured as far as the East Indies.

Dublin and Edinburgh were thought to be amongst his regular haunts, and here he would certainly have found audiences to appreciate his traditional music.

Unfortunately, it is difficult to know the true events of Jimmy's life, but it is certain that his wandering ways were eventually brought to an end in 1803. In that year, he stole a horse from Gateshead, then in the County of Durham, and was pursued north until he was captured at Jedburgh, in the Scottish Borders. He was convicted at the Durham Assizes and sentenced to death. The only alternative was to accept transportation, so ensuring that he would never set foot in Britain ever again.

However, Jimmy escaped both punishments on account of his old age and poor health. He was to live the rest of his life in the dungeon beneath Elvet Bridge, often suffering from illness in his later years.

Jimmy lived there until he passed away on the unlucky 13th of November, 1810, aged 77. A pardon allowing for Jimmy's release had, in fact, just been granted by the Prince Regent, but unfortunately it did not arrive in Durham until shortly after Jimmy's death. Today it is often claimed that Jimmy can be heard playing his pipes in the dungeon beneath Elvet Bridge, making Jimmy arguably Durham's most famous ghost.

In 1997, strange happenings were reported from a coffee shop that stands above the Elvet Bridge dungeons. These included a broken grandfather clock that suddenly chimed and an apparition of an old woman poking a fire. The dungeon where Jimmy resided was in recent years converted into a pub bearing Jimmy's name, and there have been reports of spooky activities in the bar.

On one occasion, shortly after the bar opened in December 2002, the assistant manager reported a glass that was suddenly flung from a shelf for no reason. Perhaps it was Jimmy reaching for another drink.

Old and New Elvet

Elvet takes its name from the Anglo-Saxon words Aelfet-Ee, meaning swan-island, and was first mentioned way back in AD 762 when a Bishop of Whithorn called Peotwine was consecrated there. Whithorn, in Scotland, is one of Britain's oldest Christian sites, so Elvet was probably a place of importance. It is likely that Elvet was initially more important than Durham itself, since Durham does not receive a mention until 233 years later, in AD 995, when Dun Holm, or 'hill-island' was settled by the carriers of St. Cuthbert's coffin. Dun Holm and

Elvet were both 'islands' because they were both surrounded on three sides by the River Wear.

It was New Elvet and not Old Elvet that originally formed the main street of the area. Until the 1930s, Old and New Elvet resembled each other in appearance. Today, New Elvet lives up to its name since few old buildings remain. One row of shops in New Elvet, near Hallgarth Street, show timber-framed Tudor-style woodwork, but these are clearly fakes that only date from the 1920s.

On the other side of the road is the more recent Dunelm House, or university student union building that overlooks the river. Built between 1961 and 1965, it was a winner of Royal Institute of British Architects and Civic Trust awards, but not everyone is convinced by the accolades.

One of New Elvet's most historic buildings is the Three Tuns Hotel, a former coaching inn, dating in parts to the sixteenth century. In the Victorian era it belonged to the Brown family and, according to an old saying, Mrs Brown's cherry brandy was one of the things for which Durham was famed. In times gone by lucky hotel guests were traditionally presented with a free tot of cherry brandy on arrival.

Also in New Elvet, near the junction with Old Elvet and Elvet Bridge is the Half Moon Inn and next door, the City Hotel (that has recently reverted to this old name after a stint as an Irish theme bar). Both pubs date in part to the seventeenth century. The City Hotel was a private mansion until the early nineteenth century, while the Half Moon, mentioned in the 1851 census, was once a livery stable and hiring place for horses and traps.

Sadly, with all its modern buildings and despite some recent tasteful development, New Elvet is a rather disappointing street compared to Old Elvet, although it is

nearly always swarming with students who at least give the street some life. Unfortunately, the street's extension over the River Wear, via the modern New Elvet Bridge, has given New Elvet the permanent appearance of a through road since the 1970s.

Things are, however a little more interesting at New Elvet's southern end where the street splits into Church Street and Hallgarth Street which both have visible character and history. The name of Hallgarth Street comes from the site of the priory's manor farm or Hall Garth. In 1083, Bishop Carileph who built Durham Cathedral gave Elvet, then called the Barony of Elvet, to the cathedral's priory monastery. The monastery lands were focused upon what is now Hallgarth Street.

The Hallgarth Tithe Barn (MR)

The only remnant of the priory farm is an impressive fifteenth century tithe barn, now used as a club by Durham prison officers. A tithe was a kind of taxation in which the prior's tenant farmers gave one tenth of their grain to the monastery. The barn is one of Durham's least-known buildings and fortunately only just avoided demolition in the 1970s.

Old Elvet is Durham's widest street and with the possible exception of the North and South Bailey is regarded as its most attractive. From the late nineteenth century to the 1950s, it was the home of the annual horse fair.

Most buildings in Old Elvet are of Georgian origin, but the most obvious exceptions are the Masonic Hall of 1869, the Methodist chapel of 1903 and the Old Shire Hall of 1898.

The bright red brick Shire Hall, with its green copper dome, is the most imposing building in the street and has been criticised for destroying Old Elvet's Georgian elegance. However, the hall has mellowed with age and it is now an impressive focal point for the street. It was built to house Durham County Council, a few years after the council was created in 1888.

In those days the council covered a much bigger area than it does today, encompassing places such as Stockton, Hartlepool, Gateshead, Sunderland and South Shields. It soon became apparent that the Shire Hall was not big enough to house all the departments of the council's administration.

An extension was built in 1905 for the education department but it was still not enough. Council departments gradually acquired other buildings across the street. Old Elvet became the focal point for the entire county's administration. Prior to this time the street was largely residential.

The council eventually vacated Shire Hall and its Old Elvet offices in 1963 after relocating to the purpose-built County Hall at Aykley Heads. Durham University, established in the 1830s, immediately acquired the Old Shire Hall as its administrative headquarters. It thus gained a red brick building that was more typical of a late nineteenth or early twentieth century university. Within

two or three years the University took over most of the council offices in Old Elvet.

Since the University was already a major presence in the North and South Bailey, it meant that the city's best streets were now dominated by the University. The University's acquisition of properties in these old streets has probably helped to discourage commercial and tourist developments in these aesthetically sensitive parts of Durham.

Elvet, St. Cuthbert's Catholic church (MR)

Standing close to the Old Shire Hall are Elvet Methodist Chapel of 1903 and the Roman Catholic church of St. Cuthbert which are both symbols of Elvet's long history of Catholicism and non-conformism.

John Wesley, the founder of English Methodism was a regular visitor to Durham and would often preach in Elvet. A Wesleyan Methodist Society was formed in the city in 1743 and from 1770 services were held in a converted building in Rotten Row. Rotten Row or Ratten Rawe was the old name for Court Lane which links Old Elvet to New Elvet. The old chapel building was demolished in the 1940s. However, a new chapel had been built in Chapel Passage at 57 Old Elvet behind the County Hotel in 1808.

This was eventually replaced in 1903 by the present chapel at the opposite side of the road.

The New Connexion Methodists also had a presence in Old Elvet for a time. The Old Elvet New Connexion Society was founded in 1828. It first met at 33 Old Elvet and moved later to number 15. Elvet was the heart of the city's Methodist movement but in the nineteenth century there were also chapels in Silver Street, Claypath, Waddington Street as well as in several of the surrounding mining villages and city suburbs.

Elvet was also for many centuries the home of the city's Roman Catholic community. In the years following the abolition of Roman Catholicism during the Reformation, it seems to have been one of the main Roman Catholic centres in the County.

From the reign of James I (1603) restrictions on the practice of Roman Catholicism were relaxed and Durham City was served by itinerant priests. In the 1660s the Maire family held Roman Catholic services in their house in Gilesgate and I believe these continued until the eighteenth century.

The Roman Catholic Jesuits had a chapel in Old Elvet (at number 44-45) from at least as early as 1688 because it was in that year that the building was destroyed by a mob. In those days Roman Catholics often faced persecution as papists were frowned upon by some sectors of society.

The Jesuit Chapel was on the north side of Old Elvet opposite Court Lane in a property belonging to Mary Radcliffe, daughter of the Earl of Derwentwater, a prominent Catholic.

Mary was Chaplain Resident at the chapel from 1705 to 1730. It was Mary Radcliffe that built the prominent house in Old Elvet in 1698 that later become part of the

County Hotel, or Royal County as it is known today. The Catholic chapel was vacated around 1820 when part of it seems to have become a Catholic School.

Until around 1826 there were two new Catholic churches in Old Elvet. These united in 1827 under one roof in the form of the new Roman Catholic church of St. Cuthbert. This church was constructed in 1827 by the Durham City architect Ignatius Bonomi and was built on the Court Lane side of Old Elvet. It still stands today opposite the Crown Court and prison. A spire was added in 1869.

The Royal County Hotel is arguably Old Elvet's most historic building. It developed from houses of the 1600s and 1700s that were once home to wealthy northern families like the Radcliffes and Bowes.

Today The Royal County stands at the western terminus of Old Elvet, but this was not always the case. Until 1971, there were a further two buildings in Old Elvet that joined the street with Elvet Bridge. One was the 1871 County Court and the other was the Waterloo Hotel, which stood right next door to the Royal County. Both were demolished so that the neighbouring street of New Elvet could be extended across the river via New Elvet Bridge.

Rather confusingly, in the nineteenth century, the Royal County was called the Waterloo Hotel which meant that there were actually two Waterloos that co-existed side by side. One was specifically called Ward's Waterloo Hotel to distinguish it from the hotel next door which was called Thwaite's Waterloo Hotel.

Thwaite's Waterloo Hotel, was the one knocked down in 1971. Thwaites and Ward were the respective owners, but in 1864, Ward's hotel became the County Hotel. It only became the 'Royal' County in about 1900, following a visit from the Prince of Wales.

A former temperance inn called the Dunelm Hotel stood on the Royal County's other flank. It was operated by the influential Pattinson family during the twentieth century and for a time the building included a cafe, toyshop and hardware store. It closed in the early 1960s and was used for a time by students for social events until the construction of the student union building in New Elvet. The old Dunelm Hotel was eventually incorporated into the Royal County Hotel after much alteration.

On the north side of Old Elvet to the rear of the street's properties is a large open, green area known in Durham as the Racecourse. Horseracing was held on this spot from about 1733. Previous to that time races were held at Framwellgate Moor, Brasside Moor or Durham Moor, all in the northern part of the city. Apart from in 1792 and 1793, when they returned to Framwellgate Moor, Durham's races were held at Elvet up until about 1895 when a new racecourse opened at Shincliffe.

New Elvet in 1966 looking towards Old Elvet where we can just see the old County Court and part of the Waterloo Hotel, both of these were demolished to make way for New Elvet Bridge (NE)

On 14 April, 1873 the Elvet race meeting is known to have attracted a crowd of 80,000 people. It was a two day event and with accommodation in short supply many of the city's residents offered their beds for the night.

In times gone by the open land known as the racecourse at Elvet was called the Smiddy Haughs or Smelt Haugh. A haugh is usually a riverside meadow and it is thought that the Prior of Durham established a smithy here on this riverside land back in medieval times. The land seems to have belonged to the Hostellier of the Priory of Durham Cathedral and it was here that the horses belonging to pilgrims and other visitors were tethered.

Historic view of Old Elvet

The north side of the old Racecourse is skirted by a riverside footpath. Over on the north side of the river is Pelaw Wood in the Gilesgate area of the city. The riverside footpath leads to Elvet Riverside at the western, city end of the path. Here were built the public baths that opened in 1855 but they were reopened in 1932 and presently await further development as it seems that Durham Baths will be moving to the riverside near Providence Row. The nearby footbridge dates from 1962 and is the third

successive structure to be called Baths Bridge. Earlier bridges dated from 1855 and 1898.

The south side of the old racecourse is skirted by an ancient footpath called Green Lane. This commences in Old Elvet near Whinney Hill and leads down towards the river at Hollow Drift rugby ground opposite the site known as Old Durham. The city's rugby club, founded in 1872 has been located at Hollow Drift since 1885.

Hollow Drift is a former meander of the River Wear that dried up around 1492. Green Lane narrows off at this point and branches south along the river bank around the foot of the heavily wooded Maiden Castle. It is thought that the lane was an old road to Shincliffe. It seems likely that in times gone by the road commenced near Durham Cathedral, crossed the river by a ford that is known to have existed somewhere near Kingsgate Bridge and then followed the course of Rotten Row (now Court Lane) and along Green Lane to Shincliffe.

At the Whinney Hill-prison end of Green Lane is Durham Magistrates Court. Dating from the 1960s it is built on the site of Elvet Railway Station of 1893. The actual railway which had ceased to operate by the 1950s ran close to the course of Green Lane and crossed the river by means of an iron bridge near Hollow Drift, but the bridge has long since gone.

Part of the way along Green Lane, but just before we reach the river there was once a medieval mill called Skaltok Mill. It stood on a meander of the River Wear from the twelfth century but was abandoned in 1492 after the river changed its course to form the present Hollow Drift.

Durham's racecourse is a focal point for Durham Regatta which is an important event in the city's annual calendar. This rowing event was established in 1834 but

developed from a procession of boats that took place here from 1815. It was initially a celebration of the victory at the Battle of Waterloo.

The Miners' Gala passes through Old Elvet, July 1957 (NE)

Without a doubt Durham Racecourse is best known as the annual home for the Durham Miners' Gala (pronounced Gayla) which has been held here since 15 June, 1872. This was not the first gala as that took place on 12 August, 1871 in the city's Wharton Park. Now traditionally held on the third Saturday in July the Miners' Gala or 'Big Meeting' once attracted crowds of 300,000 or more. Since the closure of all the County Durham mines the event is now only a sad reflection of what it once was and although colliery brass bands and some political leaders still attend the event we no longer have the massive crowds and seemingly endless processions wedging their way through the city's narrow streets.

Durham Prison

A visit or stay at Durham is often a pleasant experience, whether you are a tourist attracted to the cathedral or a student at Durham University. However, for some, being 'in Durham' is an altogether different experience and a one in which they have very little choice. I am of course referring to the inmates of Durham Prison.

There has been a prison of one form or another in Durham since medieval times. It is known for example that a prison cell was attached to Durham Cathedral in the area of the cloisters. A prison is also known to have existed in South Street in medieval times but there were probably others.

By 1387 Durham's main prison was located on the western side of Palace Green as we know that in that year there was a jail break. From about 1417, the prison was moved to the Great North Gate in Saddler Street and in about 1632 this jail was interlinked with a House of Correction beneath Elvet Bridge.

Conditions in these early jails were appalling and as early as 1774 some individuals were beginning to question the treatment of prisoners. In that year a prison reformer called John Howard visited Durham Jail and its associated cells and reported the dreadful situation that existed.

In 1808 a Justice of the Assize called Sir George Wood Knight instructed a grand jury to consider the existing site and condition of the prison. The jury concluded that the Jail, House of Correction and associated courts were 'insecure, unwholesome, inconvenient and wholly inadequate'. On top of it all, the narrow entrance of the Great North Gate presented a traffic hazard for travellers making their way up and down the Bailey towards Durham Cathedral.

Things were pushed into motion by the then Bishop of Durham, Shute Barrington, who promised to donate £2000 towards a new prison providing that it was commenced before April 1810. By 1809 Parliament empowered local magistrates to erect suitable new buildings. The site chosen was a field at the head of Old Elvet.

The Old Jail, part of the Great North Gate

Described as a dry, healthy spot, it was purchased by the Reverend John Fawcett, one of the men entrusted with the prison's development. Mr Francis Sandys, architect of the new jail at Gloucester was appointed to the task of building both court and jail. On 31 July, 1809, Sir Henry Vane Tempest laid the foundation stone in the presence of several local dignitaries including Ralph John Lambton, Shute Barrington and officers and brethren of the Provincial Grand Lodge of Freemasons.

Unfortunately as Mr Sandys' work proceeded it was heavily criticised and deemed insecure. He was dismissed from the job, but according to the Durham historian Surtees, he had successfully completed the court.

The prison was a different matter. A new architect called Moneypenny was appointed but Mr Moneypenny seems to have encountered difficulties, partly due to escalating costs. These were partly caused by having to remove and work around the efforts of Mr Sandys. Like Sandys, Moneypenny was dismissed but refused to lay the matter to rest. In a series of newspaper articles and circular letters he attacked Sandys' professional character. Sandys subsequently sued Moneypenny for libel and for his efforts a court awarded him £100 of Moneypenny's money.

Meanwhile, Ignatius Bonomi, a Durham architect, of Italian parentage, was given the job. He supervised the project very closely but with less attention to ornate detail than that envisaged by Sandys. Bonomi's work met with general satisfaction, except no doubt amongst the future inmates who came to reside there.

The new court opened in August 1811 but prisoners were not removed to the completed jail until August 1819. Durham's previous prison, The Great North Gate, was demolished the following year. It had been one of the most impressive medieval buildings in the city.

The cost for building the new prison, including the demolition of Sandys' work, caused outrage throughout the County of Durham. A cost of £134,684 15s 5d was to be met through the County Rate tax. This was a phenomenal amount of money in those days and attempts were made to resist the payment.

A meeting of landowners and land occupiers was held at the King's Head in Darlington on 7 June, 1813 and a circular letter was posted pleading with people not to pay the tax 'until an opinion of counsel can be obtained on the legality of this rate, by which an enormous sum of money will be raised for purposes, in the judgement of the meeting not within the intent of letter of the act of building the jail'.

The new jail pictured in the 1830s

The protests had little success and the prison and tax, were there to stay. Of course the costs of the building meant little to the inmates who arrived at their new home in August 1819. For most, their only concern was to

leave the prison as soon as they could. A few left as reformed characters, others left hardened by prison life. Some would never leave at all. For many their last glimpse of the world came from the gallows in the prison yard.

Executions in the form of hangings took place at Durham Jail from 1816 until 1958. Before this time, they had taken place at Dryburn, just north of the city. The Dryburn executions dated back to medieval times when drawing and quartering were often part of the ritual.

The last execution at Dryburn is thought to have been in August 1814 when Ann Crampton was hanged for allegedly cutting off her adulterous husband's manhood, but the details of this particular incident though irresistible are scant.

The executions at Dryburn were always in public and often attracted big crowds keen to witness those macabre events. In 1816, executions were transferred from Dryburn to the new courthouse at the front of the prison that was being built in Elvet. The gallows were situated near the steps just outside the courthouse where executions continued to attract big crowds. A nearby house in Old Elvet with an iron balcony facing the court was often rented out for the occasion, to wealthy spectators who could afford the view.

The first execution outside the courthouse was on 17 August, 1816, when John Grieg was hanged for the murder of Elizabeth Stonehouse at Monkwearmouth. Described as a stout, good-looking man of 37 years of age, his body was cut down and given to his friends for interment after the hanging. In later times, the bodies were often buried in the prison grounds or handed over to surgeons for dissection. Almost all of the executions that took place at Durham Jail or courthouse were for murder, but very occasionally executions took place for

rape. These included George Acheson, executed for the rape of a child in 1819, and Henry Anderson of Penshaw, who was executed for a rape in 1822.

William Jobling

Many executions captured the public imagination, such as that of Thomas Clarke of Hallgarth Mill, near Pittington, on 28 February, 1831. Clarke had murdered a 17 year-old maid at the mill. About 15,000 people are thought to have turned up for this execution, perhaps because it was unusual to have such a high-profile case so local to Durham City. Clarke pleaded his innocence in front of the crowd before departing from the world.

Another well-known execution was that of William Jobling, a South Shields miner, who was executed on 3 August, 1832, for the murder of a 71 year-old magistrate called Nicholas Fairles at Jarrow. Jobling had been striking in protest over conditions at a local workhouse when the incident took place. It seems that Jobling was present at the murder but evidence suggests that a colleague called Ralph Armstrong committed the actual crime.

About 100 soldiers, some mounted, were present at Jobling's execution outside Durham courthouse. Jobling intended to address the crowd but words failed him at the last minute. Just as the final bolt was to be withdrawn to release the rope, a person near the scaffold shouted "farewell Jobling', causing him to turn his head. This displaced the cord and protracted his sufferings so that they continued for some minutes. After the execution was complete, the body was hung for an hour and then taken into the jail where it was tarred with pitch. The soldiers escorted the body to Jarrow Slake where it was hung in a cage from a gibbet 21 feet high. Here the body remained until it was stolen on the night of 31 August. It was never seen again.

The practice of gibbeting was outlawed in 1834 and by 1868 public hangings had also been abolished. The last public execution at Durham was on 16 March, 1865, when Matthew Atkinson was hanged outside the courthouse for the murder of his wife at Winlaton.

Executioner William Calcraft

After 1868, all executions at Durham took place behind closed doors within the grounds of Durham prison. These included Durham's most famous execution, that of Mary Ann Cotton. Mary, who was responsible for about 15 murders, was executed at 8am on the morning of 24 March, 1873. Her executors were Thomas Askern and William Calcraft. Had this execution taken place in public it would have surely attracted unprecedented crowds.

It might be thought that the nineteenth century had tougher attitudes on the death penalty than the twentieth century but remarkably only about 36 executions took place at Durham Courthouse and Jail between 1816 and 1899, compared to 55 between 1900 and 1958. This may have been due to a preference for transportation in the nineteenth century. Transportation to Australia or other places was often considered an alternative punishment, even for very serious crimes.

In about 1890, an execution shed was erected in the prison grounds to enclose the pit, or drop, over which the Durham gallows were erected. It was superseded in 1925 by a specially built execution building with a pit inside.

It is interesting to recall some of the famous, or we should say infamous names, that have been imprisoned at Durham over the years. Some of the most notorious figures in British criminal history have resided at Durham as unwilling guests of the reigning monarch.

They have included Mary Ann Cotton, Myra Hindley, Harold Shipman, Rose West, John McVicar and Mad Frankie Fraser to name a few.

These are of course the exceptional characters of ill-gotten fame. Many other inmates, of which there were thousands during the prison's 186 year history have been forgotten. Even unfortunate individuals who ended their lives on the Durham gallows were often no more than a passing curiosity, soon forgotten by those who continued to go about their lives beyond the prison walls.

Most Durham people know little about life within the prison walls. From the outside they admire the elegant, cheerful facade of the creamy-coloured courthouse that masks the dark, grey, formidable and rather sinister looking walls of the nineteenth century prison that lurk behind.

Completed back in 1819 by Ignatius Bonomi in the shape of a quadrangle, the prison was built partly with money from the Bishop of Durham. Back in the nineteenth century, it was the Bishop who appointed the jailer or 'gaoler' in the preferred spelling of the time. Often residing in the prison along with his family and earning, in the 1850s, a salary of £300 a year – we would call him 'the Governor' today. Underneath him were the Prison Chaplain (£200), a surgeon (£40) and other staff including a schoolmaster, taskmaster, matron, turnkey, porter and a number of warders.

At the time of the 1851 census there were 225 prisoners at Durham. There were 36 women prisoners – always segregated from the men – and 11 of these described their occupation as prostitute.

Mary Ann Cotton

About 91 of the 225 prisoners in the jail in 1851 were County Durham born. These were mostly natives of larger towns in the old county like Sunderland, South Shields, Gateshead and Darlington.

Fordyce, the Durham historian writing in 1851 noted that many were from outside the county. These were said to be men of 'bad character and dissipated habits, who had sought a new residence after being driven from their native place'. It was noted that 647 County Durham residents were imprisoned at Durham during the year 1851, mostly for short term sentences but 1,178 'strangers' to the county were also sent to the prison during that year.

Prisoners came from a wide range of occupations but some occupations were more numerous in the prison than others. For example, in the 1851 census the prisoners in Durham Jail included 22 miners and 38 sailors.

Over a quarter of the prisoners in 1851 were aged 20 or under including Bridget and Ellen McQuire, two sisters from Newcastle described as Ballad Singers. They were aged only 12 and 14. The youngest prisoner in the jail at the time was an Irish born boy, James Horn, a common labourer of 11 years old.

By the time of the 1881 census the prison was holding 501 prisoners. Sixty-three of them were coal miners, 68 soldiers and 21 sailors. Offences convicted by miners were often associated with drunkenness, or occasionally violence erupting during employment disputes. For soldiers and sailors, military indiscipline was a common offence and many of those in jail were awaiting court martial. Occasionally sailors were imprisoned for refusing to sail on what they considered un-seaworthy ships.

The number of young people in prison was always a cause for concern. Following a government inspection of Durham Prison in 1851, a report noted that the inmates encountered by the young boys during their stay often influenced the future criminal activities of the boys. 'It is feared that the run-away apprentice is taught the art of picking pockets and the pick pocket is induced to become a burglar', stated the report.

Speaking further of the boys, the report further noted that it is 'pleasing' to the boys' 'precocious vanity that they become familiarised with crime and gradually, think little of the punishment from seeing their seniors along with them in prison'. It was noted that the boys often sat around all day in a room filled with up to 100 prisoners and often gave double the trouble to the officers than most of the adults.

Nineteenth century punishment of prisoners included the Cat o' Nine Tails but punishment was determined by

age. Generally boys could only be whipped in the presence of the jailer and surgeon.

Prisoners were fed on a basic diet that included, oatmeal, porridge, bread and fish each served on set days. The diet was very similar to that fed to the inmates of the workhouse in Crossgate and in truth conditions there were probably just as bad as in prison. As in the workhouse the prison inmates were kept busy at work. Prison work included weaving, mat making, cleaning, teasing rope and joinery for the men with knitting and

Durham Prison (NE)

sewing included in the work given to women. Of course occasionally prisoners kept themselves busy with escape plans, but few succeeded in this respect.

Prison escapes were once a much more common occurrence than they are today. In the 1950s and 1960s they were a constant problem in Britain. Durham Prison was seen as one of the most secure, but even it had its share of escapes. The old Durham Jail, a fortified gateway in Saddler Street set the trend. It was a formidable prison with notorious conditions but even here some prisoners managed to break out.

One of the first breaks occurred in February 1737 when two prisoners – John Dodsworth and John Penman 'viciously knocked down' the underkeeper of the jail. In March 1787 two smugglers escaped from the same jail by means of a rope.

When the new prison opened at Elvet in 1820 it proved very hard to break. There were occasional escapes, but it was considered one of the strongest in Britain for many decades. In October 1961 *The Northern Echo* noted that Durham's escape record was second to none and that there had been only been two escapes in the previous 6 years – an indication of how many escapes were occurring eslewhere.

One of the Durham escapes had occurred earlier in 1961, on 14 March, when Ronnie Heslop otherwise 'Rubberbones' or 'Houdini Hesslop' broke from the prison. Heslop, a native of Page Bank who lived at Ushaw Moor at the time excavated his way free from the prison over a period of four days using a teaspoon and kitchen knife after removing a ventilation grill from the cell floor.

Heslop, a serving soldier was awaiting trial at the Quarter sessions of the Assize Court (now the Crown Court) and jumped down from the roof of this very court during his

escape. He swam the river twice as he made his getaway in a feat emulated by Durham's more famous escapee John McVicar some seven years later. Heslop had been charged with stealing £262 from a Spennymoor lemonade factory and attempting to blow a safe at the Ministry of Labour in the same town. He was on the run for six weeks before recapture.

John McVicar

Heslop's escape made the front page of the Echo, but the paper's main story focused on political events in South Africa. Escapes were seemingly not that significant an event. In fact the night after Heslop's escape there were escapes from Thorp Arch Prison in Yorkshire and at Wandsworth which experienced a further escape on 20

March. With such frequent escapes, it is was no wonder that Durham's six year escape-free record was seen as impressive.

In October 1961 the government started to take action against prison escapes and decided Durham would hold some of the country's most difficult prisoners and particularly those prone to escape.

A specially prepared wing, described as a prison within a prison was developed. It would become the famous E-Wing and was thought to be inescapable. One man proved otherwise. His name was John McVicar.

McVicar, a Londoner once considered the most dangerous man in Britain was an armed robber who escaped from a coach taking him to Parkhurst Prison in 1966. He was on the run for four months and on recapture was taken to Durham Prison. He wasn't in for long as on the 29 October, 1968 he achieved the unthinkable, an escape from E-Wing. McVicar chipped his way through the brick wall of a shower room, replacing bricks with papier mache replicas. After working his way into a ventilation shaft he entered the exercise yard and made his escape over the roof. Two other convicts who attempted to escape with him were captured immediately.

After jumping the prison wall McVicar found himself in an unfamiliar little city, but in his autobiography *McVicar by Himself* he gives a description of streets and features encountered during his night-time escape. Durham can be disorientating to the stranger so we cannot be certain of McVicar's route but he says he passsed the police station and mentions a hump back bridge and a church with a graveyard from where he swam across the river before reaching the gardens at the rear of a college. He then says he walked along a landscaped riverside walk for half a mile until his path was blocked by a factory area. At this point McVicar swam along the river, in the direction of the current, briefly encountering a rat sitting on an exposed pipe. The pipe and occasional rat can still be seen here today.

McVicar slept the night hiding on some derelict land that was perhaps at Framwellgate Waterside or maybe across the river near the Sands. From here he recalls observing the time on a cinema clock tower which must have been the Essoldo in North Road. In the morning McVicar climbed through some building works and entered a narrow cobbled street. He also mentions what he thought to be a bowling alley frequented by kids – perhaps the ice rink. Whatever his route, within half a mile he was in open countryside and from here followed the course of the river and railway as far as Chester-le-Street where he contacted friends in London from a call box. He slept the night in a car, parked in a suburban garage and the following morning was picked up in a car arranged by some friends and taken to London. Here he remained on the run until captured in 1970. McVicar was finally released from prison in 1978. Two years later his life and escape from Durham became the subject of a film starring Roger Daltrey. It was simply entitled *McVicar*.

Church Street, Stockton Road and Mount Joy

Church Street takes its name from the neighbouring church of St. Oswald and dates from Norman times. Pre-conquest sculptures and evidence of an earlier church suggest a very long history and it is possible that St. Oswald's stands on the site where Peotwine, a Bishop of Whithorn was consecrated back in AD 762. In the post conquest era the parish of St. Oswald covered an area stretching both north and south of Durham.

At Church Street Head (the southern end of Church Street) the street forms a junction with Stockton Road, South Road and Quarryheads Lane near the New Inn.

The New Inn is undoubtedly the Durham pub most frequented by Durham University students. There was a coaching inn of this name on the site long before the university came into being in the 1830s, but it is believed that the name New Inn arose after a licence was transferred to the site from another pub further down the South Road.

St Oswald's Church (NE)

Charley's Cross pictured in the 1960s (NE)

Much history surrounds the road junction at which the New Inn stands. Hidden in a nearby field stood Charley's Cross (or Pearsby's Cross), a medieval cross on the outskirts of the old city. In the late 1500s food was left here for the poor of Durham who had been removed from Durham City and banished to Elvet Moor where they lived in specially constructed cells during a terrible plague. The cross was built to symbolise sanctuary in the city and was one of several surrounding Durham. Others included Phillipson's Cross that stood approximately where Whinney Hill roundabout is now located and of course the Neville's Cross which is forever immortalised in the name of a famous battle.

Durham Bow School founded in 1885 stands on the corner close to the Charley's Cross site and has been located on this spot since 1888. It is for boys aged 3 to 13 and since 1976 it has been the preparatory school for Durham School that stands farther north at Bellasis off Quarryheads Lane. As at nearby St. Mary's College the times are changing for the Bow School as girls will be admitted for the first time during 2006.

Stockton Road forms part of the A177 and heads east from New Inn to the roundabout at the junction of Hallgarth Street and Whinney Hill. Here the road becomes Shincliffe Peth and heads south past Maiden Castle through Houghall and Shincliffe on its way to Stockton-on-Tees.

A little less than a century ago much of the area around Stockton Road and Church Street Head was a hive of industrial activity. It was home to a colliery, an iron foundry and building works with many of the surrounding houses occupied by working class men.

The iron foundry was the Union Iron Foundry and was established around 1851 by John Mavin. It stood just off Church Street Head near the junction with Stockton Road and its proprietor lived in Union Place. Union Place is on the north side of Stockton Road and backs onto what was once the foundry site. The foundry business was still operating in the 1880s.

On the opposite side of Church Street from the foundry was an open area called Palmer's Close where coal shafts associated with the neighbouring Elvet Colliery were bored during the nineteenth century. The close was named from Pilgrims (also called Palmers from the act of prayer) who entered the city at this point in medieval times.

On the same side of Church Street, bordering the ancient cemetery of St. Oswald's church there once stood a huge cotton spinning mill. It was erected in 1796 by a member of the Salvin family and was six storeys high with 365 windows. It was one of the most imposing factories ever built in the city but burnt down only ten years later on 6 January, 1804. It must have been one of the most spectacular fires the city has ever seen. Unfortunately the Salvins had not paid their insurance premiums and the factory was not rebuilt.

Near the site of the mill on the south side of St. Oswald's churchyard is Anchorage Terrace in an area once known as Anchorage Close. A hermit or anchorite connected with the neighbouring church lived here in medieval times but nothing is known of his identity.

In the nineteenth century Anchorage Terrace was called Pit Row and housed the miners of Elvet Colliery which stood on the south side of Stockton Road where the University Library now stands. Elvet Colliery seems to have been established in the 1840s by an Elvet resident and former colliery viewer called Thomas Crawford. It was a land sale colliery, in other words coal wasn't transported by sea but was used locally. Coal from Elvet Colliery was consumed by Durham City residents for domestic use and for the creation of coal gas in the city. The colliery was already out of use by the time the first stage of the University science block was opened in 1924 and it is said that the business was closed partly as the result of a possible legal action resulting from the undermining of St. Oswald's church.

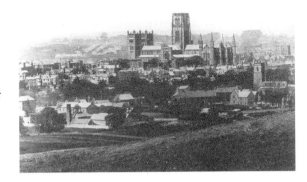

Old photograph showing Elvet Colliery in the foreground

The University Science Block was only the first of many massive university developments that took place on the south side of Stockton Road during the twentieth century. Other developments took place in the 1930s, 50s and 60s when the Science Library was added to a neighbouring site. Apart from Elvet Colliery, the area south of Stockton Road was largely open countryside until the 1920s and marked the southern edge of the city's development as it had more or less done since medieval times.

The only area of land south of Stockton Road that remains undeveloped today is that which rises in a steep hill at the eastern end of the road near Whinney Hill roundabout. This is Mount Joy Hill and lies just south of the roundabout before the road heads off to Shincliffe.

Whinney Hill is the hill on the eastern side of the roundabout. Just behind is another hill on its eastern flank with a precipice called the Scaur that overlooks the River Wear. On a level area at the top of this heavily wooded hill is Maiden Castle – the site of an ancient fort that probably dates from the Iron Age.

Whinney Hill roundabout is overlooked on its north side by the impressive curve of Mount Joy Crescent along the course of the Stockton Road. It was built and resided in by a man called Thomas Coates who owned a large builder's business just behind the terrace in Hallgarth Street where a nursing home now stands.

Mount Joy Crescent was no doubt intended as a showcase for Coates' workmanship. The crescent was reputedly built with stones from Durham's racecourse grandstand. It is the first street in the city to be encountered by motorists as they enter Durham from the south. Coates originally lived in Gilesgate and established his business at 79 Claypath in the 1880s before moving to Elvet at the very beginning of the twentieth century. By the 1920s his business was involved in building,

timber, carting and somewhat surprisingly he also served as an undertaker. With a ready supply of timber such a diversification was not as strange as it sounds. The building business was still going strong at the outbreak of the Second World War.

The actual hill called Mountjoy is situated on the south side of the Whinney Hill roundabout and it was here according to legend that more than a thousand years ago the monks carrying St. Cuthbert's coffin gained their first glimpse of Durham. The monks were no doubt overjoyed with their find but it is more likely that Mount Joy really derives from the old French term 'Mont Joie'.

Mount Joy Crescent (DS)

In France a 'Mont Joie' was a place where pilgrims heaped stones when they gained sight of the end of their pilgrimage. Perhaps a similar practice occurred at Durham.

Today the area called Mountjoy stretches much farther south than the hill from which it is named. Much of the area south of the hill between Little High Wood and Grey Wood is also called Mount Joy and incorporates the Mount Joy Research Centre. Affiliated to the University of Durham it stands out of the back of Grey College in an area of Durham known as Bucks Hill.

South of the research centre is the beautiful Great High Wood which sits on a high ridge that bends to form a nook within which we find Mount Joy Cottage and a covered reservoir. The reservoir dates from the 1840s and served Durham City but was not always covered. It was connected to a pump house (now a restaurant) across the other side of the wood at Houghall. A cottage near the reservoir was built for the 'Turncock', or man that looked after its maintenance and management. Houghall, Old Durham and neighbouring Shincliffe are featured in the accompanying book on the Durham City villages.

Chapter Seven

South Road and the Colleges

By the end of the nineteenth century suburbs had developed to the north, east and west of Durham City but the area to the south of Elvet remained largely open countryside. Beyond the tip of Durham's River peninsula the scenery was typified by country lanes, woodland and a scattering of houses and cottages all within easy reach of the road from Farewell Hall.

Today this road is the A177 or South Road that commences at the Cock of the North roundabout near the junction with the Great North Road. With the exception of a small, recently developed housing estate near the roundabout this area is still largely void of suburban housing development. Nevertheless hundreds of people live and work in this area today because it is the part of Durham most dominated by the colleges and departments of Durham University.

From Mount Oswald (north of the roundabout) to Mount Joy on the outskirts of Elvet there are dozens of university buildings. Built in a variety of architectural styles and often in landscaped grounds, they have all cropped up in the area since the end of the Second World War.

However the first educational establishment encountered as we proceed north from Farewell Hall is not a University building but Durham High School for Girls. Founded in 1884 its first head was Miss Elizabeth Gray, but in those days it was situated at number 33 Claypath and was a rather small establishment. It moved to Haughton Hall South Bailey in 1886 and around 1910 to new premises at Leazes House near Claypath. It was not until 1968 that it moved to the present purpose built buildings near Farewell Hall.

The first Oswald House

As the A177 continues north from the High School towards Mount Oswald it takes on the rather peculiar name of Money Slack. The name is something of a mystery, but was originally designated to a marshy area in the vicinity of neighbouring Blaids Wood on the eastern side of the road. 'Slack' was certainly an old word for marsh, but why money? Perhaps it was a person's name or maybe coins were found here years ago. Another story is that highwaymen relieved (or slackened) travellers of their money in times gone by.

Mount Oswald stands in parkland on the western side of Money Slack and with the exception of Burn Hall near

Croxdale is perhaps the most impressive mansion in the Durham City area. Originally called Oswald House, it was a small villa built around 1800 for a London merchant called John Richardby. The architect is unknown but the house was named from its location in the Elvet parish of St. Oswald.

Richardby sold the property to Thomas Wilkinson of Brancepeth in 1806. Thomas Wilkinson was a one time Alderman and Mayor of Durham but the house didn't develop into a palatial mansion until after 1828 when he sold the property to his cousin, the Reverend Percival Spearman Wilkinson of Belmont.

The Reverend, who was a one-time curate of Ainderby Steeple in North Yorkshire, employed Phillip Wyatt the architect of Wynyard to convert the villa into a grand scale mansion called Mount Oswald.

Mount Oswald's architectural style has been attributed to the Durham City architect Ignatius Bonomi (who built Burn Hall for the Salvin family) but records confirm that it was Wyatt who built Mount Oswald. Wilkinson may have had reasons for overlooking Bonomi in Wyatt's favour. Wyatt had built Wynyard for the Marquess of Londonderry and like the Marquess, Wilkinson was a staunch Tory.

Bonomi had undertaken work for the rival Whig statesman Lord Lambton, so party politics may have played its part in the choice of architect. Although Thomas Wilkinson, sold the property to his cousin Percival in 1828, Thomas seems to have owned additional land on the opposite side of the road to the north of Mount Oswald. Here his son George built a mansion called Oswald House, a name easily confused with the earlier building at Mount Oswald.

The architect and date of the second Oswald House is unknown but George was certainly in residence there by

1838. George's son, another George Wilkinson was born in this house and went on to become the Bishop of Truro and St. Andrews. When George senior accidentally shot himself dead in 1866 Bishop George sold the property to his sibling Thomas Chandler Wilkinson.

Later in the century Oswald House was occupied by a coal owner called Robinson Ferens, a JP connected with the firm of Ferens and Love. In 1916 Oswald House served as a hospital but during the 1920s, 30s and 40s it was occupied by Mr C. J. Sadler, a member of a well-known family of North East industrialists. Unfortunately Oswald House suffered severe fire damage in 1960 and was subsequently demolished. Since the early 1970s, the site has been occupied by Durham University's Collingwood College.

Meanwhile at Mount Oswald, the Reverend Percival Wilkinson had fathered 8 children and died (probably in a state of exhaustion) in 1875. His son, a JP who was also called Percival Spearman Wilkinson, succeeded him to the property but in the 1890s it seems to have passed into the hands of the North Brancepeth Colliery Company.

Captain Rogerson

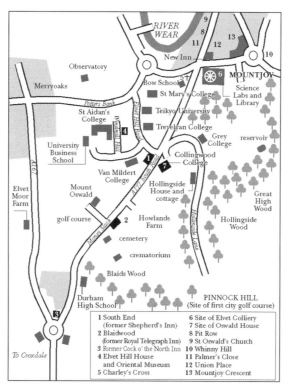

College Area Map (NE)

In 1898 Mount Oswald was leased to Captain John Edwin Rogerson (1868-1925) who was son of John Rogerson of Croxdale.

Rogerson was a JP, Deputy Lieutenant, High Sheriff of Durham and director of the Weardale Steel Coal and Coke Company amongst other industrial concerns. He was also noted for being the Master of the North Durham Foxhounds.

In the late 1920s Mount Oswald became the home of Durham City Golf Club. The club was established in 1887 but was initially located at Pinnock Hill or Pinker

Knowle as it is also known. Pinker Knowle is located near Houghall and is across the road from Mount Oswald beyond the Crematorium. The golf club moved from Pinker Knowle to Mount Oswald in 1928 and was based there until 1974 when it moved across the river to Littleburn near Meadowfield. However, Mount Oswald's owners, North of England Estates continued to operate a golf course on the Mount Oswald site.

Mount Oswald itself has no obvious connection with Durham University but a small cottage facing the estate on the opposite side of the road has a slight link. Previously called Mount Oswald Cottage and now called Blaidwood after a nearby wood, it was home in the 1930s to William Robert Gray, the official robe maker to Durham University. Gray, who later moved to the manor house at Shincliffe was the proprietor of a tailoring business in Durham.

In the 1880s, Blaidwood Cottage was home to a gardener but in the early nineteenth century it was known as Telegraph Hall. Until the 1830s it served as an inn called the Royal Telegraph.

Mount Oswald (DS)

South End and Elvet Hill

The first university buildings to be encountered alongside the A177 north of Mount Oswald are those in the Howlands Farm area on the eastern side of the road. The actual farm was built here on University land during the early twentieth century but most buildings on the site only came into being in 1998. They are part of Durham University's Postgraduate Society or Ustinov College as it has been called since 2002 and around 1,400 postgraduate students are members with more than half originating from overseas.

Newton Wynne Apperley

Howlands Farm is presently an important area of development and is the home to Durham University's sixteenth and newest college, due to open in October 2006. This is Josephine Butler College named after Josephine Butler (1828-1906) a nineteenth century social reformer, who had a huge influence on society's view of women's health and education. Butler was born at Milfield Hill in Northumberland and her father's cousin was Earl Grey the

Victorian Prime Minister whose name is commemorated in another of Durham's University colleges.

South End, once the site of the Shepherd's Inn (DS)

The Howlands Farm area is also a pick up point for Durham's Park and Ride scheme that is designed to reduce traffic congestion in the city centre.

The actual farm at Howlands is not particularly old but there are a number of older houses hidden amongst the modern colleges just to the north. They include buildings like Hollingside House and Elvet Hill House.

One of the first of the older properties we encounter heading north is South End. This stands on the western side of the A177 at the junction of Elvet Hill Road near Van Mildert College. In the early nineteenth century it was a coaching inn called The Shepherd's Inn, a name that reminds us of the rural nature of this area in those earlier times.

By the 1860s the inn became a collection of dwellings called South End where residents included Charles Hodgson, an iron merchant who owned a business in Durham's North Road. There were other residents at the house but Hodgson was still a resident here in the 1880s.

In the 1890s and early twentieth century South End was home to the Australian born Newton Wynne Apperley JP (1846-1925). Apperley who rather vainly called his house Newton Wynne, was Private Secretary to the Marquess of Londonderry, a Chairman of St. Oswalds Parish Council and the author of a book on fox hunting.

Today the houses of South End belong to Durham University and recent occupants have included the Institute for Middle Eastern and Islamic Studies and the University's Conference and Tourism section. It is currently occupied by part of Durham University's Sports department.

The most prominent modern building in the South End area today is Van Mildert College that stands alongside the older buildings. Opened in 1966 it was built by Middleton, Fletcher and Partners and features a large ornamental lake in its grounds. The lake was apparently the architect's response to a drainage problem encountered during construction of the college.

Van Mildert College is named after William Van Mildert who was technically the last Prince Bishop of Durham. He was the founder of Durham University in the 1830s and presented Durham Castle to the University as its first college. Van Mildert College and South End stand near the entrance to Elvet Hill Road that leads up a hill towards a building of 1820 called Elvet Hill House. It lies hidden amongst the modern colleges.

Now attached to the University's Oriental Museum, Elvet Hill was built by the famed Durham City architect (of Italian parentage) called Ignatius Bonomi as his own home. Bonomi's house was initially called the Rising Sun and was laid out with splendid gardens complete with peacocks, but the architect doesn't seem to have lived there very long. Before 1838 it became home to John Fogg Elliott, a Director of the North Eastern Railway, a company for whom Bonomi undertook a considerable amount of work. Elliott's widow, Sarah was still residing at the house in the 1890s.

Elvet Hill (DS)

In the 1950s Durham University purchased the house from a local solicitor and it subsequently became home to the School of Oriental Studies, later called the Department of East Asian Studies. Elvet Hill House was modified to accommodate university needs but is still largely the work of Bonomi and includes his original sundial on an exterior wall.

Today the Elvet Hill area is more or less a university campus incorporating a number of university buildings and colleges. They include Trevelyan College, a structure of large hexagonal blocks that opened in 1967 and St. Aidan's College that has excellent cathedral views. Founded in 1947 as St. Aidan's Society, it was initially based in Shincliffe Hall but became a college in 1961 when Sir Basil Spence, architect of Coventry Cathedral, erected the present building on the edge of Elvet Moor.

Just east of St. Aidan's is the rather stark Durham University Business School building of 1978. This and St. Aidan's both stand on Mill Hill Lane, an old country lane named from a windmill that stood near Elvet Hill House as recently as 1820. A road through the campus area called Windmill Hill climbs to the site of the mill.

Buck's Hill and Hollingside

Buck's Hill lies on the eastern side of the A177 and as at Elvet Hill on the opposite side of the road there are some older country houses hidden amongst the late twentieth century colleges of Durham University. Here we find Grey and Collingwood Colleges which are both named from famous Northumbrian figures. One was Admiral Collingwood of Tynemouth who fought alongside Nelson at Trafalgar and the other was Earl Grey of tea fame. Grey was the Prime Minister of Britain in the 1830s when Durham University came into being.

Grey College and Durham Cathedral. The college is named after the Northumbrian born Prime Minister Earl Grey (NE)

Collingwood College is a dark brown structure of square brick blocks constructed in the early 1970s by Richard, Sheppard, Robson and Partners. It stands on the site of the mansion called Oswald House that burned down in the previous decade. Nothing remains of the mansion except for the garden lake that is now incorporated into the college grounds.

Grey College dates from 1959-61 and has been described by the architectural historian Nikolaus Pevsner as resembling a housing estate of sub-Georgian houses. The college stands on Hollingside Lane, a pathway that is yet another remnant of pre-university days. It was once an ancient thoroughfare called Butterby Lane and skirts the western fringe of the beautiful Great High Wood. Eventually terminating south of Pinnock Hill (or Pinker Knowle) it crossed the River Wear by a ford to reach the moated farmhouse of Low Butterby to the south. Hollingside House was one of the main routeways in and out of the city.

Hymn writer John Bacchus Dykes

Durham's Great High Wood occupies a mile long ridge on the edge of a river plain that separates Houghall in the east from the university campus area to the west. The southern half of the wood is called Hollingside and this is also the name of an early nineteenth century cottage and house that stand alongside the lane.

Hollingside was once home to John Bacchus Dykes (1823-1876) a renowned hymn writer. Later residing at Old Elvet he was a Canon and Precentor of Durham Cathedral until he became Vicar of St. Oswalds at Elvet in 1862. He was the composer of some 300 hymns including *St. Cuthbert, St. Oswald, Lindisfarne* and *Hollingside*. His most famous work was 'Melita', better known as *Eternal Father Strong to Save*. The hymn is known in the United States as the naval hymn because it is traditionally sung at the naval academy there.

Across on the eastern side of the A177 from Buck's Hill we find Trevelyan College, Elvet Garth, St. Mary's College and the Teikyo University of Japan occupying the northern half of Elvet Hill. The oldest building in this area is Elvet Garth house formerly called Elvet Villa. In the 1850s it was home to Richard Cail the engineer who along with a Mr Harrison constructed the impressive viaduct in Durham's city centre. Today Elvet Garth serves as a residential block occupied by staff members of Durham University.

Trevelyan College known to students as 'Trevs' occupies the land behind the old house and was completed in 1967. It is named after the famous Cambridge historian George Macaulay Trevelyan (1876-1962), a former vice chancellor of Durham University who had strong family links to Wallington Hall in Northumberland. Trevelyan was best known for his *History of England*, published in 1926. Trevelyan College consists of numerous inter-linked hexagonal buildings.

Close to Trevelyan College is the Teikyo University of Japan in Durham, linked to Durham University but actually an overseas campus for the Teikyo University in Japan. The college in Durham was established in 1990 and gives Japanese undergraduate students an opportunity to study in an English academic environment.

St. Mary's College is the most northerly of the Elvet Hill colleges as we head towards Quarryheads Lane and Stockton Road. The college is also the oldest of the group, tracing its origins back to 1899 when it was established as a Women's hostel for Durham University. It was once situated at Abbey House on Palace Green but moved to the present location at the northern extremity of Elvet Hill in 1952. October 2005 was an historic month for the college, as it opened its doors to male students for the first time.

St. Mary's College (DS)

Quarryheads Lane and South Street

Quarryheads Lane is a busy road that skirts its way around the southern tip of Durham's river peninsula at the top of the river gorge. It commences at The New Inn where it forms a junction with Stockton Road and curves around to the North West where it is joined by Potters Bank.

Quarryheads Lane should not be confused with Quarryhouse Lane in the Neville's Cross area but like that part of the city was once associated with the quarrying of sandstone used in the construction of Durham Cathedral. Stone for the cathedral seems to have come from Kepier Wood near Gilesgate and from Baxter Wood just off Quarryhouse Lane in Neville's Cross, but stone quarried around the Quarryheads area seems to have been used in the construction of the monastic buildings of the Cathedral Priory and at Durham Castle.

Quarryheads Lane is certainly within reach of the cathedral site and stone could have been easily transported across the river. As the lane curves to the north beyond Potters Bank we find an old gateway called the White Gates that probably date from the early nineteenth century. A pathway leads down to the river at Prebends Bridge and here we can stand and admire the cathedral stonework for ourselves in one of the most famous views of the city.

After Framwellgate Bridge and Elvet Bridge, Prebends Bridge is Durham's third oldest. Located near the tip of the peninsula on which Durham Cathedral stands it links Quarryheads Lane to the Baileys on the peninsula across the river to the east. It is used mainly by pedestrians as traffic is virtually excluded.

The bridge opened on 11 April 1778 and was built by George Nicholson, the architect to Durham's Dean and

Cathedral and Fulling Mill viewed from South Street banks (NE)

Chapter. Quarryheads Lane terminates a little north of the Prebends Bridge area at Durham School. Here in the vicinity of the school are two quiet streets called Pimlico and the Grove that branch off from the lane to form a triangle at the southern end of South Street.

Pimlico was named after Pimlico in London, but the reason for the Durham name is unknown. In the nineteenth century the neighbouring street called the Grove was home to the famous oversized actor called Stephen Kemble. He died in 1822 and was buried just across the river in the Cathedral's Chapel of the Nine Altars. His friends included the tiny Polish dwarf called Joseph Boruwlaski who lived nearby in the Bailey.

From Pimlico, South Street runs north to south along the bank top of the sylvan gorge formed by the River Wear. This is the western edge of the Durham river peninsula and there is little room for houses on the eastern side of the street which is just as well because South Street provides one of the best uninterrupted views of the cathedral.

South Street is one of the oldest thoroughfares in Durham and the fact that it uses the word 'Street' rather than 'Gate' as in the case of most ancient streets in the city has led some historians to believe it was once a Roman road. The suggestion is that it was once the main north-south route through Durham and there are other good reasons to believe this may be the case. The fact that it is called South Street when it clearly lies to the west of the cathedral and city centre is one reason to believe the theory. It is also important to remember that Framwellgate Bridge was built before Elvet Bridge, so anyone coming into the city from the south who wanted to cross a bridge would have had to head up South Street to reach the old bridge.

People have certainly lived in South Street since medieval times and there are in existence burgage records that name some of the landholders in South Street way back in the 1200s. They include Isolda daughter of Reyncoce the Scot, Hustinge the Fuller, Robert Quarrington, Simon Filius Simonis Nigri and Peter De Walibus the Rector of Crathorne.

On the river down below South Street are the wooded South Street Banks at the bottom of which stand the redundant South Street Corn Mill. Occupying a site dating back to medieval times the mill was once used by the Priors of Durham. It perches on the western end of the noisy weir that cuts across the river towards the more famous Fulling Mill that sits humbly beneath the cathedral on the opposite bank. South Street Mill can be reached by footpath from Prebends Bridge or Framwellgate Bridge. It is worth the walk because it provides the best known and most photographed riverside view of Durham Cathedral.

South Street is one of the most sought after streets in Durham City and is noted for its expensive town houses.

South Street pictured in 1968 (NE)

It offers one of the most unusual 'side on' views of Durham Cathedral.

Despite its wealth of attractive Georgian houses the street was not always the most desirable place to live and in the nineteenth and early twentieth century properties in this street, particularly at the northern end were regarded as squalid. One particular part of South Street located at this northern end called the Curtain was an especially unfavourable slum.

Perhaps the first inkling that South Street was destined for better times came in 1894 when two derelict houses were purchased and subsequently demolished at the northern end of the street. On 28 July, 1899 of that year the foundation stones of a new school were laid on the site.

The school owed its origins to the bequest of a Scotsman called James Finlay Weir Johnston (born 1796) who had departed from this world almost half a century earlier in 1855 and knew nothing of the school that would bear his name.

The Durham Johnston Technical School when it was located in South Street (MR)

Johnston was a graduate of the University of Glasgow who moved to Durham in 1826 and resided for the rest of his days at number 55 Claypath in the city. He established an academy in Saddler Street and taught English, reading, writing, arithmetic and geography for an annual subscription fee. For an additional charge Latin, Greek, Mathematics, Italian or French could also be taught.

This was an exceptional range of subjects for an academy of this kind. The school proved a successful venture but seems to have closed around 1829 when Johnston started to concentrate his efforts in other areas, particularly experimental chemistry. In the 1830s he became a founder of the British Association for the Advancement of Science and a reader in chemistry and mineralogy at the burgeoning University of Durham. He was handsomely paid for his lectures by clients that included the Newcastle Literary and Philosophical Society and the London Lead Company whose northern headquarters was at Middleton-in-Teesdale.

When he died in 1855 he left a bequest in his will that upon the death of his wife (who would pass away in 1862) a sum of his money should be applied to literary, scientific or educational purposes as considered appropriate by his appointed trustees. Part of this bequest was invested in the Johnston Laboratory at what would later become the University of Newcastle upon Tyne but by the end of the century the bequest was largely untouched. What remained was eventually invested in the foundation of the Johnston Technical School in South Street. This school became the first secondary school in the city and remained on this site in South Street until the early 1950s when it moved to its present location at Crossgate Moor near the top of Redhills Lane. The lower school for the Johnston is located at Whinney Hill.

Whilst the Johnston may be the oldest secondary school in the city, the award for oldest school in both city and county of Durham goes to Durham School, a private school on Quarryheads Lane near the southern extremity of South Street. The school has only been located on this site since 1844, but its origins go back to at least 1414 when Cardinal Thomas Langley, the Prince Bishop of Durham established the institution on Palace Green.

Durham School 1962 (NE)

After the Reformation the school was re-established by Henry VIII but it is widely believed that Langley had merely re-established Durham Cathedral's old almoner's school. This school was located somewhere in the Bailey near the Cathedral cloisters from perhaps as early as AD 995. It was probably re-founded from an earlier monastic school that had once existed on the island of Lindisfarne.

Whatever its origins Durham School moved into an existing nineteenth century house called Belasis House and was adapted as a school by the architect Anthony Salvin between 1843 and 1844. The house, that originally belonged to a surgeon called William Cooke, was further extended in the 1850s and 60s. During the nineteenth century the school was often known as Belasis Grammar School and thus retained a name that had been applied to this part of Durham since Norman times. Belasis is French and means 'beautiful site' but it once belonged to a family called Belasis who were also associated with Belasis near Billingham.

Belasis in Durham encompassed much of the land around Clay Lane to the south west of the Durham peninsula out towards Durham Observatory. Remarkably this area is still a relatively undeveloped part of the city to this day. Durham School stands at the northern end of Quarryheads Lane which makes a sudden turn to the west at this point to become Margery Lane.

Margery Lane is linked to Clay Lane which is the home of the former Nevilles Cross College near the Great North Road. Clay Lane and another historic pathway called Blind Lane encircle the area of Neville's Cross formed by a hill on which we find St. Margaret's Primary School and the streets of Copeland Court and Archery Rise.

Copeland was the name of the man who captured King David of Scotland at the Battle of Neville's Cross. Archery Rise may also take inspiration from the battle but in truth this hill seems to have been situated outside the battlefield area. An archery club once existed near the present tennis courts at the top of the hill and may have provided further inspiration for the street name.

Margery Lane like Quarryheads Lane is actually a busy road and makes a sudden turn to the north where it is joined by Clay Lane. Here Margery Lane heads north towards traffic lights at the junction of Crossgate, Crossgate Peth and Alexandria Crescent. Here we have left the quiet seclusion of Durham School, Quarryheads Lane and Clay Lane far behind and we have to negotiate the busy Durham traffic in the vicinity of the Colpitts pub.

Margery Lane takes its name from St. Margaret as this is part of the Crossgate area of the city in the parish of St. Margaret. There are modern housing developments on the west side of Margery Lane at Briardene, Summerville and Nevilledale Terrace and neo-Jacobean style buildings of the nineteenth century on the east side of the road that form boarding houses belonging to Durham School.

Much of the land on the eastern side between Margery Lane and South Street once formed gardens belonging to the priors of Durham and now include St. Margaret's churchyards and St. Margaret's allotments. At the north eastern end near the junction of South Street and Crossgate were once located the Prior's 'stews' or fishponds used by the Cathedral Priory in medieval times. Remnants could still be seen in the nineteenth century.

St. Margaret's Church stands on the corner of South Street and Crossgate (DS)

The Cathedral from South Street (DS)

The Medieval Hospital of Kepier pictured across the river from Frankland Lane (DS)

St. Margaret's Church, Crossgate (DS)

Mount Oswald, South Road (DS)

The Gilesgate Penitentiary (DS)   *Neville's Cross (DS)*

St. Cuthbert's Hospice (DS)

Leazes Place, Gilesgate (DS)

Durham Cathedral – The Cloisters (DS)

Bishop Cosin's Hall and Almshouses, Palace Green (DS)

Bishop Cosin's Hall, Palace Green (DS)

Bishop Cosin's Almshouses, Palace Green (DS)

Water pump at College Green near Durham Cathedral (DS)

Walkway, Durham Cathedral Cloisters (DS)

Durham Cathedral pictured from Gilesgate (DS)

Chapter Eight

Lowe's Barn to Crossgate Moor

The Cock of the North roundabout stands at the junction of the A167 or Great North Road and the A177 Money Slack Road near Mount Oswald a mile south west of Durham. Near the roundabout is a group of old farmhouses that were historically associated with the Salvin family. The farms are called Farewell Hall and are found on both sides of the great road.

It is said that in early times they were the place where visitors to Durham were given the farewell by friends as they set off home. However they also seem to have been called 'Fair well' at one time or another. Until the early nineteenth century Farewell Hall incorporated a coaching inn called the Durham Ox.

The Cock of the North pub on the north side of the roundabout was a well-known landmark named after a locomotive but was demolished in the summer of 2005. The pub dated from the 1930s and although there was no earlier coaching inn on the site its loss will be lamented as it was a familiar welcome home. The site is now a housing development.

The Duke of Wellington, Lowe's Barn (DS)

Heading up the Great Road into the western outskirts of Durham City we reach Potters Bank and Lowe's Barn where the houses are mostly post war. Those in Merryoaks west of the road around Balliol and Percy Squares are of the 1950s and 60s but St. Cuthbert's Hospice, the one time BBC Radio Durham building occupies a much older cottage.

East of the A167 is an estate with Dickensian themed street names around Mill Lane. They back onto Durham University Business School and date from the 1980s. Lowe's Barn lies at the southern extremity of Neville's Cross on the boundary of the old boroughs of Crossgate and Elvet.

Mr Lowe seems to have been the name of a farmer whose farm stood on the south side of Lowe's Barn Bank which joins the A167 from the west. The Lowe family were later farmers at Mount Joy. The farm at Lowe's Barn was created after enclosures on Elvet Moor in the 1770s and by 1805 was owned by the Reverend Davidson and Reverend Britton.

During the nineteenth century part of the farm became the Duke of Wellington, a coaching inn on the Great Road. First listed in a Durham trades directory of 1861 its proprietor was Mr Robson. The inn still exists but underwent a major facelift in 2002. Maps of the area prior to suburban development show a pattern of little rectangular fields around Lowe's Barn. Some are to the west along Lowe's Barn Bank but most are to the east along Potters Bank where there was once a tollgate. The fields represent the eighteenth century enclosures of Elvet Moor.

Before that time the moor was unfenced common land belonging to the residents of Elvet and was used for grazing. In this respect it was similar to Framwellgate, Crossgate and Gilesgate Moors that were used by the residents of those districts. When Elvet Moor was enclosed, the land was distributed amongst householders in Elvet and properties like Bells Folly on Potters Bank now occupy the fields.

Observatory (NE)

Neville's Cross College

Potters Bank joins the A167 east of the Duke of Wellington and is an old thoroughfare named, it is thought, from city potteries that may have existed here in medieval times. The road terminates at Quarryheads Lane near the tip of Durham's river peninsula.

Clearly visible from Potters Bank is Durham University's Observatory, built just to the north in 1839. Its architect was the famed Anthony Salvin, a distant relative of the Croxdale and Farewell Hall Salvins. It was designed to house astronomical implements collected by Dr Hyles of the Royal Astronomical Society.

The observatory is situated on Clay Lane, an old pathway linking Quarryheads Lane to Neville's Cross. Clay Lane is also the site of two large and impressive red brick Edwardian buildings that housed Neville's Cross College until very recently.

Neville's Cross College opened in 1922 and was a teacher training college that merged in 1977 with Durham Technical College at Framwellgate Moor to become New College Durham. New College was a dual site college but in late 2000 the Neville's Cross site was sold and the remaining college at Framwellgate Moor was completely rebuilt.

The Neville's Cross college site is now an area of residential and office development. It is intended that one of the Edwardian buildings called Neville House will feature 67 apartments whilst the other called Sheraton House will accommodate offices. The whole development called Sheraton Park includes several new streets of over 200 houses surrounding the former college buildings.

Two old lodge houses associated with the college entrance near Clay Lane on the A167 will remain. Just north of Clay Lane a street called Ellam Avenue joins the A167 and is named from a rather unfortunate event.

The Reverend George Ellam (MR)

Ellam was the Reverend George Sydney Ellam MA, the assistant curate to the Rector of St. Margaret's church in Crossgate. He was a well-known character and was effectively vicar of St. John's Church at Neville's Cross where he held the post from 1894 until 17 April, 1905. On that day he became Vicar of Satley in western Durham but unfortunately did not hold the post for long. A few weeks later on 13 May, he was tragically killed in a motorcycle accident at Neville's Cross, only a stone's throw from the street that is named in his memory.

West of the Duke of Wellington, Lowe's Barn Bank descends towards the River Browney where it joins the foot of Neville's Cross Bank before crossing the river towards the Stonebridge Inn. This inn has been around for over 200 years but man knew this area in much earlier times. In 1899 Bronze Age urns were found in a field at the foot of Lowe's Barn Bank and another urn and hoard of medieval coins were discovered in a field to the north a decade before.

A Roman road that branched off from Dere Street at Willington crossed the Browney near here, but the exact course from thereon is uncertain. Perhaps it ascended Lowe's Barn Bank to form the missing link to another Roman Road at Shincliffe.

Neville's Cross and Crossgate Moor

Crossgate Moor and Neville's Cross form the western suburbs of Durham City but Neville's Cross is the slightly older and more southerly of the two. It grew around the crossroads now occupied by the Neville's Cross traffic lights. Here the A690 Crossgate Peth changes into Neville's Cross Bank as it descends towards the valley of the River Browney in the west.

The Great North Road or A167 also changes name here. South of the crossroads it is called Darlington Road but is called Newcastle Road to the north. Until the 1960s, this junction was not a crossroads but a dogleg where travellers from Darlington made an awkward right turn up Neville's Cross Bank for a hundred yards before turning left to continue north. The left turn is now St. John's Road, a quiet street terminating in a cul-de-sac at Redhills railway cutting. Here the Great North Road crossed a bridge over the line.

St. John's Road includes a rather intriguing stone house of 1902. It was apparently built as a shop and warehouse that later served as a wartime fire station and church hall. Built by an architect called Forster, it is thought to incorporate stones from Durham's demolished racecourse grandstand. The building looks as though it was built to be a church and its history is something of a mystery.

The medieval stump of Neville's Cross overlooks the A690 near the junction with St. John's Road close to where a tollhouse once stood. Shown on the 1850s map and depicted in an early nineteenth century drawing, (below) the tollhouse was later removed. The cross itself was here long before the fourteenth century battle with which it is often associated and is now caged in with iron railings.

Across the A690 is St. John's church, built as a mission church in the late nineteenth century and just to its east is the upper part of a street called the Avenue leading down a steep bank into the city. Here at the top of the Avenue are nineteenth century villas like Farnley Towers which belonged to Durham's Victorian businessmen.

The villas represent late nineteenth century development at Neville's Cross but there were earlier developments of a more modest kind to the west of the present traffic lights. Here Neville's Cross consisted of three terraces by the mid-nineteenth century. Two remain, namely Alma Terrace on the western side of Neville's Cross Bank and an opposing terrace incorporating the former coaching inn that was until recent times the Neville's Cross Hotel. The building, now a restaurant is identified by its peculiar green dome.

Neville's Cross Primary School of 1908 stands near Alma Terrace and a Methodist church and co-operative store of the same era once stood close by. The old co-operative laundry buildings remain and date from about the time of the First World War. They are now operated by a firm called Sunlight and include some modern extensions.

A third terrace stood on the eastern side of Darlington Road below what is now Geoffrey Avenue but was demolished in the 1960s. Other terraces like Prospect Terrace on Neville's Cross Bank and Cross View Terrace in Darlington Road came later in the nineteenth century, but one building now occupied by a motorcycle garage has a distinctly 1920s appearance.

The old tollgate near the stump of Neville's Cross. The old Newcastle road is hidden to the left of the toll collector. Neville's Cross Bank is in the foreground with Crossgate Peth and Durham Cathedral beyond the gate

Crossgate Moor and the Browney

After the Great North Road crosses the main railway line we head north into the city suburb of Crossgate Moor. The Victorian settlement of Crossgate Moor is situated at the top of Redhills Lane which branches to the east of the great road. Named from the surrounding moorland that was enclosed in 1769, the settlement or village of Crossgate Moor faces out onto the A167. It did not come into being until the second half of the nineteenth century and consisted of the terrace overlooking the main road and another tucked behind it called Neville Terrace that still bears a date inscription of 1877. A new housing development called Red Hills Mews has recently been constructed behind this terrace.

The two terraces of the original Crossgate Moor lie south of Durham Johnston School, but the school itself has only been here since 1952. It was relocated from an earlier site in South Street (see page 82) near the city centre. Until recent decades a large public house called the Redhills Hotel stood close to the school in Crossgate Moor but it has now gone.

Compared to the settlements of Framwellgate Moor and Gilesgate Moor that came into being in the 1830s, Crossgate Moor was a rather tiny latecomer. It wasn't a pit village like Framwellgate Moor or a scattering of little pit terraces like Gilesgate Moor, although a significant number of nineteenth century residents in Crossgate Moor were coke workers at the neighbouring colliery villages to the west. In truth Crossgate Moor really only developed as a suburb in the twentieth century. Urban growth took place during the 1940s, 50s and 60s when housing developed to the south in and around a new street called St. Monica Grove.

In the nineteenth century the Durham suburbs of Crossgate Moor and Neville's Cross were barely big enough to call villages. There were no more than 30 to 40 households in each place by 1881. Crossgate Moor consisted of the two mentioned terraces and a few other scattered houses close to where Durham Johnston School now stands. Its population in 1881 included 11 coke workers, two miners, four stonemasons, three joiners, four general labourers, three laundry workers and three print compositors. There was also a butcher, wood keeper, cartman, shoemaker and dressmaker.

The coke workers probably worked at collieries around the River Browney like Bearpark but the joiners and masons are likely to have worked for William Rutter, a builder of Rose Villa. At number 8 Neville Terrace lived John Simpson, one of three noted mustard manufacturers in Durham.

In the 1881 census there were four people employed in making clothes at neighbouring Neville's Cross, three railwaymen, seven labourers, a blacksmith, publican, iron moulder, cartwright, gamekeeper and millwright. However the most significant group of workers were the papermakers.

Papermaking involved mashing old rags into a watery fibrous pulp. The pulp was rolled onto a flat felt surface and dried from a heated furnace. At least one 1881 resident of Crossgate Moor was a paper mill furnace stoker. Better quality white rags or a bleaching agent were required for white paper. Rags were brought into Brandon railway station from all over the region and distributed to the local paper mills along the River Browney.

Eleven papermakers resided at Neville's Cross and a further six at Crossgate Moor. They were employed in paper mills west of Durham along the River Browney where four separate paper mills were established in the late 1700s at Stonebridge, Langley, Relly and Moorsley Banks.

Moorlsey Banks was the most northerly of the paper mills. Situated on the Browney off Toll House Road near Crossgate Moor, the history of the Moorsley Banks mill is sketchy, but was probably established by the Ord family in the late eighteenth century.

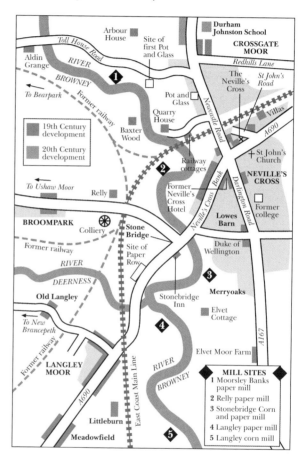

Crossgate Moor Map (NE)

By 1851 Anwick Smith and sons owned the mill, but it subsequently passed to John Davison in the 1860s and then to John Binns in the 1870s. The Binns family moved here from Lancashire but Mr Binns later committed suicide.

By 1881 his widow, Ellen resided at Tenter House near Durham's St. Godric's church and continued running the business with the assistance of a manager.

The Old Pot and Glass (MR)

She employed 14 men, two boys, four women and four girls at the mill. Most workers lived in Neville's Cross or Crossgate Moor but the mill ceased operating at the end of the nineteenth century. It was powered by water with a sluice gate and millrace connected to the Browney river.

Just east of the mill site is a small wooded copse alongside Toll House Road that marks the site of the first Pot and Glass Inn. First shown on the 1830s tithe map, but in existence long before, it was no doubt popular with the paper workers. The pub closed around 1938 when its licence transferred to a new establishment called the Neville Dene on the Great North Road in Crossgate Moor. The Neville Dene stood close to the site of an earlier pub called The Three Tuns that appears on an 1850s map. Yet another tollgate, this time Redhills Tollgate, stood near the Three Tuns but both pub and toll have long since gone. However the Neville Dene

remains and has been known as the Pot and Glass for many years. The building that housed the original Pot and Glass was demolished about 1950.

The history of Neville's Cross and Crossgate Moor is closely connected to that of the River Browney that flows along the western edge of the suburb. The valley is reached on foot from the A167 via Quarryhouse Lane. An eighteenth century house that gave the lane its name is still there. Quarrying ceased in the early twentieth century but took place hereabouts from medieval times. Some stone for Durham Cathedral was quarried at the neighbouring Baxter Wood.

Baxter Wood stands on the opposite bank of the Browney to Quarry House and is reached by a footbridge. A popular walking area, it was known as Bacstane Ford in medieval times. Bacstane means 'bake stone' as the flat stones of the Browney riverbed were ideal for baking bread. Interestingly, the opposite bank of the river south of Quarryhouse Lane was called Bakehouse Whins.

Railway Cottages, Quarryhouse Lane (DS)

During the 1100s Augustinian monks from Guisborough established a small priory at Baxter Wood at

the invitation of Henry Pudsey, the son of a powerful Bishop of Durham. It was unusual because Benedictine monks at Durham Cathedral Priory owned all the monastic establishments in County Durham. When Bishop Pudsey died, the influential Benedictines persuaded Henry to give them Baxter Wood and the Augustinians were forced to leave.

Remnants of Relly paper mill (DS)

As part of the deal the Benedictines established a new priory in 1196 on the site of a monastic cell at Finchale and agreed to declare Henry as its official founder – thus ensuring his place in heaven. Baxter Wood remained in Benedictine hands and later monks operated a coal mine here during the medieval period. Perhaps the attractive Baxter Wood farmhouse incorporates stones from the old monastery.

From the late nineteenth century the area immediately south of Baxter Wood was home to four major railway junctions. Here the main North Eastern Railway was joined by the Bishop Auckland, Deerness Valley and Lanchester Valley branch lines, the last of which followed the Browney valley for much of its course.

St. Cuthbert's Hospice. Once BBC Radio Durham. In the nineteenth century it was home to a paper making family (DS)

Baxterwood, Relly Mill, Bridgehouse and Deerness Valley railway junctions were operated by signalmen residing along with plate layers and a railway inspector in an isolated terrace called Railway Cottages just across the river in Quarryhouse Lane. The terrace can still be seen but a similar terrace called Deerness Junction Cottages built alongside the railway junction was demolished in the 1970s.

Only the main line remains today as the other railways now form three long distance footpaths that converge at Relly. However if we ignore these routes and take an adjoining riverside footpath we reach the remnants of Relly Paper mill just south of Baxter Wood Farm.

Here are the remains of an impressive dam, weir and an adjoining ditch that was once the millrace. The race can be traced a quarter of a mile south and passes under the railway viaduct. It eventually cuts straight across a field (now filled in) formed by a meander of the Browney near the mill itself.

The former millhouse, now a private house can still be seen. The mill site including millhouse can also be glimpsed from the passing train. Like Moorsley Banks Paper Mill at Aldin Grange, Relly Mill seems to have belonged to the Ord family in the late 1700s or at least before 1819 when Benjamin Ord was its proprietor. It belonged to the Taylors in the 1820s and to William Granger in the 1830s and 40s.

By 1851 Relly Mill belonged, like Moorsley Banks to Anwick Smith and sons. The Smith Brothers (presumably Anwick's sons) were proprietors in 1879 when the mill specialised in making brown paper.

It was still operating during the first decade of the twentieth century by which time the Smiths were selling stationery that was presumably made of white paper. The mill eventually lost out to larger competitive mills in other parts of the country.

There had been five Smith brothers involved in the Relly paper mill business in 1881 and four of them were born on the Durham side of the Browney at Elvet Cottage near Merryoaks. Later renamed Park House, Elvet Cottage, was home in the 1960s and 1970s to BBC Radio Durham whose presenters included Kate Adie. It is now St. Cuthbert's Hospice.

The youngest Smith Brother at Relly Mill was born at Langley Grove, the house at Langley Paper Mill. This mill and house have gone but Langley Grove was later home to Martin Holliday, manager of North Brancepeth Colliery Company. He gave the adjoining land to the people of Langley Moor and it now forms the picturesque Holliday Park on the outskirts of that village where the waters of the River Browney and River Deerness converge.

Langley paper mill was established about 1777 and early owners included Mr Eggleston and Mr Chilton, but the

Smiths owned it from around 1803. It was probably the largest Browney mill and I believe it made white and brown paper. Workers initially resided in a nearby street on the main road called Paper Row (later Langley Cottages) but these were demolished by the 1960s.

Langley Paper mill ceased trading in the late 1870s when the Smiths concentrated their efforts at Relly. The family does not seem to have been involved in another Langley Mill situated further south near Littleburn as this was a corn mill. Nor were they connected with Stonebridge Paper Mill, half way between Relly and Langley.

Situated on the Lowe's Barn side of the river, quite near Elvet Cottage, Stonebridge Paper Mill was operated by White and Teasdale in the 1820s and became a corn mill before 1834. It was operated by the Selby family in the early twentieth century. The valleys of the Browney and Deerness and their associated places are featured in the accompanying village book.

The River Browney and Deerness converge near the site of Langley Mill (DS)

The Battle of Neville's Cross

The Battle of Neville's Cross was rooted in a long-running economic and military struggle between England and France that came to be known as the Hundred Years War. The war commenced around 1336 and a major turning point came in August 1346 when the English king, Edward III and his son Edward the Black Prince, resoundingly defeated the French at Crecy.

It was a victory against the odds. The English were heavily outnumbered in the battle and victory was largely due to the skill and astonishing range of the English longbowmen. Following the victory King Edward besieged the French port of Calais with the intention of capturing it for the English. It was a siege involving many English ships including 17 from Newcastle, five from Hartlepool and one from Bamburgh that together carried a total of 460 North Eastern men. Also in France were knights and soldiers from County Durham who served in the army of Thomas Hatfield, the war hungry Prince Bishop who fought alongside the King at Crecy. Calais was eventually taken in August the following year, but not before King Philip of France called on his ally, David, King of the Scots, to invade England.

Philip and David believed England was not adequately defended in Edward's absence but this proved to be a fatal error of judgement as Edward had left many capable soldiers behind including at least 10,000 longbowmen.

In October 1346 King David II, the son of Robert the Bruce, confidently began the Scottish invasion of England with 15,000 men. Entering England through Cumberland in the west he sacked Lanercost Priory before moving to Northumberland where Hexham Priory suffered a similar fate. Hexham itself escaped the ravages, because the Scots intended to use the town as a storehouse for their plunder.

After crossing the River Derwent the Scots entered County Durham at Ebchester and headed south to the Prior of Durham's park at Beaurepaire (Bearpark) on the banks of the River Browney. Here they encamped for the night, destroyed the prior's manor house and plundered the game and livestock for which the park was renowned.

The stump of Neville's Cross (DS)

Meanwhile, the English gathered an army of 10,000 men at Richmond and headed for Barnard Castle. They consisted mostly of skilled longbow archers, with 1,000 from Lancashire alone. They were strong, stocky men capable of shooting deadly arrows to a range of 300 yards at an astonishing rate. If the Scots were expecting to meet the raw and undisciplined elements of a standby English army, they were in for a terrible shock. According to most sources William de la Zouche, the Archbishop of York was in overall command but there were units commanded by Ralph Neville, Henry Percy, Lord Mowbray and Thomas Rokeby. From Barnard Castle they proceeded to Auckland Castle Park and camped for the night on 16 October.

The following morning the English set out for the prominent hill at Merrington near Spennymoor where they surveyed the surrounding land and observed Scottish movements in the hills to the west of Durham. Advancing east to Ferryhill they encountered a rather surprised party of foraging Scots under Sir William Douglas that were revealed by the sudden lifting of a dense fog.

These Scots were pursued north as far as Sunderland Bridge near Croxdale and a skirmish ensued in which perhaps half of the Douglas men were slain. The skirmish is thought to have taken place at a site near Hett village called Butcher Race that lies close to the A167. Those who escaped the slaughter retreated north to join the main body of Scots at Beau Repaire but some no doubt fled. Perhaps they were wise, as this skirmish was nothing more than a prelude to the battle that took place later that morning.

It is well known that the Battle of Neville's Cross was fought on land now occupied by the western suburbs of Durham City and if we head south through this area on the A167 we reach Neville's Cross. A sign helpfully informs the motorist that this was the site of the battle and with a stretch of imagination we can picture the bumps and braes of the open countryside that existed in 1346.

However, if truth is to be known, we are in the wrong place. To find the real battle site we need to head north, because historians agree that it was the northern part of Crossgate Moor and not Neville's Cross that formed the true heart of the battle. This explains why the battle was once called the Battle of Redhills and was still occasionally known by this name in the nineteenth century. It became the Battle of Neville's Cross through a long-term association with the medieval cross that stands to the south.

In fact the cross in question was located here long before the battle, but Lord Ralph Neville apparently erected a new one after 1346 to commemorate the encounter. The higher ground of Crossgate Moor west of Redhills Lane formed the most southerly section of the battlefield close to where Durham Johnston School now stands. From here the battlefield stretched about half a mile north to just beyond the prominent farmhouse called Arbour House that overlooks the valley of the River Browney. It was here in this area that the Scottish forces amassed.

Topography played a major part role in the battle so it is important to know the true location. The whole battlefield consisted of a narrow ridge of raised but broken ground little more than half a mile wide with valleys to the east and west.

On the west were the slopes of the Browney and to the east the steep and boggy-bottomed Flass Vale from which Redhills Lane ascends. The valleys would effectively hem in the opposing parties on both sides of the battle and helped to determine the result.

Sometime in the morning of the 17 October, 1346 the Scottish army assembled in three units on the hills of Crossgate Moor. The positions of the armies are approximate but it was clear as the Scots approached the battlefield, that the English had seized the better ground.

This was significant because the English were numerically inferior to the Scots with a force of about 10,000.

Neville's Cross as it once appeared

Leading the Scots was King David II, assisted by Lord Robert Stewart on the east and William Douglas on the west. Stewart's men assembled somewhere near Whitesmocks but it was the western flank that was most vulnerable. Here Douglas's men who had suffered severe losses in a skirmish earlier that day must have felt particularly nervous. Now teamed with the Earl of Moray, Douglas held a risky position on a prominent hilltop where Arbour House Farm now stands. The land falls sharply around this hill with the Browney valley on one side and a slope near Toll House Road on the other. Such topography would seriously impede the momentum of an advancing charge and English archers could easily pick them off.

The battlefield of Neville's Cross is not easy to imagine because so much now lies amongst housing developments around the A167. However the Scottish positions were located in what is still open countryside today. It was the English right flank under Henry Percy and Ralph Neville that stood in what is now the built up area occupied by upper Redhills Lane and Durham Johnston School.

The Archbishop of York seems to have been in overall command of the English but some sources place Neville at the helm. Whoever was in charge, the English centre stood approximately where the A167 now runs between two footbridges while the western flank under Thomas Rokeby and Lord Mowbray stood in what is still countryside above the Browney.

Unbeknown to the Scots, the English also had a card up their sleeve in the form of a reserve cavalry under Edward Baliol hidden somewhere near Crossgate Peth. Ironically this reserve was the only unit on the entire battlefield that was actually located in what we would call Neville's Cross today.

Who knows who made the initial move in this six-hour battle but as English archers blackened the sky with thousands of deadly arrows many Scots knew the end was near. The whistling of this lethal weaponry instilled chaos and fear amongst the Scottish ranks but although many horses bolted, the determined Scots continued their rapid advance towards their English foes with an almighty charge.

Stewart's eastern flank gained ground quickly causing the ranks of Percy to run. This entire English flank pivoted backwards and inwards behind the English centre. Stewart sensed Scottish success and closed in on the retreating men and the deafening clash of steel, in hand to hand combat quickly ensued. However, in the heat of the moment Stewart had not noticed the English reserve under Baliol closing in on him. He was soon under attack on two sides with the steep and boggy Flass Vale hindering movements to the east.

It was there in that ancient vale that the Durham monks led by Prior John Fossor erected the holy cloth from St. Cuthbert's tomb on the Maiden's Bower. Here on this Bronze Age burial mound the monks knelt and prayed. Others watched nervously from the cathedral tower, but in truth little could be seen of the battlefield from up there.

On the western flank the terrain around Arbour House, coupled with fenced enclosures and a severe onslaught of English arrows completely destroyed the Douglas advance and here the battle was soon all but over.

Back on the east many of Stewart's men fled but the disciplined English troops resisted the temptation to chase in hot pursuit. Instead they focused their attention on King David and the vulnerable Scottish centre.

It was not long before the King himself was under threat. His armour bearer soon numbered among the slain and David, severely wounded, fled from the battlefield. As the English claimed victory the leaderless Scots fled north and the battle diminished into a series of sporadic skirmishes, most notably at Findon Hill near Sacriston.

The wounded David headed west and took refuge under the arch of Aldin Grange Bridge on the River Browney. Here, according to legend he was betrayed by his reflection in the river, a discovery that fell to John

Coupland (or Copeland) a Northumbrian who had set out with his men in search of foraging Scots. The King fiercely resisted the attempts to arrest him and dashed out two of Coupland's teeth in the struggle. David, the hostage was eventually taken to King Edward who rewarded Coupland with a handsome fee and a knighthood. Coupland seems to have used part of the reward to purchase Crook Hall in Durham City.

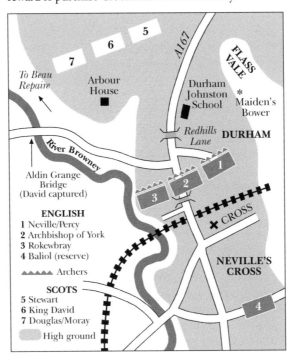

Battle of Neville's Cross 1346 Map (NE)

As for King David he was held hostage in the Tower of London for about 11 years until handed over to the Scots for a ransom worth about £15 million pounds in today's money. However as far as I know, the canny Scots never paid the fee.

Not one, but two crosses were built to commemorate the victory of 1346. One was a wooden cross erected at the Maiden's Bower in Flass Vale that existed in some form or another until it was removed in the mid-sixteenth century. More famous was the actual Neville's Cross erected by Lord Ralph Neville to commemorate the battle.

It is generally agreed that Neville erected the cross on the site of an earlier one that marked the boundaries of sanctuary in the city long before the battle. Whatever its origin, only the base of the cross and part of a shaft remain, now caged in with railings near a busy road. Neville for his part in the battle became the first laymen to be buried in Durham Cathedral and his tomb can still be seen there to this day.

Redhills and Flass Vale

Redhills Lane is a steep climbing street that links Crossgate Moor and Nevilles Cross to the more central areas of Durham City and has done for many centuries. The top of the lane terminates at the A167 or Great North Road in Crossgate Moor but across the main road is the closely associated Toll House Road, the main route to Bearpark.

The actual hills called Red Hills once belonged to Durham Priory and Red Hills Lane more or less follows the course of a medieval route called the Prior's Path. This headed east to the prior's retreat at Beau Repaire. Toll House Road was part of the Prior's Path but was later renamed from a tollgate that stood nearby. The Prior's Path veered off from Toll House Road near Arbour House Farm which stands prominently on a nearby hill. From here the ancient path continued north towards Beau Repaire.

In 1857 a railway was built that cut straight through the middle of the Red hills. This railway line is now the London to Edinburgh route and runs parallel to the lower parts of Redhills Lane. For most of its course Redhills Lane is a one-way street accessible to ascending traffic only. Here however we will descend the lane in a route that would have to be taken on foot. At the top of the lane are the terraces of the original Victorian settlement of Crossgate Moor and modern housing developments called Redhills Mews.

Former Barnardo's Home, Redhills Lane (DS)

Just to the north is Durham Johnston School and as we head east along the lane we encounter two large cottage-like buildings. Once called the Cottage Homes, these were formerly the girls' and boys' blocks of a Barnardo's home and were separated from each other by a fence. Tucked behind is a small building of a later period incorporating a little observatory that I understand was formerly used by the Johnston School.

Redhills Villa belonged to Mr Blagdon (DS)

Continuing east along the lane there is a short nineteenth century terrace called Gray Terrace which I believe was named after a one time Mayor of Durham. Here there is a kink in Redhills Lane with a blind corner of which motorists and pedestrians should be wary. The lane narrows here and begins to descend. Despite the one way traffic restriction, these sections of Redhills Lane are still precarious for cars and pedestrians. It was also a rather precarious place to be in 1346 as it was somewhere around this point that the forces of Neville and Percy formed the right flank of the English army during the Battle of Nevilles Cross.

It is at this point in Redhills Lane that we reach a graveyard and former mortuary chapel dedicated to St. Bede. It is wedged in between the railway line and the lane. Dating from 1866, but now deconsecrated and forming a private house, it was once the chapel and cemetery belonging to St. Godric's Roman Catholic Church. St. Godric's church is located in the city's Castle Chare area but there was no available space for a graveyard there.

There are some houses in Redhills Lane at this point forming Redhills Terrace, but they date from the late nineteenth century.

Redhills railway cutting divides Durham's suburbs into two parts with housing in Crossgate Moor and Redhills Lane on one side separated from Hawthorn Terrace, The Avenue and Neville's Cross to the south. For the train traveller entering Durham, the cutting blocks off approaching views of the city until the very last minute. Trains emerge from Redhills cutting to reveal the breathtaking views of cathedral and castle.

Near the foot of Redhills Lane are a number of large houses or villas. The first and most westerly of the group is a large white painted house of the late nineteenth century. This is the oldest of the villas and was built for Mr Blagdon, the proprietor of the huge Blagdon's Leather works that were situated on Framwellgate waterside. Close to the villa, but of a later period are two large red brick villas that once belonged to the officials of the Durham Miners' Union. These two villas were of course associated with the famous Durham Miners' Hall of 1915 that dominates the foot of Redhills Lane.

The Miners' Hall, Redhills Lane (DS)

The red brick Miners' Hall with its architecture designed by H. T. Gradon has been described as Edwardian Baroque in style. In the grounds are four statues of mining leaders called Crawford, MacDonald, Forman and Patterson that were relocated from the earlier miners' hall in North Road. A lodge house stands at the entrance to the present hall's grounds at the foot of Redhills Lane.

Membership of the union increased in the late nineteenth century and this necessitated the construction of the Redhills Hall. The most remarkable feature of the building is its impressive debating chamber that was considered a potential headquarters for an assembly during a recent regional government referendum.

The villas, Red Hills Terrace, former chapel and miners' hall can all be seen from the passing train if the inquisitive traveller resists the temptation to view the cathedral in the opposing window.

At the foot of the bank Redhills Lane becomes Flass Street which is named from the marshy low lying land just to the north called Flass Vale. The name Redhills is also connected with Flass Vale. The blood of battle slain Scotsmen defeated at Neville's Cross is often cited as an explanation for the name of Redhills but in truth Redhills probably means Reedy hills from the reeds that grew on the banks of the neighbouring vale.

Joining Flass Street on land that was once part of the vale are a number of short nineteenth century terraces wedged between the city's railway viaduct and County Hospital. They include Mowbray Street, named after Sir J. R. Mowbray, a nineteenth century Tory MP for Durham City who was known as the Father of the House of Commons. Neighbouring Waddington Street is named after a Dean of Durham Cathedral who was involved in the foundation of the nearby County Hospital. The street runs along the edge of the hospital grounds and appears

on the 1850s Ordnance Survey map as a short, unnamed lane without houses. It developed into a terrace later in the century.

The principal feature of Waddington Street is the United Reformed church, previously a Presbyterian church, that dates from 1878.

At its eastern end Waddington Street terminates at Ainsley Street, named from the Ainsley family who manufactured Durham mustard. Ainsley family members lived in South Street and Atherton Street but Waddington Street was home to their mustard manufactory.

A treeless Flass Vale as it appeared in the 1920s

On the 1850s map Ainsley Street was part of an undeveloped country road called Flass Lane. The lane was a continuation of Margery Lane but in the north became Back Lane or Back Western Hill as it is still called today. Flass Lane should not be confused with Flass Street, the nearby terrace that stands close to the site of a spring called Flass Well.

Close to the junction of Ainsley Street and Waddington Street is the King's Lodge, pub and restaurant occupying a building that was formerly the Rose Tree Inn. It was known by the name Rose Tree from at least as early as the

1850s but parts of the building date back to the eighteenth century.

A public footpath alongside the pub leads into Flass Vale, which is one of Durham's biggest surprises. Within seconds of walking along the path you find yourself in a deep wooded vale almost half a mile long and within a hundred yards there is not a building to be seen. It is hard to believe you are in the middle of a city and there is no sign of the nearby terraced houses.

The trees in the vale form Shaw Wood but most trees were cleared at the beginning of the twentieth century for farming. It is only in recent decades that the trees were re-established. On the north side, Flass Vale's banks rise steeply towards Back Western Hill. This bank was once called Gibbet Knowle where dead and probably limbless bodies of criminals were left hanging after execution at St. Leonards near Dryburn. If this is not eerie enough, Flass Vale's south bank is one of the Red Hills allegedly named from the flowing blood of massacred Scotsmen who fell at the Battle of Neville's Cross back in 1346. Flass Vale is clearly not a place for the squeamish.

Flass is an old Scandinavian word meaning 'marsh' and the boggy vale was once bigger than it is today. It stretched into what is now the North Road area of the city and was drained by a stream called the Mill Burn. Many of the city's terraces were built in the vale, as was the city's impressive viaduct. With such boggy land to contend with the engineers of the viaduct encountered many problems during the building of this structure and its opening was hailed as a remarkable achievement. It was an achievement that would change the face of Durham.

Adjoining Waddington Street and Flass Street near the foot of Redhills Lane is the northern part of Sutton Street along with Lambton Street and Bridge Street which nestle beneath the railway viaduct.

The County Hospital

Close by and dating from 1849-50 is the Durham County Hospital. It officially opened to patients in 1853 on land called Hill Field that was presented to the city of Durham by the influential Thomas Wilkinson. Built to resemble an Elizabethan house, it was situated in something of a rural oasis at the time and its situation was encouraging to the health of patients. It superseded an earlier hospital of 1793 that was located in Allergate.

The new hospital was initially called Durham Infirmary and was the initiative of George Waddington, Dean of Durham Cathedral who with other wealthy notables provided the funds. Around 139 inpatients and 514 outpatients were treated in the early part of 1850, but treatment was generally for the privileged. Most patients received treatment on the recommendation of subscribers but the Durham historian Fordyce writing a few years after the hospital opened noted that 'sudden accidents or diseases requiring immediate help of the surgeon are received at any hour without recommendation.'

On the immediate north side of the viaduct part of the original Sutton Street survives close to where it is joined by Waddington Street and Flass Street. It turns east and skirts the grounds of the County Hospital. Here, near the

Century Chinese takeaway, another nineteenth century terrace called Lambton Street joins Sutton Street.

Lambton Street is a rather attractive street with shuttered windows. It was one of the many terraces built in Durham in the years following the opening of the viaduct in 1857 but isn't built with the usual red bricks that typify the terraces of the area and looks like a rather neat colliery terrace.

Bees Cottage (DS)

Nearby and close to the takeaway is a creamy coloured stone cottage called Bees Cottage that predates the surrounding terraces. It was perhaps associated with the family of Jacob Bee, a well-known diarist who lived in Durham until his death in 1711 but this is not certain. In the nineteenth century the cottage was home to a wool spinning business. In the 1920s it became the site of Luke's Bakery who owned bakery shops and a cafe in the city. In recent times the cottage has served as a guesthouse and it is now privately owned.

Chapter Nine

Crossgate, North Road and Castle Chare

South of the viaduct, Sutton Street becomes Alexandria Crescent near the Colpitts Inn linking Sutton Street and Allergate with Crossgate Peth and Margery Lane. Alexandria Crescent is now part of the A690 but in the 1850s was an undeveloped country lane.

The two ancient streets of Crossgate and Allergate join the crescent on the eastern side and on the west are the nineteenth century streets of Hawthorn Terrace and The Avenue. In the early nineteenth century a brick works stood near here and clay for the bricks was excavated in the region of John Street near Hawthorn Terrace.

The Colpitts pub and associated Colpitts Terrace date from the 1850s and are named from a local family who were public house proprietors in Durham. The first proprietor of the inn was George Colpitts but around the same time, John and Thomas Colpitts were respective landlords of the Puncheon on Framwellgate Bridge and Wheatsheaf on Elvet Bridge. John was also involved in brewing while another Colpitts called James was proprietor of the lucrative True Briton coach service that transported passengers from Old Elvet's Waterloo Hotel

to Newcastle. All three men hailed from the Bishop Auckland area.

The Colpitts family ceased to be landlords of their eponymous pub by the end of the nineteenth century but operated the Criterion on Framwellgate Bridge at the beginning of the twentieth. The family then described themselves as a wholesale retail wine, spirit, ale and porter merchants involved in the bottling of Bass's ale and Guinness's stout.

The Colpitts with Hawthorn Terrace to the rear (DS)

The long terraced streets of Hawthorn Terrace and the Avenue run back to back and separate the busy centre of Durham from Neville's Cross at the top of the hill. They are situated in what was until the 1870s entirely open countryside called Coddesley or Codeslaw. First mentioned in the 1500s this land belonged to the Almoner of Durham Priory.

The lower half of the Avenue consists of an attractive row of town houses but several scattered, detached villas or little mansions were built for Durham's wealthy

merchants and businessmen around the top of the Avenue at Neville's Cross.

There were at least 10 such villas at the top of the Avenue by the 1880s but others followed later. The villas can still be seen and all are built in different architectural styles. Some stand alongside the Avenue itself but others are to the north between the Avenue and the nearby railway.

These prominent villas are now dotted in amongst twentieth century streets of various decades like Farnley Hey Road, St. John's Road and Percy Terrace. Without a doubt the most prominent villa is Farnley Tower. Situated in the Avenue itself, it was formerly called The Tower and is the first villa encountered upon reaching the brow of the hill beyond the row of houses.

Built around 1870, Farnley Tower was home to the Durham architect John Forster, who built the Avenue and many houses in and around North Road. Farnley Tower provides a wonderful and rather unusual towering view of the city looking towards the viaduct and St. Godric's church. Today the house is a successful bed and breakfast guesthouse and has served this role for about five years. In previous times it has served as a doctor's surgery and a residential care home.

Other villas in the area include Percy Villa, that was home to a retired grocer called John Chapman in 1881 and a house called Neville Court that then belonged to John Hardings Veitch, a Durham printer and stationer. Near St. John's Road is Rokeby Villa of 1881 that was home to Henry Dodd, Secretary of the Weardale and Shildon District Waterworks, whose office was based in North Road.

Immediately opposite Farnley Tower are villas called Avenue House and Dunster House. Avenue House was home (in 1881) to John Tuke, a Lay Clerk of Durham Cathedral who made his fortune from a piano and music business. His next door neighbour at Dunster House in the early 1880s was Tom Hugh Harrison, a Master Organ Builder. Harrison and his family seem to have moved to 24 the Avenue later in the decade.

Farnley Tower (DS)

Number 24, was the largest house at the end of the Avenue before it was extended and was originally called Codeslaw House. In 1923 it became home to Durham Football Association who moved there from Tenter Terrace. They relocated in 1970 to Ferens Park on the Sands and took the name Codeslaw House with them. It is often mistakenly thought Codeslaw was connected with the rules and regulations of football, but as we have already mentioned, Codeslaw was the ancient name for this part of Durham. In 2005 the Durham Football association relocated to Chester-le-Street and took the name with them once again.

In the 1880s Thomas Hugh Harrison employed around 20 men at his famous organ factory in Hawthorn Terrace that was only a short walk from his home in the Avenue. In 1861 at the age of 22, the London born Harrison had started an organ business at Rochdale in Lancashire and developed a reputation for the quality of his work.

Thomas Harrison

With encouragement from John Bacchus Dykes (1823-1876) the renowned hymn composer, (who was vicar of St. Oswalds in Elvet), Harrison relocated to Durham in 1872.

Joined by his brother James, the Harrisons purchased an eighteenth century mill of some kind or another from John Forster. The mill, located in what was then Cross Street was extended to meet Harrison's needs. Cross Street is now the lower part of Hawthorn Terrace near the Colpitts Inn. Hawthorn Terrace seems to have come into being during the 1870s and I believe it was initially called Avenue Terrace.

In 1896 Harrison's sons Arthur and Harry took over the organ building firm. Harry was the designer and Arthur the voicer, who determined the sound and quality of the organs. Over the years Harrison and Harrison came to build organs for cathedrals and churches across the length and breadth of Britain as well as in the United States. Of particular note were organs built for Durham Cathedral, the Royal Albert Hall, King's College Cambridge and Westminster Abbey.

Following Arthur's death and Harry's retirement after World War Two, Harry's son Cuthbert Temple Harrison succeeded to the company. However, Cuthbert was dismissed by his uncle, apparently because there were two many Harrisons involved in running the business. Cuthbert went on to serve in the military in India and became Major Cuthbert Harrison before returning to the firm upon his uncle's death in 1936. Cuthbert was still closely connected with the business up until his death in 1991, but Mark Yenning has been Managing Director of the firm since 1975.

Harrison and Harrison vacated Hawthorn Terrace in 1996 after 124 years when they relocated to their specially designed workshop at St. John's Road, Meadowfield. The nearby church of St. John in Meadowfield is appropriately the home of one of Harrison's organs. The attractive former organ factory building in Hawthorn Terrace can still be seen and has now been converted into apartments and offices.

The former organ factory as it appears today (DS)

Hawthorn Terrace is no longer the hive of industry that it once was and most of the employment in Hawthorn Terrace today can be found a little further up the street where council offices occupy a building that was yet another of the Victorian businessmen's villas.

This particular stone villa stands on raised ground above the street and was called Almoner Villa when it was built in the late nineteenth century. In 1881 it was home to a 61-year old Cumberland born man called Richard Ferguson who made his money from land and houses. Later in the century it was home to Councillor James Fowler JP, who owned a well-known grocery business in Claypath. The villa was renamed Byland Lodge in the early twentieth century and currently (in 2006) houses offices belonging to Durham City Council.

A nineteenth century sketch of Harrison's organ factory

Crossgate and Allergate

Crossgate is an attractive street with a number of Georgian houses but is a fairly quiet thoroughfare where rickety cobbles and a one way system deter all but the necessary traffic. It is one of the oldest streets in Durham and commences at Framwellgate Bridge near the junction with South Street and North Road.

St. Margaret's church, dating from Norman times stands nearby and is the historic focal point of the street. It incorporates much work of the fifteenth century and underwent significant restoration in Victorian times. The church was originally dependent on St. Oswald's church in Elvet but in 1431 St. Margaret's became an independent parochial chapel with a parish all of its own.

Crossgate Moor, Millburngate and the entire Framwellgate area as far north as Finchale were part of St. Margaret's parish until the nineteenth century. In more historic times Crossgate had formed part of Durham's Priory lands which included an orchard in the vicinity of the street. The prior's orchard is thought to explain the name Grape Lane, a medieval back lane that runs through the site. At the junction with Crossgate this lane is now lined with modern houses but emerges in rural surroundings behind St. Margaret's Church. The name suggests the Priors grew grapes here, but streets called Grape Lane can also be found in historic cities like York, Bristol, London and Oxford where they derives from a rather intriguing and unexpected source.

Grape was an old pronunciation of 'grope' and in the case of the cities I have mentioned was used in conjunction with a rather rude word to describe an illicit activity. It may be that Durham's Grape Lane had a similar origin. If this is the case then many old guidebooks have skirted around the explanation and some have even claimed that the name was a corruption of Grey Plain. Whatever the meaning, there was no sign of illicit activity by the time of the 1881 census when the lane's residents included a cow keeper, butcher, labourer, bookbinder, shoemaker, gardener, cabinet maker, blacksmith, Chelsea pensioner and an organ pipe maker.

Grape Lane joins Crossgate near the Elm Tree pub. This pub along with the Angel Inn, on the opposite side of the street is one of Crossgate's best-known features. Pubs

called The Angel and Elm Tree have existed in Crossgate since at least the eighteenth century.

Durham Castle from Crossgate.

An historic view of Crossgate (MR)

However Crossgate's most prominent feature can be found up at the top end of Crossgate before the traffic lights near the junction with Margery Lane and the A690. Here we find a large Victorian building that was until recently St. Margaret's Hospital.

Now incorporating various offices, the building was originally Durham's Union Workhouse and was built in 1837. It housed the destitute residents of Durham City and surrounding 'Union' that covered a district encompassing places as far apart as Willington, Pittington, Kimblesworth and Quarrington. The workhouse was managed by a Board of Governors and in the 1860s and 70s had a master with the almost Dickensian sounding name of Mr Buddle.

Intended for around 125 inmates the workhouse consisted of 10 sleeping apartments, a large dining hall and rooms for the sick. By the time of the 1881 census there were 183 pauper inmates of which 44 were aged 60 or over and 82 aged 16 or under. Many of the children were orphans or illegitimate. Workhouse meals were strictly planned and only children or the sick were given alternative diets.

In the 1850s breakfast in the workhouse consisted of a pint of oatmeal porridge and milk for the men and a pint of coffee with bread for the women. Supper for the men was a pint of boiled milk or gruel, with oatmeal and bread, whilst women made do with bread and tea. Set dinners were assigned to each day of the week but consisted of nothing more elaborate than combinations of broth, stew, rice, potatoes, pease pudding and bread. On Mondays and Wednesdays dinner was treacle and suet pudding, which must have seemed something of a treat for the hardworking inmates.

Outside the workhouse the residents of the street of Crossgate seem to have been predominantly working class. Many ironworkers lived in Crossgate finding employment in two separate iron foundries belonging to James Lumsden and a family called Pepplo that stood opposite the workhouse. Lumsden's son James Junior was landlord of the Angel Inn in the 1850s and was succeeded by John Pepplo Lumsden sometime before 1881.

Pepplo's and Lumsden's iron foundries existed from at least as early as 1827 but Pepplo's business seems to have

passed to William Coulson in the 1840s. The Coulsons were later involved in establishing the Grange Foundry at Carrville around 1867 and one member of the Coulson family became an iron master at Tudhoe. Hauxwells, an iron foundry based in Atherton Street took over one or both of the Crossgate foundries in the 1870s.

In the upper reaches of Crossgate beyond the road junction and traffic lights Crossgate changes name to Crossgate Peth, the part of the street that was outside the historic built up area of the city.

The former Union Workhouse (DS)

The original Crossgate Peth terminates at Neville's Cross and is now simply called the Peth. It is now a rather quiet back road. The street called the Avenue runs parallel to the Peth to the north whilst the A690 runs parallel to the south. This section of the A690 is now offically, but rather erroneously called Crossgate Peth.

In times gone by coachmen who stopped to allow their horse to drink before climbing the original Peth often complained of inexplicable drops in temperature as they continued their journey west. As they proceeded they encountered the presence of a sombre looking woman with a new born child in her arms. She sat in the coach until reaching Neville's Cross where she disappeared out of sight. She is thought to have been either the ghost of a young woman who lost her husband at the Battle of Neville's Cross or that of a girl who was thrown to her death down the steps of the Victorian workhouse. Her assailant was a visiting soldier.

Crossgate's neighbour, Allergate, is one of the least known of Durham's Streets, but also one of the oldest where people have lived since at least the 1200s. Along with Crossgate and Millburngate, it formed part of the 'Old Borough' of Durham and belonged to the Priors of Durham Cathedral in times gone by.

In appearance Allergate closely resembles Crossgate but is a shorter street and there are no pubs. Some houses in the street date from the eighteenth century but there are earlier features behind the facades. One house of particular note is number 22 Allergate that is of great interest because it incorporates a late medieval timber framed building. In Medieval times this house stood on the fringe of Durham's built up area. Timber framing in the house dates from the late 1400s or early 1500s and I believe the original roof timbers are still intact. A seventeenth century kitchen wing and late eighteenth century staircase were added later at the rear. Incidentally, not far away, at number 7 Crossgate, is a similar, but smaller medieval building. This one has an eighteenth century rear staircase extension.

Allergate's name is something of a mystery. In early times it was called Alvertongate or Allertongate, from some uncertain connection with the Yorkshire town of

Northallerton. Northallerton was formerly called Allerton or Alverton and the surrounding district called Allertonshire belonged to the Bishops of Durham in medieval times. Allergate could mean road to Northallerton but this is a bit of a puzzle since the street has an east-west orientation. Perhaps Allergate was once longer in extent and connected via Grape Lane or some other route to South Street that was the ancient thoroughfare en route to Yorkshire. It is possible that the name Allertongate was shortened to Allergate through association with the French 'aller' meaning 'to go'.

The little-known street of Allergate (DS)

Allergate is more or less an offshoot of neighbouring Crossgate and it is at this point that Neville Street links the two older streets to neighbouring North Road. North Road didn't come into being until 1831 and Neville Street was built slightly later in the 1840s. Neville Street is an attractive street of nineteenth century stone houses much smarter in appearance than North Road itself. This is rather fortunate as it doesn't detract from the two older streets to which it is linked.

In times gone by most of the houses in Allergate were situated on the north side of the street and behind them were long gardens and plots of land that terminated on the banks of the stream called the Mill Burn. East Atherton Street now occupies most of this area and the stream now runs in a culvert beneath the ground. The stream ran parallel to the land plots and was in historic times the boundary between the Durham Prior's Borough of Crossgate and the Bishop's Borough of Framwellgate.

In Victorian times much of the land behind the houses on the south side of Allergate belonged to Durham's Poor Law Guardians who operated the Union Workhouse in Crossgate, but on this same side of the street Allergate had an institution all of its very own in the form of a hospital.

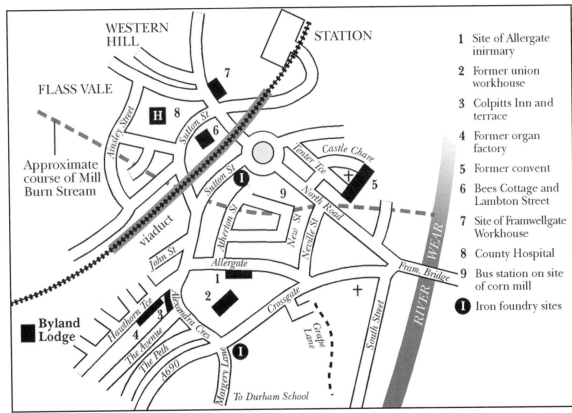

1 Site of Allergate inirmary
2 Former union workhouse
3 Colpitts Inn and terrace
4 Former organ factory
5 Former convent
6 Bees Cottage and Lambton Street
7 Site of Framwellgate Workhouse
8 County Hospital
9 Bus station on site of corn mill
I Iron foundry sites

North Road Area Map (NE)

Durham's old Hospital or Infirmary was established in Allergate in 1793. It had originally opened as a dispensary in Silver Street in 1785 but proved such a successful venture that the trustees moved to the larger Allergate site seven years later. The wealthy benefactor Mr Wilkinson presented them with the land that was then occupied by a house and a garden.

Two surgeons served the hospital and there were two physicians. One of the physicians was William Cooke who resided at Belasis House in the Quarryheads Lane area of the city. His house is now part of Durham School. The Allergate Infirmary served Durham for 60 years but it was decided around 1849 that a new, larger hospital, was required. In 1853 this resulted in the opening of a new Durham Infirmary in open countryside to the north. This building, is now the County Hospital in North Road.

Around North Road

Most of the main streets in Durham's city centre including the lost Millburngate and Framwellgate can be traced back to medieval times. The Market Place, Silver Street, South Street, Saddler Street, Old Elvet, New Elvet, Gilesgate, Claypath and Crossgate all have medieval origins. There are two very obvious exceptions to this rule. One is the new High Street formed by the Prince Bishops Shopping Centre but the other is the street in the centre of the city that is called North Road.

Until the Shopping centre was built it was the nearest thing Durham City had to a high street and although it may seem as if North Road has been there since time immemorial it was only built in 1831. Until that time, the streets of Millburngate and Framwellgate were the main entry points to the city from the north and they formed part of the route of the Great North Road

through the city. Unfortunately Millburngate and Framwellgate were steep, dilapidated streets and were unpopular with travellers.

When plans were made for the Great North Road to bypass the city altogether, the people of influence in Durham decided that a new street needed to be built within the city area as part of the route to the north. The result was the street of North Road, built a little to the west of Framwellgate.

The lower part of North Road, within the city centre was originally called King Street and some older residents of the city may still remember this name. Commencing at the western end of Framwellgate Bridge, the street was named after King William IV, who became King at about the time of its construction.

North Road at night looking south towards the castle as pictured in an old postcard (MR)

Further to the north, the street was simply called North Road, up to the junction with Framwellgate Peth near the Garden House Pub or Woodman as it used to be known. King Street and North Road became a focus for Victorian development and a number of terraces were built around it, particularly after 1857 when the viaduct and station was built above the street. King Street became the main pedestrian route into the city for passengers alighting from trains in the new railway station. For travellers it was often their first view of Durham.

Before 1831, the area now occupied by North Road was open marshy land with overflowing springs and a stream called the Mill Burn. The Mill Burn gave its name to nearby Millburngate and once operated as a mill race for a medieval flour mill called the Clock Mill. This stood close to the Wear where The Gates (Millburngate) Shopping Centre stands today. The stream was diverted beneath North Road by means of a culvert, but in the decades that followed, development was often plagued by flooding.

Until the 1920s another corn mill stood in the North Road area, roughly where the bus station stands today. It was called Robson's Steam Corn Mill or the City Mill and it had a prominent chimney. From the 1840s it belonged to a man called John Robson who also owned the Market Place Mill of which remnants can be seen near the old ice rink near the Sands. Nothing can be seen of the North Road Mill however.

Like the ancient Clock Mill, the North Road mill was powered by means of the Mill Burn stream. This stream now flows in a culvert beneath the city's streets and can still be seen in Flass Vale. From this point it flows underground, roughly following the course of Waddington Street. It then passes beneath the terraces at the rear of North Road and then underneath North Road itself. It eventually enters the river by pipe at Framwellgate Waterside directly opposite the site of the city mill.

The former Miners' Hall in North Road

In the 1860s the North Road corn mill business was taken over by Mr Hill but by 1873 Hill moved to the Market Place Mill and North Road was back in the hands of the Robsons. However by the end of the 1870s Hill was listed as miller at both establishments and like his Robson predecessors resided at Neville House, the grounds of which now form part of the bus station. It is the big house used by the bus station for offices and dates from 1842. Hidden behind North Road with Neville Street to its rear, it has a distinctly Georgian appearance.

Durham City Bus Station is undoubtedly the busiest spot in North Road today. It was built in 1928 and was best known for its ornate iron and glass arcade. Built by the architect Albert Fennell, of Chester-le-Street, the arcade was removed in 1976 and taken to Beamish Museum for preservation.

On the same side of the street as the bus station, the most prominent building in North Road is undoubtedly the former cinema, with its tall green copper domed tower. For most of the twentieth century it served as a cinema but it was not built for that purpose. It was originally the Durham Miners' Hall, which was the headquarters for the Durham Miners' Association. It was built in 1874 on the site of a block of earlier houses called Monk's Buildings and the architect was T. Oliver of Newcastle.

The hall opened on 3 June, 1876, and one of the first meetings discussed the coal owners' proposed reduction of Durham miners' wages by 10%. The building incorporated statues of the mining leaders Alexander Macdonald, W. H. Patterson and William Crawford. It was Crawford who established the Miners' Gala in the city in 1871. A statue of another leader, John Forman, was added to the building in 1906.

The membership of the union increased rapidly during the late nineteenth century and by the beginning of the twentieth century, the building was no longer suitable for the task. In October 1915, a much larger miners' hall was opened at Redhills and the statues were moved to the new site.

The old hall became a cinema around 1934, but was not the only cinema in North Road. An earlier cinema called the Globe, built in 1913, was built on the opposite side of the street, but further to the north.

North Road looking north towards the viaduct as pictured in an old postcard (MR)

Durham City was a mass of back-to-back terraced houses laid out in the typical grid iron style of the nineteenth century. If it were not for the cathedral and castle the view could be of any northern industrial city. In reality the terracing is only typical of Durham City around the viaduct and North Road to the west of the station. This densely terraced area was still almost wholly open countryside in the 1850s and although the housing development was spurred on by the opening of the railway and station in 1857, the associated developments were never on the same scale or as aesthetically grim as in other northern cities.

Many of the terraces in this part of Durham are clustered around the street of North Road that dates from 1831. The street has been compared to the shopping street of a typical mining village but there was never a colliery in its immediate vicinity. However the North Road area was once a hive of industrial and commercial activity and many of the workers lived in surrounding terraces. A number of tightly packed terraced houses occupy the area around the bus station between North Road and neighbouring Allergate. These are early twentieth century terraces built of red brick and are named New Street, Mitchell Street and East Atherton Street. The name of New Street is not what it seems. It is named after the Eaglescliffe born Mr William New, who was a resident of Flass Street. New was a prominent member of Durham's co-operative movement that built some of the terraces hereabouts.

East Atherton Street is an offshoot of the original Atherton Street and dates back to the nineteenth century. It was named after Sir William Atherton, (1806-64) a one time resident of the city who became Durham's MP in 1852. In 1859 he became Solicitor General for the nation and was noted as a proponent of electoral reform. Atherton Street dates from the 1860s but large sections of the street adjoining North Road were demolished in 1970.

Other prominent buildings in North Road include the Bethel Chapel of 1861 that was paid for by the local coal owner, Joseph Love. This is one of the grandest Methodist chapels in the Durham City area and stands near the entrance to the bus station. Joseph Love lived in a house that is now part of St. Leonard's School and had considerable mining interests at places like Shincliffe and Brandon.

Love was a staunch Methodist, but had a reputation for uncompromising attitudes in his dealings with the miners. His chapel was perhaps the grandest building in North Road until it was overshadowed by the construction of the miners' hall in 1874. This fact was probably not lost on the miners' union.

One of the joys of travelling on the train from London to Edinburgh is the spectacular view of Durham Cathedral and Castle that can be seen as the train enters Durham Station across the viaduct from the south. Many people who have not even visited Durham are familiar with this view but although it gives a taster for Durham's medieval joys it also gives a rather misleading impression of the city.

If we remained on the train and viewed the city landscape beneath the viaduct we could very well believe that

Atherton Street in the winter of 1966. Hauxwell's iron foundry can be seen behind the advertisement (NE)

In times gone by Atherton Street was principally famed as the home of Hauxwell's Iron Foundry and Engineering Works, that was one of the best known firms in the city. Situated at number 8 Atherton Street, the firm was established by George Hauxwell, who was born at Great Ayton around 1826. He moved north to Durham from the Yorkshire town of Yarm and established his works near Durham viaduct around 1860. In the 1870s the firm acquired a rival foundry in neighbouring Crossgate.

In his later years Hauxwell's three sons William, Robert and George Junior assisted George in the business that came to be known as George Hauxwell and Sons. By the time of the 1881 census George described himself as an Iron Founder and Engine maker employing 22 men and eight boys.

Most foundry workers seem to have lived in the Crossgate area of the city. Over the years Hauxwell's was involved in all kinds of industrial activity. They were colliery engineers, millwrights, iron founders, farriers, heating engineers and welders. One particular legacy of the firm

was their manhole covers that can still be seen across Durham today.

George Hauxwell became a JP and Alderman in Durham and died in 1897 but his firm continued to operate into the second half of the twentieth century. The building that housed the old foundry was a part of Atherton Street that was demolished around 1970. Demolitions also affected parts of Sutton Street where the A690 now cuts through part of the foundry site.

Castle Chare: The Catholic Corner

Castle Chare, called Castle Chair on a 1754 map is attached to the northern end of North Road and was one of the main roads into Durham in times past. Back in the eighteenth century it was a narrow country lane leading to Witton Gilbert and though linked to that village via Back Western Hill and Whitesmocks it was not as important a thoroughfare as neighbouring Framwellgate and Millburngate.

Framwellgate and Millburngate formed part of the Great North Road and Castle Chare was linked to them. Old Framwellgate and Millburngate have now gone and the south end of Castle Chare that joined Framwellgate is now a dead end where steps lead down to the Millburngate roundabout.

We will see that the crowded houses that once dominated Framwellgate and Millburngate were removed in slum clearances in the 1930s but other demolitions came later in the century. Co-operative Terrace overlooking Castle Chare, was demolished in the 1960s to make way for the road developments that include the two nearby roundabouts.

A small part of Castle Chare north of the viaduct near County Hospital was cut off from the rest of the street by

one of these roundabouts and lives on as an attractive little group of houses called Parkside right below the railway station. The Parkside houses stand opposite the Bridge Hotel and occupy the site of an early nineteenth century workhouse marked on John Wood's 1820 map of the city. The workhouse served Framwellgate but was superseded in 1837 by the larger workhouse at Crossgate that served the whole city.

The street of Framwellgate has gone and is now the A691. Here the recently completed period style housing development called 'Highgate' has created a new version of the street but the part of Highgate alongside the A690 more or less follows the course of Castle Chare where Co-operative Terrace once stood.

Castle Chare – left to right the former convent (or Wheatsheaf), Convent school and St. Godric's Church (DS)

Highgate is linked to the original Castle Chare, or at least what remains of it, by the new Highgate pedestrian footbridge across the A690. Here we find a stone wall and a street sign that are the only real remnants of the ancient steeply climbing street. Chare could be an old word for a steep winding lane, drop, or alley and the name certainly occurs in this respect along the quayside at Newcastle upon Tyne.

Durham's Castle Chare was probably named because of its impressive views of the castle across the river but 'chare' could simply mean 'seat with a view'.

Castle Chare could be described as Durham's 'Catholic Corner' because the notable buildings that remain all have strong Roman Catholic connections. The most obvious is the church of Our Lady of Mercy and St. Godric.

St. Godric's as it is known for short has a rather cat-like appearance as it sits on an island of high ground between two streets and two roundabouts, silently surveying the surrounding city. Featuring prominently in the famous railway station view of Durham, it was built in 1864 by E. W. Pugin, initially as an offshoot of the increasingly overcrowded St. Cuthbert's Roman Catholic church in Old Elvet. St. Godric's served the northern half of the city whilst St. Cuthbert's in Elvet (dating from 1827) continued to serve the remainder.

Little remains of the ancient lane called Castle Chare (DS)

St. Godric's fire and Tenter Terrace in 1985 (NE)

The expanding mining community at New Durham near Gilesgate Moor was initially considered as the site for the church, but in the end Castle Chare was chosen. The proximity of many Irish Catholic immigrants in the neighbouring Framwellgate slum may have been one important factor influencing the choice.

Early photographs of St. Godric's reveal there was no tower and it then looked rather like a huge stone shed. Funds for its construction were severely stretched and the tower was not added until 45 years later in 1909 when the church was finally completed in its full Gothic splendour.

The only major setback to St. Godric's architectural appearance came later in the century, in 1985, when the church fell victim to a serious arson attack. It was subsequently restored and while repairs were undertaken, parishioners attended special services in St. Cuthbert's Anglican Church near Durham County Hall.

When the Catholics purchased the land at Castle Chare back in the 1850s, they also took over a large, impressive

Georgian town house dating from 1750. Before that time this house served as a coaching inn called the Wheatsheaf and is best remembered as the Castle Chare Art Centre of more recent times.

This distinct and currently creamy coloured Georgian building now holds apartments called St. Anne's Court, but for most of its history it was a convent. The building was initially used for church services whilst St. Godric's was being built, but in 1860 the Sisters of Mercy at Sunderland were invited to establish a convent here in return for educating Catholic children in Durham City.

The building was used as a convent and school but at the end of the century a large purpose-built school building was constructed next door. Called St. Godric's school this imposing red brick building now forms apartments called St. Godric's Court. However the school itself lives on at a new location in Carr House Drive near the entrance to Newton Hall housing estate on the northern outskirts of the city.

Tenter Terrace and Tenter House (DS)

On the southern flank of St. Godric's church we find Tenter Terrace which separates the church from the city's

North Road. Two pubs called the Railway Hotel and Royal Hotel once stood either side of the junction of Castle Chare and Tenter Terrace but have long since gone.

Tenter Terrace was built on the site of the Tenter Fields, named from the Tenter Hooks stretching process used in the cloth making industry of Framwellgate. Tenter Terrace is one of the earliest nineteenth century terraces in Durham and is built of local stone rather than the typical red brick that dominated the later terraces around the viaduct after 1860.

At the south end of the terrace, next to the church is a larger house called Tenter House that was once the presbytery or priest's house. Today it belongs to the Roman Catholic Mill Hill Missionaries who once resided at Burn Hall near Croxdale. In 1881 it was home to Mrs Binns, a paper manufacturer who employed paper workers in the Neville's Cross area of the city.

Parkside looking towards St. Godric's church. Parkside is the upper part of Castle Chare and was the site of the Framwellgate workhouse (DS)

The former convent, Castle Chare (DS)

The modern Highgate development pictured from Castle Chare (DS)

Chapter Ten

Framwellgate, Aykley Heads and Dryburn

Framwellgate Bridge is the oldest of Durham City's bridges and was known until the sixteenth century as Old Bridge. Ranulf Flambard, a very powerful Bishop of Durham built the bridge and he was in his time one of the most influential men in England. Flambard had been principal advisor to King William Rufus and was responsible for bringing great wealth to the King by heavily taxing the barons and postponing the appointment of bishops. This enabled the King to reap the revenues of the bishoprics.

In 1099 Rufus rewarded Flambard for his service by making him Bishop of Durham, and a rich reward it was, since the Bishops of Durham were Prince Bishops, holding political and ecclesiastical powers in Durham as virtual rulers of the see. Unfortunately Flambard's position was weakened in 1100 when King William Rufus died during a hunting accident in Hampshire's New Forest. The King's brother, Henry, another of William the Conqueror's sons, quickly seized power and became King Henry I.

Framwellgate Bridge as pictured in an old postcard

King Henry had accompanied Rufus on the hunt and some historians believe he is implicated in the death. Whatever the cause, Flambard must have been a worried man. The Bishop was well remembered for his money making schemes and was hated by the wealthy and powerful who pressurised the King to have him punished.

After taking advice from council, the King had Flambard arrested in 1100 and Flambard became the first person in history to be imprisoned in the Tower of London. The following year Flambard made another important entry into the Tower's record books when he became the first man to escape. Flambard fled to France where he supported the claims to the throne of the Conqueror's eldest son, Robert Curthose, Duke of Normandy. Robert, Henry's brother, was no stranger to England and during an earlier visit in 1080 had established the famous New Castle on the Tyne.

Although King Henry backed down from confrontation, Robert did not seize the throne. Instead the King was forced to pardon Robert and his supporters, enabling Flambard to return to Durham.

At Durham Flambard embarked on the building of St. Giles Church in what became Gilesgate and he actively encouraged the development of trade in the city. He fortified the castle moat and strengthened the riverbanks but his most important work was undoubtedly Framwellgate Bridge, which commenced in 1128.

In Flambard's time, the Market Place was the hub of Durham, as it is today, but it is likely that there was also commercial development to the west of the river at the junction of South Street, Crossgate and Millburngate.

By that time Durham was divided into four boroughs called St. Giles; the Bishop's Borough; Elvet Borough and Old Borough. The Old Borough was centered upon the street of Crossgate and stretched as far north as Millburngate. However, the adjoining street of Framwellgate was part of the Bishop's Borough, as was the Market Place, on the other side of the river. It is probable that a ferry linked the two parts of the borough together.

Flambard would have recognised that this was unsatisfactory and set about building a bridge. It would be misleading to assume Framwellgate Bridge is entirely

Flambard's work because it has seen much renovation and rebuilding over the centuries. Today it consists of two prominent wide arches with a span of 90ft, but these are not Flambard's work. There is, however, a third, smaller land arch hidden from view beneath the buildings of Silver Street and this may be one of Flambard's originals. It is likely that the original bridge had five or six arches and would have more closely resembled Elvet Bridge than it does today. The original arches were most likely swept away by a flood in the year 1401 when Bishop Langley rebuilt the structure.

If there had been five or six arches on Framwellgate Bridge in earlier times then they had certainly gone by the sixteenth century when the antiquarian John Leland recorded only three. A chapel occupied the middle section of the bridge in medieval times but it is not recorded when or why it was removed. The bridge also had fortified gateways at each end. These ensured that the bridge did not compromise the natural defences of the city.

The gateway at the Millburngate end of the bridge was probably demolished some time before the seventeenth century, as it is not shown on Speed's map of 1611. The gateway at Silver Street is, however, shown on the map and was demolished in 1760. Two houses on one end of the bridge were washed away during a great flood in 1771.

Framwellgate Bridge was widened in 1828 to cope with traffic and has undergone much repair work in recent years. During renovation in 1828, it is recalled that workmen recovered a live toad embedded in the bridge's masonry. How it came to be there remains a mystery.

Framwellgate and Millburngate

For most of their history, the ancient streets of Framwellgate and Millburngate were part of the main road from London to Edinburgh, known as the Great North Road. The two streets probably traced their origin to the construction of Framwellgate Bridge by Bishop Flambard in 1121.

Framwellgate took its name from an ancient well that stood nearby and Millburngate from a stream that now flows in a culvert beneath Durham's North Road. Millburngate has gone altogether, with its site now occupied by The Gates (formerly Millburngate) Shopping Centre. Millburngate was a short street that led off from Framwellgate Bridge, with an offshoot called Horse Hole leading down to a ford across the Wear.

The street of Millburngate headed northward out of the city and its continuation was called Framwellgate. Historic houses could be found along the entire length of the street called Framwellgate until it started to climb into steeper open country, roughly where the railway viaduct is now situated. From this point Framwellgate was called Framwellgate Peth, from a northern word peth, meaning climbing hill or street.

Historic view of Framwellgate Bridge showing the Castle and Cathedral

The lost street of Millburngate pictured from Framwellgate (MR)

Until the seventeenth century, Millburngate and Framwellgate streets were home to Durham merchants and traders. Workers living there included tinsmiths, silversmiths, brewers, and tanners.

Framwellgate's ancient leather tanning trade was remembered in the name of the Tanner's Arms that stood in the street near the junction with Sidegate until the 1960s. Indeed, one major nineteenth century remnant of the trade

called Blagdon's Leather Works, still remained in the street near Framwellgate Waterside until the late 1960s.

By the early nineteenth century the streets of Millburngate and Framwellgate had fallen out of favour and became notorious for their slums. From 1831, the two streets were increasingly overshadowed by a new road called King Street, or the lower part of North Road as it is known today. For a time this would have provided a new main route north to Newcastle, but was largely superseded by the Great North Road that bypasses the city to the west.

Millburngate and Framwellgate were in desperate need of revival but unfortunately rather drastic measures were taken when almost all of the houses in the two streets were demolished in the late 1930s. This was despite outcries from building conservationists concerned with their preservation. There was special concern over two, small half-timbered sixteenth century cottages, but they were condemned and demolished with the rest. In fairness, the two streets were no longer fit for human habitation. A novelist called Joan Conquest who visited the area in 1933 described them as the worst slums she had seen in Britain.

Waterside near Horse Hole showing Blagdon's works (MR)

The Fram Well superstructure with Highgate in the distance (DS)

Millburngate is now remembered in the name of a shopping centre called the Gates and in the name of the modern Millburngate Bridge. This road bridge stands alongside Millburngate House which is surely one of the most controversial landmarks in Durham City. More commonly known as the National Savings Office it is, architecturally speaking, the biggest blot on Durham's landscape.

In the late 1980s, the architectural historian Alec Clifton Taylor reflected many people's views when he described Millburngate House as 'an assertive lump of hideous concrete that could only have been put up by a Government department exempt, as it should certainly not be, from obtaining planning permission; and it is a disgrace'. There is however another side to the story and in the late 1960s the construction of the office was anticipated with great excitement because of the jobs it would bring.

The relocation of the Post Office Savings Certificate Division from an Edwardian office block in Manor Gardens, London, to a new office in Durham was announced in 1962. The Durham MP, Charles Grey welcomed the announcement with glee. He had campaigned to bring much-needed jobs to County Durham and wanted to see a major government department located in the region.

In London, 2,000 employees were given the choice of moving to Durham or finding work elsewhere within the government. By March 1963 only 350 of the London staff had volunteered to relocate to Durham but the number who eventually made the move was probably smaller. From as early as 1963 some of the key workers arrived in the city, settling in places like Belmont, West Rainton and Framwellgate Moor. The first local people to join the workforce were Jean Pigg, 16, of Esh Winning, and Carole George, 18, of Belmont. Local people eventually outnumbered the newcomers and were situated in temporary offices at Aykley Heads and in Church Street, Elvet.

The National Savings Building pictured during its construction in 1968. It is often criticised for being one of the most unsightly landmarks in the city. The offices created a number of jobs in the city (NE)

Workers moved into the first section of the new building on Millburngate waterside in January 1967 and by the time of its official opening by Princess Alexandra in March 1970, about 1,300 people worked there.

The jobs were welcomed but some were still angry about the appearance of the building. No members of the public, not even the City of Durham Trust, had been allowed to see plans for the building. On the positive side two rather ugly gasometers were removed from what had been the city's gas works to make way for the building, but criticisms arose about the appearance of the National Savings Office as it took shape. In 1968 City of Durham Trust member Roger Norris described the building as a 'sore thumb' and a 'thorough disappointment'. The trust was not entirely opposed to modern concrete structures however and cited Dunelm House, which houses Durham University's Students' Union, as a good example of a modern building.

Crook Hall to Aykley Heads

Crook Hall is a hidden gem situated within easy reach of Durham City centre in beautiful cottage gardens. Reached by car from Framwellgate waterside or on foot from Sidegate and Frankland Lane, the building is noted for the impressive fourteenth century hall at its eastern end. As an example of medieval domestic architecture it is of great importance to our region but other parts of the house give an interesting insight into architectural history with the whole middle section of the house dating from the fifteenth and sixteenth century while the westerly wing is of Georgian origin.

Crook Hall's history is inseparable from Sidegate, one of Durham's oldest streets. Historically called the manor of 'Sidgate', Crook Hall was its manor house. Sidegate is a narrow, cobbled street that climbs steeply from Crook

Hall and Frankland Lane to join Framwellgate Peth (A691) below the railway.

Crook Hall (picture by Mary Hawgood)

Buildings in the street are no earlier than the Victorian era but stone walls along the street may be striking reminders of earlier days. Sidegate was literally a side entrance to the medieval city, but 'gate' was an old word for a street rather than a gateway. 'Sidgate' (as it was then spelled), was first recorded in 1217 and was held by Gilbert De Aikes of Aykley Heads. He sold it to Aemeric, son of Aimer, Archdeacon of Durham. Aemeric's sons Richard and Emerie took the name De Sydgate, but succeeding descendants throughout the world have been known by the surname Emerson.

In the later 1200s Peter Del Croke acquired Sidgate manor. Presumably connected with Crook in Weardale, he set about building the manor house during the 1300s and the oldest parts of Crook Hall date from his time. It seems likely that Peter gave his name to the hall, but crook could also refer to the bend in the nearby river.

During the middle 1300s parts of the property were divided but were later held by William De Coxhow (Coxhoe) and John Coupland, the knight who captured King David of Scotland at the Battle of Neville's Cross in 1346.

In 1372 Coxhow sold Crook Hall and Sidegate to the Billingham family who owned it until the 1650s. It was one of their number, Thomas Billingham, who granted the use of a spring on his estate for supplying Durham City with water. The spring was the well that gave its name to the street of Framwellgate. The well's inaccessible site is now located on the south side of the main line railway west of Crook Hall, but the superstructure that covered the well can be seen near the junction of Sidegate and Framwellgate Peth where it was placed in 1959.

Residents of Durham were indebted to the Billinghams for the supply of their water until 1631. In that year the temperamental Cuthbert Billingham indignantly cut off the supply to the city and redirected the pipes to a mill on his land. He was later forced to restore the pipes. A ghost called ''the White Lady'', that reputedly haunts the Jacobean sections of the hall is thought to be Cuthbert's niece.

Cuthbert's successor, Thomas Billingham held the estate until the 1650s when it was seized because of damages Billingham owed to a man called Walton. The Hall then came into the hands of James Mickleton and his wife Frances who were given the estate as a wedding gift from James' father Christopher Mickleton, a lawyer of Cliffords Bar. In 1736 the hall was purchased by the Hoppers of Shincliffe and it was through this family that it passed, in 1793, to the Reverend Hopper Williamson, the Recorder of Newcastle.

From 1834 to 1858 the Reverend leased his property to the noted antiquarian Canon James Raine whose guests at Crook hall included William Wordsworth and John Ruskin.

By 1887 the Crook Hall estate belonged to John Fowler who used the hall for bottling beer. His son, a farmer, resided here until the 1920s when it came into the hands of Alderman Pattison who owned a shop on Elvet Bridge.

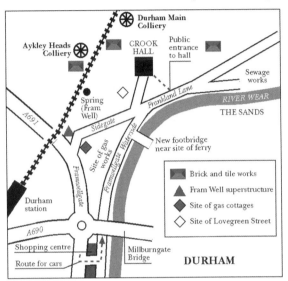

Crook Hall area Map (NE)

From 1930 until the 1970s Crook Hall was the home of John Cassels, Principal of Houghall Agricultural College and it was his widow Muriel who developed the gardens. In 1979 John and Mary Hawgood bought the hall but Margaret Bell has been the owner since 1995 and it is now regularly open to the public.

Crook Hall is set in a rural oasis that takes us back to Durham's early days, but there was plenty of industrial activity in the Sidegate neighbourhood in decades past.

From 1824 until the 1970s the site now occupied by Millburngate House National Savings Office just below Sidegate was the city gas works. Until the 1950s a row of

houses called Gas Cottages was situated in Framwellgate near the junction with Sidegate and housed some of the workers.

In the second half of the nineteenth century, a colliery called Durham Main opened alongside the railway just north of Crook Hall but closed in 1924. A footbridge linked it to another colliery on the Aykley Heads side of the line. There was also a succession of three brick works in the Crook Hall area.

The first brick works established before or during the 1850s was located on the Crook Hall side of the railway. The second, of the late nineteenth century, was on the Aykley Heads side, but the third and largest was on the north side of Frankland Lane near the Barker's Haugh sewage works. It came into being in the mid-twentieth century but the sewage works opened in the early 1900s.

Some of the workers in these various industrial concerns may have resided in a terrace called Lovegreen Street built in the late nineteenth century and named after a local ferryman. Demolished in the 1960s its site is now occupied by Sidegate car park near Crook Hall. For many locals and visitors to Durham, the car park is their only acquaintance with the ancient manor of Crook Hall and Sidegate.

Much of the land north of Crook Hall and Sidegate was historically part of Aykley Heads. Aykley was first mentioned in the twelfth century when it belonged to Gilbert De Aikes whose property faced out towards the cathedral and castle. He was by no means the first inhabitant of the area as a Bronze Age Barrow discovered in what is now Aykley Heads business park points to habitation in much earlier times.

The present Aykley Heads House is an attractive honey coloured building near the entrance to the business zone and though it is mostly eighteenth and nineteenth century, there are parts that date from 1680. It incorporates the offices of Connexions County Durham and the Bistro 21 restaurant that occupies the former kitchens of the old house.

Inside Crook Hall (NE)

Historically, Aykley was connected with Crook Hall and, in the 1600s, belonged to the Billingham family of that manor. It was later granted to the Reades who conveyed it in turn to the Dixons in the early 1700s. In 1763, it passed to the Johnsons, who held it into the nineteenth century when Francis Johnson was the owner. In the later nineteenth century, there were mining developments at Aykley Heads, mostly near Crook Hall, carried out at one stage or another by the Framwellgate Coal and Coke Company, Aykley Heads Colliery Ltd, and Galgate Ltd, of Barnard Castle.

Aykley Heads Colliery opened in the 1880s and mining was undertaken until about 1949. Durham Art Gallery and Durham Light Infantry Museum stand near the site of a drift mine associated with this colliery.

Today, the most dominant feature of the Aykley Heads area is Durham County Hall that was built in 1963 to the south of Aykley Heads House. The new County Hall replaced the Shire Hall in Old Elvet and is one of the most imposing buildings in the city. Fortunately it is far enough away from the city centre not to spoil the view. The County Hall is one of the biggest employers in the city, but many city residents work in other offices that are scattered around the Aykley Heads area.

Today's Aykley Heads includes a business park that houses amongst other offices the North East Chamber of Commerce. Also of significance is Durham Police Headquarters and a little to the north in Framwellgate Moor is the city's fire station. There is a housing development in the area called Aykley Vale close to the site of Carr House Farm and nearby a classical looking building without a roof occupied by a solicitor's office. It was once an electricity substation dating from about the 1920s. One other major employer in the area is of course the University Hospital of North Durham (UHND), that lies just across the road from Aykley Heads at Dryburn.

Aykley Heads House (NE)

Much of the area between Aykley Heads and Framwellgate Moor was historically known as Durham Moor and there appears to have been a settlement here from at least the 1500s. It was a small hamlet on the Great North Road and was in existence long before the former mining village called Framwellgate Moor came into being. Durham Moor hamlet was clustered around the area now known as the Black Boy Roundabout near the entrance to the old Dryburn Hospital. Black Boy was the name of a pub that once stood here.

Dark and Dirty Days

Dark, dangerous, disease-infested streets were once the norm in Durham City. It is hard to believe it today, but this picturesque city could quite literally sicken its nineteenth century visitors with its cess pits, open sewers and unmade roads.

Arriving at night would have been particularly horrific. Inadequate street lighting left the city's narrow medieval thoroughfares cloaked in darkness. Visitors and locals who cared to wander the night time streets might have wondered what they were stepping into and whom they might meet.

The more unruly, nocturnal natives of the city lurked in alleyways waiting to relieve pedestrians of their worldly goods, but in fairness, Durham was not the most crime-ridden place in County Durham. That honour fell to the larger industrial towns. However, quite remarkably in the 1840s Durham City did achieve the dubious distinction of having the poorest health record in County Durham. In fact its mortality rate was even higher than those parts of Tyneside and Teesside that then fell within the County's jurisdiction.

Durham was not the most heavily urbanised place in the county but the mass of overcrowded slums that crammed into the city's alleyways coupled with appalling sanitary conditions made Durham a less than desirable place to live.

A typical Durham slum. This one was called 'the Curtain' and was situated on the corner of South Street and Crossgate. Note, the timber framed buildings (MR)

Legislation did little to improve conditions. Paving Acts of 1773 and 1790 set out the jurisdiction for pavements, sewers, drains, watercourses, footpaths, carriageways and street lamps. These amenities fell under the wing of a countywide commission of 257 people, mostly magistrates, whose work was severely stretched by the population growth of the early nineteenth century.

In 1816 Durham's city streets, were described as being 'soft as an Irish bog', being badly paved or not paved at all. Flagging covered paths in places but it was often useless in wet weather and made worse by drip from eaves and filth from houses.

The City Gas Works (centre) pictured in the 1960s (NE)

An act of 1822 switched the onus for flagging and sweeping to nearby house owners, but the streets remained a problem. They were muddy quagmires. Cobbling improved things, starting in 1830 at Claypath and Gilesgate and was generally complete by 1840.

Early nineteenth century street lighting in Durham came from oil lamps filled with whale oil shipped from Shields and Hull. There were about 180 lamps in Durham but they were thinly spread across the city and rather dim. Lamps were poorly maintained, often vandalised, stolen or simply not lit at all. Responsibility for lighting was contracted out on an annual basis but winning tenders varied in their reliability.

In 1824 Durham switched to gas lighting when Mr West, who had recently supplied Stockton, set up a gas works in the city. The works were situated on Framwellgate Waterside roughly where the National Savings office now stands and they were Mr West's property. West resided in Durham, at West Hall, a large house at Western Lodge in the north west of the city.

The arrival of gas was a major event: 'we behold' wrote the *Durham Advertiser*, 'a city long notorious for its nocturnal darkness become at once one of the best-lighted towns in the kingdom'. West's gas works supplied fuel for the city's lamps until superseded by electric street lighting in 1901. A Tyneside based electricity company erected a sub-station near Aykley Heads to supply the city. The building is now a solicitor's and can still be seen.

The sanitary conditions of the city in the early nineteenth century were shocking to say the least. A report made by a government inspector, George Clark, in line with the Public Health Act gives an unsanitary insight into the state of the city in May 1849.

Former electricity station at Aykley Heads (DS)

Mention is made of houses with privies emptied into middens or open cess pools that often overflowed. Dirty water flowed in gutters filled with refuse in front of the city's houses. The number of privies per household fell well short of the report's recommendation of two (male and female) for each 10 houses and most privies in the city were unisex. Disposal of waste was often a problem, as many streets had no sewage facilities.

Mention is made of specific streets including the 'open and offensive gutters' of Grape Lane, a shallow cesspool at Allergate and a spot called Horsehole on Millburngate waterside with a 'filth outflow' below the weir. It was used, apparently as a 'general receptacle for refuse of all kinds.' Even the very heart of the city near St. Nicholas Church had an exposed stagnant ditch and a pile of street sweepings that included soil and filth from houses.

The report was, however, full of praise for the city's water supply. This was not altogether surprising. The water supply had been improved by the opening of the city's first waterworks at Houghall near Shincliffe. These works opened on 1 May, 1849 at more or less the same time as the report was published. The works pumped and filtered water from the River Wear into a reservoir at Mount Joy and distributed it across the city via a main pipe line that followed the course of Hallgarth Street. The city's water supply was taken over by the Weardale and Shildon Water Company in 1880 who brought in water from Waskerley Reservoir but the old pump house at Houghall still survives and is now a restaurant.

A re-sewering scheme was introduced in 1852 but did not do enough to improve sanitation with sewers still entering the river at 17 different points. The city's current sewage works at Barker's Haugh at the foot of Frankland Lane, opened in the early 1900s and improved things once and for all. The works stand only a short walk along the riverside from the gasworks site. Scented odour from the sewage works is occasionally carried to surrounding areas by a passing breeze. It provokes the rather unpleasant thought that Durham must have once been a very smelly city.

Dryburn, Western Hill and Whitesmocks

In the nineteenth century much of the area around Aykley Heads and Dryburn was open hilly land that formed part of the historic 'Township of Framwellgate'. This township included the area called Western Hill that saw significant housing development during the middle of that century.

Centered on the newly-built Princes Street and Albert Street, Western Hill was one of the few middle class Victorian suburban developments in the city. If you climb these steeply inclined streets today, you still get a feel for their Victorian heyday. It was the kind of better class town house development found in the middle class areas of growing industrial towns and cities like Darlington, Newcastle and Sunderland, but in Durham City, a place little affected by industry, these developments were not so extensive. The new streets at Western Hill grew up alongside a much older lane called Back Western Hill

North of Western Hill and mostly originating in the 1800s were a small number of mansions that were lived in by some of the more wealthy and influential Durham citizens. They included Dryburn Hall, now part of Durham's hospital, Springwell Hall, (now part of St. Leonard's School), a house called North End and another called Western Lodge.

In historic times, the name Dryburn was notorious across the Bishopric of Durham as the site of the city gallows where criminals, catholics and gipsies met their unfortunate end. It was a prominent location overlooking the main road, but its use as a place of execution may have had something to do with the similarity of the name Dryburn to Tyburn, where criminals were traditionally executed in London. When hangings first took place in Dryburn is uncertain but a hill called Gibbet Knowle is mentioned around 1397 and a gibbet is a kind of gallows. In the 1300s, Dryburn was the site of a dwelling called Dryburn House that was held here by a man called John De Bamburgh, whose land encompassed 61 acres.

A medieval hospital called St. Leonard's stood nearby and was certainly in existence by 1292. In the 1100s, the sister of St. Godric of Finchale is thought to have died here. The location of the hospital was possibly in Spittals field, a corner of land between two roads, now opposite Durham County Hall. In 2005, a new housing development is currently underway on this site just south of the University Hospital of North Durham.

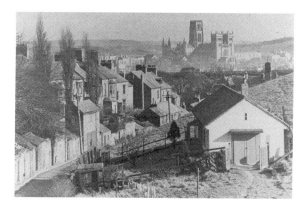

Historic view of Back Western Hill (MR)

Parts of the medieval hospital building may still have been in existence in 1652 when there is a record of a payment to labourers for the demolition of 'Spittle House' here. Also nearby was St. Leonard's chapel, probably in another corner of land between two roads near the present Garden House pub. On old maps, this land was called Chapel Close long before it came to be occupied by the present Victorian church of St. Cuthbert.

The precise site of the gallows in the Dryburn area is open to question It could have been on the old Spittal field where there is now a housing development, or perhaps on the land opposite, or maybe they took place in what is now Wharton Park or where the hospital now stands.

Significant clues may be found on the tithe maps. A tithe map of the Dryburn area compiled in 1839 shows an old field called Gallows Field, that seems to have been referred to elsewhere as the Gallows Flat. It was located on the spot now occupied by St. Leonard's Roman Catholic School.

Springwell Hall now part of St. Leonard's School stands on the site of the Gallows Field (DS)

The same map also shows a quite separate area called Gilbert Knowle, presumably the 'Gibbet Knowle' referred to in other sources. It lies on a hill on the western flank of Back Western Hill the ancient thoroughfare behind Albert Street. The knowle or knoll overlooks Shaw Wood and the boggy bottoms of Flass Vale. Although it is possible that more than one site was used for hanging I think it is probable that the actual executions took place on the Gallows Field at St. Leonards.

I suspect that the Gibbet Knowle was where the practice of gibbeting was carried out. A Gibbet was where the dead and decomposing bodies were left hanging following an execution as a warning against crime. The top of the slope at Back Western Hill was certainly a prominent location and any bodies that were hanging there could be viewed from parts of the city centre.

Most executions involved criminals and seem to have taken place here up until the early 1800s, but hanging and quartering was particularly prolific in the 1590s during the reign of Queen Elizabeth I when Catholic priests and their sympathisers were regular victims. Many of the men came to be recognised as Catholic martyrs and it is probably no coincidence that the Roman Catholic Diocese of Hexham and Newcastle bought the Gallows Field land in 1935 for the construction of their Catholic school which still stands here today.

In the nineteenth century the name of Dryburn was synonymous with a family called Wharton. The Whartons originated from Kirby Thore, in Westmorland, moved to Yorkshire and acquired property in County Durham at Old Park west of Spennymoor in the 1600s.

The Whartons were certainly men of influence in the Durham City area. Robert Wharton (1690-1752), of Old Park, was a mayor of Durham City, as was one of his sons, while a grandson was an MP for Durham City between 1802 and 1812.

The Whartons purchased Dryburn from the Hutchinson family in about 1760, but it was not until 1824 that Dryburn Hall, now part of the hospital, was built as the family seat by Robert's great-grandson, William Lloyd Wharton (1789-1869).

William Lloyd Wharton was High Sheriff of Durham, a director of the North Eastern Railway and a coal mine owner at Coundon, near Bishop Auckland, where the main street is still called Wharton Street. Wharton was keen to impose his mark on the landscape around Dryburn and developed a large garden on a hill at the southern extremity of his property. Durham railway station opened below this hill in 1857 and at about the same time William constructed a mock military battery resembling a castle above the station for purely ornamental purposes. It highlighted a wonderful panoramic view of Durham Cathedral and castle.

The Battery at Wharton Park

The opening of the railway station would have set in motion the growth of Durham as a city and there were already signs of growth on the hillsides in the 1850s with the emergence of housing at Western Hill. Wharton ensured that the neighbouring hill occupied by his garden was protected as open land for posterity and encouraged the residents of Durham to use it as a public park. It is the Wharton Park that we know today.

The Grey Tower (DS)

It is possible that Wharton was also responsible for the construction of another castle-like structure that lies alongside North Road near the northern fringe of the park. Here I am referring to the enigmatic Grey Tower, which has the appearance of a medieval tower house. It was certainly within Wharton's land and was called Wharton's Tower at the time of the 1851 census, when it was the home of Edward Greatorex, the Sacrist of Durham Cathedral.

In the 1880s the tower was inhabited by the editor of a newspaper called the *Durham Chronicle*. His wife, Mrs Linneaus Banks, wrote novels called 'Stung to the Quick' or 'The Waif of the Wear', and her stories gave rise to the tradition that the tower was haunted.

John Lloyd Wharton

Local people often referred to the tower as the haunted house and a ghostly face was said to occasionally appear in the upper window. In the mid-twentieth century the tower was the home to Frank H. Rushford and his wife Hannah, who was the first female Mayor of Durham. Frank Rushford was the editor of the *Durham County Advertiser* and an author of several books about the local history of the city.

Despite its apparent antiquity, most experts believe the Grey Tower is of early to mid-nineteenth century origin or possibly late eighteenth century. However, the experts also admit that the building's true origins are something of a mystery. There is a suggestion that the cellar may have medieval origins and Rushford mentioned that the eminent antiquarian, Canon William Greenwell, had suggested the building may be of some antiquity.

Greenwell said it had been built to guard against a band of brigands who apparently inhabited a cave on the opposite side of the road. In fact the cave is more of a hollow and is actually a redundant gravel pit. Nevertheless stone artefacts of possible medieval origin have been uncovered in the tower's vicinity. They were possibly connected with the medieval chapel or hospital dedicated to St. Leonard that is known to have stood nearby.

The Whartons have links to yet another towering structure that stands on land above the old gravel pit across the road. I am referring here to the Durham Obelisk, built in 1850 on Wharton's land and presented by him to Durham University Observatory. The Observatory itself opened in 1840 but is situated much further to the south, near Durham School. The obelisk was designed to assist with astronomical observations by allowing the observatory to pinpoint the location of the Meridian North. It stands close to Princes Street and Obelisk Lane in the city's Western Hill suburb.

William Wharton's brother, John Thomas Wharton, inherited Dryburn in 1869 but died two years later. It then passed to John's son, John Lloyd Wharton (1837-1912) who was an MP for Durham City in 1871 and 1874 as well as being a JP and Deputy Lieutenant. Wharton was also an MP for Ripon in North Yorkshire from 1886 to 1906. Dryburn was described as his family seat, but in truth he usually resided at Boston Spa near Wetherby. He was chairman of the North Eastern Railway from 1906 until his death in 1912.

Colonel Waring Darwin

In the early twentieth century Dryburn was the home of John's daughter, Mary Dorothea, and her husband, Colonel Charles Waring Darwin (1855-1928), who was somehow related to the famous naturalist Charles Darwin. It was Mary that officially presented Wharton Park to the City of Durham in 1913 though it had been used as a public park for some time.

The Waring Darwins lived at Dryburn until during or just after the First World War when Colonel Cuthbert Vaux, of Vaux Breweries fame, acquired the property. During the inter-war years, Dryburn was acquired by Durham County Council to be utilised as a public assistance hospital, but during the Second World War it became an emergency hospital for wounded servicemen when German prisoners numbered amongst its patients. Part of the hospital was also used for young people suffering orthopaedic difficulties who had been evacuated from a London hospital during the Blitz. In recent years Dryburn Hospital was rebuilt on an adjacent site and has been renamed the University Hospital of North Durham, but it still incorporates Dryburn Hall, the former home of the Whartons.

Dryburn Hall is now part of a hospital (DS)

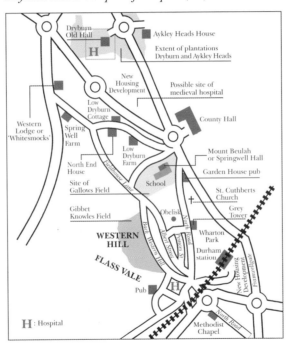

Map showing features around Dryburn, Western Hill, Whitesmocks and North End (NE)

The medieval hospital, chapel and gallows of Dryburn may have long since gone, but a scattering of prominent eighteenth and nineteenth century buildings still lie hidden among the housing developments of recent times. The County Hall of 1963 dominates the area today, but 100 years earlier the most prominent building of the area was St. Cuthbert's Church, with a parish that encompasses most of the area.

Built in 1863 to serve the expanding population north of the city, this church probably occupies the site of St. Leonard's medieval chapel. It may also stand on the burial ground of executed criminals, whose remains were not claimed by their families. The architect of the church was E. R. Robson, apparently better known for his board schools. Nikolaus Pevsner, the architectural historian, describes his work here as 'extremely odd', but it is quite an attractive church.

St. Cuthbert's is modelled on a church in Normandy that was destroyed during the Second World War, and is one of the grandest Victorian churches in Durham City. Its atmospheric graveyard, wedged in a corner of land between two busy thoroughfares, only adds to the church's character.

The Waring Darwin family at Dryburn Hall

St. Cuthbert's Church (DS)

The Springwell Hall Lodge House (DS)

West of St. Cuthbert's are Grey Tower, North Road, Western Hill and the towering obelisk of the 1850s, but immediately north of the church at the junction of the two roads is the Garden House pub. A well-known Durham landmark, it is as much a focal point as the neighbouring church. Formerly called the Woodman Inn, it became the Garden House Hotel in the latter part of the nineteenth century, possibly because of its proximity to the gardens of Dryburn and Springwell Hall. Close to the pub, the two roads – North Road and Framwellgate Peth merge in a roundabout at the eastern entrance to St. Leonard's Roman Catholic School.

The stark stones of Mount Beulah can be seen amongst the present day buildings of St. Leonard's School. Built in 1859, this house was the home of Joseph Love, a coal owner and Methodist preacher who previously lived on Gilesgate bank.

Love owned mines throughout Durham, but despite his name, Love was occasionally something of a hate figure as he was often uncompromising in his dealings with miners. The impressive Methodist church near the bus station in North Road is Love's legacy, but his old house at St. Leonard's though large is much less appealing.

Now part of the school and stuck next to the roundabout, this former house of Love barely lives up to its name of Beulah, a word that signifies a place of peace and abundant beauty in sight of heaven. A later owner of the house, Colonel Reed JP, was unimpressed. When he moved here in the 1880s, he renamed it Springwell Hall.

Springwell was a name already associated with the area and the hall was only one of a number of places that had this name.

Close by and overlooking the roundabout is an intriguing white painted cottage in two sections, called Springwell White Cottage. It occupies the site of a tollhouse that served the Framwellgate turnpike and may even incorporate stones from that building. In the late nineteenth century it seems to have been occupied by a gardener. A small stone building immediately south of the cottage within the school entrance was once the lodge or gatehouse of Springwell Hall.

Low Dryburn Farm (DS)

Old photograph showing North End House

Springwell Hall and its cottage that we have just mentioned are situated at the city end of a street called North End that joins the main road opposite County Hall. North End continues north west from here towards the A167 and here we find the areas of the city called North End, Whitesmocks and Western Lodge.

Halfway along North End is an eighteenth century white painted cruck-framed farmhouse called Low Dryburn Farm, a reminder that this area was once open farmland. Formerly part of the Dryburn Hall estate, Low Dryburn was farmed in the nineteenth century by the Steadman family. Another house, called Low Dryburn Cottage once stood opposite and was inhabited by a gardener, but this area is now occupied by the St. Leonard's housing development that has recently sprung up near the University Hospital of North Durham.

Further west along North End is North End House, now a National Health Service establishment. Built in the late nineteenth century, it was once home to John Francis Bell of Witton Gilbert. He was a proprietor of the corn merchant's firm called Bell and Adamson that was situated in Durham's North Road.

John Francis Bell of North End House

Continuing west, North End eventually becomes a street called Whitesmocks, which terminates at the A167. Whitesmocks was originally the name of an inn, that was apparently named from the clothing of coachmen or waggoners who passed this way. According to the Durham historian Surtees, writing in 1840, Whitesmocks was once also called Well Springs House. It was owned in 1669 by Richard Wiseman and by Thomas Hopper in 1828.

Fordyce, a Durham historian writing in the 1850s, says that Whitesmocks was the old name for Western Lodge, the grand house with a delightful collection of cottages adjoining it on the north side of the Whitesmocks road. An inn was still in existence at Whitesmocks in the 1830s and it is notable that one of the cottages at Western Lodge is called the old brewery.

During the mid-nineteenth century Western Lodge was home to James Atkinson West, who established Durham City Gas Works alongside the river at Framwellgate in 1823. By the 1870s, the main house at Western Lodge (Grey Lodge) was home to John Shields, a county magistrate.

On the south side of the Whitesmocks road opposite Grey Lodge is yet another place called Springwell, this time a former farmhouse called Springwell Farm.

Opposite Western Lodge on the western side of the busy A167 – which is virtually impossible and rather dangerous to cross when traffic is busy – is Aden Cottage probably named after the former British colony seized during the 1830s. The cottage was once the home of Lieutenant James Monks JP, general merchant and a major of a rifle regiment.

The Whitesmocks Inn

During the early twentieth century, the Durham suburb of Whitesmocks developed on the edge of the Aden Cottage grounds on this western side of the great road. It should not be confused with the street of Whitesmocks on the east side of the road. However at this point we have reached the western limits of Durham City's

suburban development and can look out over the open countryside to the west. Much of the land we can see was once the medieval park known as Beau Repaire Park. It stretched from what are now the outskirts of Langley Park and Witton Gilbert south towards the present village of Bearpark that commemorates the name. Here we have entered an area covered by the accompanying book on the Durham City Villages.

The Obelisk is a prominent feature of the Dryburn area (DS)

Albert Street, Western Hill (DS)

Chapter Eleven

Framwellgate Moor

In times gone by Framwellgate Moor was literally an area of empty moor consisting of common land that was not enclosed into fields until the early 1800s. An open track ran through this undulating land, forming the Great North Road that in parts came to be the Front Streets of new mining villages called Framwellgate Moor and Pity Me.

The Framwellgate moorland formed the most northerly part of a rural tract of land called the Township of Framwellgate and stretched over a mile from the centre of Durham City taking in places like Dryburn and Aykley Heads.

Until the nineteenth century the street of Framwellgate in Durham City centre had formed the northern edge of Durham's built up area but was demolished in the 1930s. Framwellgate, the street had given its name to Framwellgate Moor but the street is now the site of a housing development called Highgate just below Durham railway station.

However, the village of Framwellgate Moor is quite different to Framwellgate the street. The former pit village of Framwellgate Moor developed on the moor from which its is named and has now grown to become one of Durham's most populated suburbs.

The pit village of Framwellgate Moor came into being in the middle of the nineteenth century and as a result of Durham's continuous growth in the twentieth century has been swallowed up along with Pity Me to become part of Durham's city growth. Both places are now regarded as suburbs but older residents regard them as two separate villages.

The grave of John Richardson in the 1960s (NE)

Framwellgate Moor was still separated from Durham by about three-quarters of a mile of open countryside until 1940 when the building of Dryburn Hospital bridged the gap. The hospital was followed 20 years later by County Hall that has similarly bridged the division of city and suburb.

In the early 1800s the rural tract of land called Framwellgate Moor was home to around 18 farms, but no major village. Farms included Woodbine Farm near Pity Me, East Moor Leazes Farm, Union Hall Farm near Brasside, Cater House Farm, near Durham Moor and Low and High Carr Houses near Newton Hall.

Cater House at Durham Moor stood until the 1960s on the western side of the Great North Road where Durham's New College now stands. The farmland that once existed on the western side of Framwellgate Moor Front Street belonged to Cater House before the first terraces of Framwellgate Moor pit village were built in the 1830s.

Cater House was first recorded in 1564 under the name of 'Cadehouse' and was apparently named from a man called Geoffrey de Catden. It was also known in the sixteenth century as the 'Scite House', pronounced with a 'sh' sound that referred to a house of dung. In 1840, Surtees, the Durham historian, described the house in more idyllic fashion as ' an ancient single tenement shaded by a row of tall sycamores a little to the west of the great road' .

Cater House was previously part of a larger farming estate called The Hagg, that belonged to the Bowes family. It was centred around Hagg (or Hag) House Farm that is now incongruously situated across the main road from McDonald's restaurant near Arnison Retail park. Part of the Hagg farmland is currently scheduled for a housing development.

Prior to 1564, the Hagg was part of the Newton estate and by this I mean the farmland on which the modern Newton Hall housing estate now stands. When the Hagg estate was divided in 1567 the south west portion called Cater House came into the possession of a family called Atkinson but in the 1640s it passed through marriage to a maltman and tanner of Framwellgate called John Richardson.

Richardson was found guilty of some kind of misdeed that deeply offended the Bishop of Durham. We know this because the Bishop ordered Richardson's excommunication. When Richardson died in September 1684 he was refused interment in a Christian burial ground and had to be buried in his own orchard. When his wife later died at Stockton, in 1690, she was buried next to him. Richardson's grave could still be seen in the 1960s when it was photographed by *The Northern Echo*. It stood alongside a barn in the vicinity of what is now New College but the grave is nowhere to be seen today.

Despite his apparent aberrations Richardson's descendants remained in possession of the Cater House estate until the early 1800s when it was conveyed to the Reverend John Fawcett. Land on the immediate eastern side of the great road (Framwellgate Moor Front Street) belonged to the Reverend Robert Hopper-Williamson. This side of the road saw very little initial development, possibly because Hopper-Williamson wouldn't make the land available.

In Victorian times nearly all the houses in Framwellgate Moor village were on the western side of the street near Cater House. Only a church, a school and a pub called the Granby were built on the eastern side of the street.

Framwellgate Moor began as a mining village in around 1838, and was surrounded by open fields. At the north end of the village was built St. Aidan's church to serve the community. It is still there today, tucked away behind the street and was originally the last building in the village.

The old Salutation (MR)

Beyond lay the separate village of Pity Me, which was at that time half a mile across fields to the north. At the south end of Framwellgate Moor village was the Salutation Inn, not the pub of today, which dates from 1960, but a predecessor. The inn appears on the first edition Ordnance Survey map back in the 1850s but probably came into being at least a decade earlier.

Front Street as we have noted, was part of the Great North Road, the region's busiest highway, but the part of Front Street near the Salutation is now restricted access with only buses allowed to make the full journey along the street. This means that the Salutation is now slightly isolated from the rest of the former mining village.

Framwellgate Moor's actual colliery stood half a mile north east of the village and could be reached from the Salutation crossroads (now the roundabout) along an open country road called Pit Lane.

Houses now stand along the course of Pit Lane, that now goes by the name of Finchale Road and Priory Road. It is now the main road of what might be termed 'new Framwellgate Moor'. The road is the headquarters for Durham County fire brigade (erected in 1957 on the approximate site of High Carr House Farm) as well as

being home to several shops and a pub called the Happy Wanderer. Most of this area represents suburban development of the 1950s and 60s and should not be confused with the earlier Front Street of the original Framwellgate Moor pit village to the north of the Salutation.

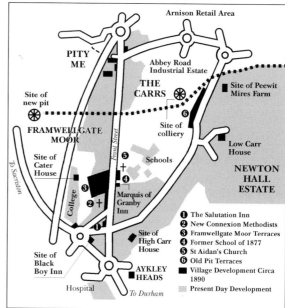

Framwellgate Moor Map (NE)

Further along Pit Lane heading towards the Arnison Shopping centre we find near the entrance to Newton Hall housing estate a collection of old houses of early Victorian origin. They once housed a mining community that was linked to Framwellgate Moor. The community was known locally as Old Pit, and stood right alongside Framwellgate Moor Colliery. The colliery itself was also often called Old Pit. The old houses of Old Pit are in marked contrast to those on the modern Newton Hall estate just across the road. Nevertheless amongst the modern houses of that estate we can see a remnant of an even earlier age. It is Low Carr House Farm that now serves as Newton Hall Community Centre. It can just be seen amongst the estate's modern houses and bears the date 1751 above the door. It is, rather sadly, scheduled for demolition.

Old Pit Lane, Framwellgate Moor (DS)

Old Pit's houses comprise of terraces called Old Pit Lane, Old Pit Terrace, Cross Row and some former colliery houses called The Carrs. Colliery officials like the pit manager and chief engineer would have lived in this area. Much of the area along this stretch of the road now contains light industries like car sales but much activity has been centred upon Durham County Council's repair depot. This site is currently up for sale and occupies the site of the colliery itself.

The Northern Coal Mining Company sunk a colliery here in 1838 on land belonging to the Reverend Hopper-Williamson, but the company failed due to rising costs. Quick sand in alluvial strata deep below caused particular problems sinking the pit. Fortunately the mine's development was taken over by new owners and

the pit finally opened in 1841. J. Bell and Hunter and Lord Londonderry and possibly Lambton seem to have been early owners but before the 1890s it was under the ownership of the Framwellgate Coal and Coke Company Ltd.

In 1894 a second pit, a mile to the west, was added to the colliery and was variously known as Caterhouse Pit, Dryburn Grange Colliery or New Pit. The site of this pit lies in a wedge of land between the A167 Pity Me bypass and the Sacriston road. New Pit and Old Pit were linked by a wagonway that ran through the fields that lay between Framwellgate Moor and Pity Me. It formed a line of demarcation between the two communities. A colliery locomotive called Cetewayo, named after a Zulu warrior, served the wagonway for many years.

Housing development in recent decades has caused Framwellgate Moor and Pity Me to virtually merge, but

the course of the wagonway (now a path) can be seen crossing the Front Street between the two villages.

On the western side of Framwellgate Moor Front Street the path runs from the site of New Pit alongside the Pity Me electricity station where it emerges onto the street. Here the wagonway crossed the road by means of a level crossing that has now gone. In early days a cabin stood here in which a man controlled the road traffic. He also apparently doubled up as a school attendance officer or 'kid catcher' and looked out for truants.

Unfortunately in June 1905 the driver of a fish cart was killed at this crossing after colliery trucks travelling between the two pits struck the cart as it made its way along the road. East of Front Street the wagonway was built along a raised embankment straight through the boggy, low-lying land called the Carrs that is still there today. The Carrs separated Pity Me and Framwellgate Moor from the community at

Framwellgate Moor Front Street showing the Marquis of Granby Inn and the former school (DS)

Old Pit. Dryer land on the south side of the old wagonway is however now occupied by Framwellgate Moor's secondary school. The path of the old wagonway emerged at the colliery site and then crossed Pit Lane by another level crossing. The wagonway's course from here can be traced between Bolton Close and Raby Road in Newton Hall housing estate before it disappears amongst estate streets like Litchfield Road and York Crescent. It eventually crossed the River Wear by a wooden bridge at East Moor Leazes near Finchale Priory and later (after 1857) by the great stone viaduct that still crosses the river near Brasside. It was from here that the coal was transported to coal staithes near Sunderland.

We have seen that there were a few scattered houses in the Framwellgate Moor area prior to the development of the colliery in the 1830s and 40s but there were also a few houses at Pity Me which was at that time a hamlet to the north.

Early Victorian maps show that there was also another small settlement to the south of Framwellgate Moor. This was the hamlet of Durham Moor Houses consisting of two farms and some cottages clustered around a crossroads west of the Salutation. The crossroads at Durham Moor is now a roundabout with branches to Sacriston, Framwellgate Moor, Durham and the A167. The roundabout at Durham Moor is sometimes called the 'Black Boy' or 'Blackie Boy' roundabout and the neighbouring bus stop, often used by visitors to the hospital goes by this name. Black Boy was the name of a pub that occupied a building on the crossroads that appears on the 1850s map. It was demolished around 1910 and it is thought that the name referred to the coal dusted pit boys.

As early as the 1850s miners who wanted to drink could walk in minutes from the Black Boy Inn to the Salutation at the south end of Front Street. From there they could proceed along Framwellgate Moor Front Street for a tipple in The Thunderstorm, Victoria Bridge, Jolly Butcher, Queens Head and Marquis of Granby. Framwellgate Moor wasn't an especially large mining village nor was it a particularly drunken one and the large number of pubs may have been partly influenced by the village's location on the Great North Road.

St. Aidan's church Framwellgate Moor (DS)

The Jolly Butcher is not on the 1890s map and by this time The Thunderstorm had been renamed the Travellers Rest. It retained this name until the 1960s when the business moved premises to Finchale Road and became The Happy Wanderer. The remaining three Front Street pubs are still there, but the Queens Head has been a real ale pub called the Tap and Spile since 1986. The Victoria Bridge was built around 1838, the year in which the magnificent Victoria Bridge railway viaduct was built at Washington. This bridge was part of the main line north and Framwellgate Moor Colliery was linked to this network.

The Marquis of Granby was probably the first pub in Framwellgate Moor and was built sometime between 1809 and 1837. It was named after a popular soldier of the eighteenth century. The pub was originally linked to an adjacent house by an arch through which a hand ball alley could be reached behind the pub. The arch and pub yard were popular meeting places where amusements like biscuit eating competitions took place.

The Marquis of Granby is on the eastern side of the road, but as we have already mentioned most of the early houses in the pit village were built on the western side near Cater House in front of the land now occupied by New College.

Six long terraces called 'the rows' were built (initially of stone) at right angles to Front Street. From north to south they were called Dyke Row, Newcastle Row, Close Row, Pump Row, Smoky Row and Durham Row. In the 1920s most of 'the rows' were demolished and some were rebuilt. The present North Terrace occupies the site of Dyke Row while Durham Row and Newcastle Row live on as Durham and Newcastle Terraces. At around the time of the demolition new rows were built on the opposite side of Front Street. They were rather unimaginatively called First, Second, Third and Fourth Avenues, but the first two were later renamed Lund and Gray Avenues after local councillors.

The spiritual needs of the miners were catered for by a number of places of worship. In 1856, the colliery owners built a Wesleyan Methodist chapel but this moved to Pity Me in 1904. A Primitive Methodist chapel was built in Close Row in 1870 but neither chapel survives. However a third chapel called the New Connexion or Ebeneezer Methodist chapel of 1870 can still be seen tucked away behind Front Street near the Victoria Bridge Inn.

For Anglican worshippers St. Aidan's church was built on the western side of Front Street in 1871 as the daughter church of St. Cuthbert's church in North Road. St. Aidan's is set back from Front Street behind a church hall. Between the church grounds and the Granby Inn is the old red brick school of 1877 which also served the communities of Old Pit and Pity Me. Before this year some of the pupils may have been educated in a building near the church but this is uncertain.

New Infant and Junior Schools were built near the Carrs area of Framwellgate Moor in 1957 followed by the senior school on a neighbouring site in 1965. This made the Victorian school redundant and it is now used as the Framwellgate Moor Community Centre.

In November 1924, Framwellgate Moor Colliery had closed. It employed around 200 miners many of whom moved on to coastal pits as far away as Ashington. Others transferred to more local pits like Kimblesworth or Bearpark.

After the colliery closure, later Framwellgate Moor residents would have to find alternative forms of employment. Two Framwellgate Moor boys that did so in a most notable way were the footballers William 'Ginger' Richardson and George Camsell. Richardson scored the two winning goals for West Bromwich Albion in the 1931 FA cup final victory over Birmingham and still holds West Brom's record for the most goals scored in a season. Camsell who was signed by Middlesbrough from Durham City in 1925 still holds Middlesbrough's club record of 345 goals in 453 games.

Framwellgate Moor has grown beyond the bounds of the original village and has increasingly become a suburb with many of its inhabitants working in Durham City and further afield. It is remarkable that today few people remember it as an active colliery village.

Pity Me

No one knows for sure how Pity Me village, north of Framwellgate Moor received its intriguing name. One theory derives it from 'miserere me', a phrase chanted by pilgrims who travelled this way. Another suggests the deceased St. Cuthbert somehow whispered 'pity me', when monks accidentally dropped his coffin at the site. Others say it was a pilgrim's inn, or the protests of prisoners taken to gallows at Dryburn. Even 'Pitty' a reference to abundant coal pits has been suggested. Many theories incorporate water of some kind. The French 'petit mare' or 'little sea' is often suggested, but the English word mere (a lake) seems more plausible.

The Carrs as Pity Me may give the village its name (DS)

Variations on the water theory include 'pitted swamp' or 'peaty lake'. It was certainly a marshy area and the boggy land called the Carrs still located to the west is a likely setting for a mere. Another possibility was a large medieval fishpond that stood north of Pity Me. An embankment called a 'stank' once formed this medieval pond known as the Vivarium de Kimblesworth and is remembered in the name of Stank Lane near the Pity Me plant nursery.

Place-name experts are largely unmoved by such explanations and see Pity Me as nothing more than a wry name given to an exposed or desolate locality. Such names are quite common and often arose after land enclosures in the 1600s or 1700s when farm buildings were erected on newly enclosed fields.

At least four localities in County Durham were called Pity Me and there were others in Northumberland. Durham examples stood at Bradbury Carrs near Ferryhill, at Dubmires near Houghton-le-Spring and just south of Escomb near Bishop Auckland. All were single buildings featured on the first Ordnance Survey map around 1850. All have been demolished, but were standing in the mid-twentieth century and (perhaps most significantly) all were situated in boggy locations.

Two factors contributed to the particular fame of Framwellgate Moor's Pity Me. Firstly it was on the Great North Road and secondly it developed into a mining village some time after 1840. If it had remained a hamlet or a farm it might have gone unnoticed. In fact, before the miners came it was not even consistently called Pity Me; 'Borough House' and 'Red Briar' were alternative names for the hamlet.

Pity Me had no colliery of its own. Its first miners worked at Framwellgate Moor Colliery that opened across the Carrs in 1841. Notably, this colliery stood on the edge of bogs near Peewit Mires, a farm that was later renamed Tewit Mires. In the 1880s this farm was home to a man employed as a whipper of foxhounds. The farm has now gone but Raby Road on Newton Hall housing estate occupies the site. Perhaps Peewit Mires, named from the call of a Lapwing, is somehow linked to the name of Pity Me.

The hamlet of Pity Me is clustered around the crossroads (recently made into a little roundabout) at the junction of Potterhouse Lane and Front Street. Some buildings here predate the nineteenth century, including the Lambton Hounds, which is a former coaching inn. Once called The Fox and Hounds, it is at least 250 years old. In the 1750s its inn sign depicted a fox being chased by hounds. A diarist of the time suggested that the fox was the inspiration for the name Pity Me, but it is equally possible that the place-name inspired the sign.

The Lambton Hounds at Pity Me (DS)

In the late nineteenth century the inn was renamed The Lambton Hound (singular) but is now The Lambton Hounds. The pub bar, installed quite recently comes from the sister ship of the Titanic. Other Pity Me pubs existing by the nineteenth century included The Red, White and Blue , the North Durham Beer House and the Coach and Horses Inn but The Lambton Hounds is the only one that remains.

Just across from the pub is the well-known North East firm of J. G. Paxton and Sons, agricultural engineers, whose firm started their business in Pity Me back in 1853. It is a strong reminder of Pity Me's rural origins.

Potterhouse Terrace joins the old crossroads from the west and is part of Potterhouse Lane, a footpath of medieval origin. This lane linked Finchale priory to monastic sites at Bearpark and Sacriston.

East of the crossroads, the old lane to Finchale is now called Abbey Road and is the home of an industrial estate on land reclaimed from the boggy Carrs. It is tucked behind the Arnison Shopping Centre.

Back on the west side, Potterhouse Terrace is detached from the rest of Potterhouse Lane by the A167 Pity Me bypass that diverts traffic on the Great North Road behind Pity Me Front Street. The remaining part of Potterhouse Lane is now a road and can be reached from the big roundabout to the north of the village. The road leads to a civic amenity site at a spot called Folly Bridge. Further along is Potter House itself. First mentioned in the 1620s it once, apparently, belonged to a man called Mr Potter.

Pity Me was still a small hamlet a decade after the opening of Framwellgate Moor Colliery in the 1830s but Potterhouse Terrace had come into existence by the 1850s. A further two terraces called the Old Rows, built for the Framwellgate Moor miners came slightly later. These were Demolished in the 1960s but were located west of Front Street where Folly Terrace now stands.

In Queen Victoria's jubilee year of 1897, the owners of Kimblesworth Colliery, (opened 1873), built houses for their miners in front of these rows along Pity Me Front Street. Called Jubilee Terrace and Victoria Terrace they became part of the Front Street.

Jubilee Terrace was situated in front of the Old Rows with Victoria Terrace to the south. A Reading Room and Institute also opened in 1897 near Jubilee Terrace.

Available to the miners for a penny a week, the fee was automatically deducted from the Kimblesworth miners' wages. Unfortunately Framwellgate Moor and Kimblesworth Collieries closed respectively in 1924 and 1967, but Pity Me is still a thriving community that has increasingly developed as a suburb of Durham City.

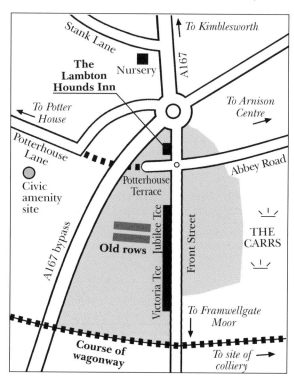

Map showing history of Pity Me (NE)

Newton Hall, Brasside and Frankland

The Framwellgate Moor area of today now encompasses one of the largest private housing estates in Europe. Situated on the hills formed by the moors of Framwellgate it is clearly a recent addition to Durham's ancient skyline but the word 'new' in the name of Newton Hall is deceptive as the name goes back to at least the twelfth century.

In 1183 Newton was first mentioned in the *Boldon Buke* which was Durham's equivalent of the *Domesday Book*. It records that Newton was a farmhouse or settlement belonging to William, a former abbot of Peterborough.

Newton became Newton Hall in 1730 when a Georgian mansion was built on the site for Sir Henry Liddell, Lord Ravensworth. His successor, Thomas, sold the house in 1812 to William Russell, the son of a Sunderland banker who was the richest commoner in England. Russell, who was a coal owner, also owned Brancepeth Castle.

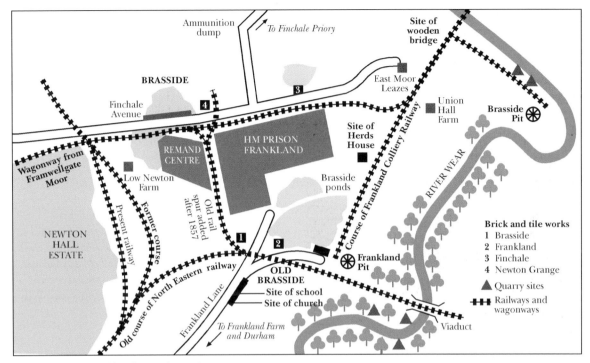

Around Newton Hall and Brasside (NE)

Newton Hall was demolished in 1926

By the 1830s Newton Hall passed to the Spearmans and then in the 1880s to the Maynards, a Yorkshire family who made their fortune from ironstone mining. The Maynards virtually owned the town of Skinningrove on the east Cleveland coast. In the later part of the nineteenth century, Newton Hall ceased to be a private residence and was taken over as a branch of County Durham's hospital for mentally ill patients, based in Sedgefield and known as a 'lunatic asylum' in the terminology of the time.

The fate of the hall in the early part of the last century was similar to that of many historic houses. It was used as a barracks during the First World War and then fell into disrepair. The hall was knocked down in 1926 and a

tragic incident occurred during its demolition. A 14-year-old boy by the name of John Arnison was accidentally killed by a falling joist dropped by a workman called Littlefair. Arnison had left school only three days earlier and his first job involved cleaning the bricks that had been removed from the hall for recycling.

In 1988, the teenager was immortalised in the name of a neighbouring retail development, the Arnison Centre. His name was chosen as the result of a competition to name the site.

The main body of the actual hall at Newton Hall was located roughly where the housing estate's Brancepeth Close stands today, but the hall and its walled gardens covered a much wider area. A tower-shaped gazebo was located on the edge of the gardens, where Eggleston Close is now located. Some old cottages just off Carr House Drive that incorporated part of the hall's stable block remain amongst the modern houses and the ditch of a picturesque avenue that was once part of the garden can just be traced in places.

A long driveway linked the hall to Framwellgate Moor and Durham City and more or less followed the course of Carr House Drive, now the housing estate's principal road. The thickly wooded section of this road is a remnant of the hall's gardens while the community centre near the shops is a former farmhouse called Low Carr House Farm. The farm is scheduled for demolition.

Brasside Ponds (DS)

Work on building the housing estate started in the mid-1950s but the earliest properties in the Bek Road and Langley Road area were initially local authority houses. A major stimulus for the growth of the estate was the relocation of the Post Office Savings Certificate Office to Durham from London. When *The Northern Echo*

interviewed several Newton Hall residents in the mid-1960s a surprising number came from outside the North East. The private houses were built mainly in the late 1960s and early 1970s but developments continued into later decades. These properties have attracted people from all over County Durham and the North East and some have splendid views of Durham Cathedral. It was these views that inspired the builders of the original hall.

Brasside and Frankland are on the north side of the River Wear in a wedge of open countryside formed by the valley that lies between the Durham suburbs of Gilesgate and Newton Hall.

The Frankland area can be reached on foot from Durham City centre via Framwellgate waterside. From here you pass Crook Hall before proceeding east along Frankland Lane, a valley pathway that was once used by monks travelling from Durham to Finchale. Farmhouses called Frankland Farm and Frankland Park stand either side of the lane recalling the name of a deer park that once belonged to the Prince Bishops of Durham. In earlier times this land belonged to a person called Frankleyn.

Historically, Brasside was a further three quarters of a mile along the lane near to where Frankland Prison now stands. Brasside means 'broad hillside' and was mentioned in the 1300s. There was no village here until the nineteenth century, but a stone house called Herd's House was built for a horse herder in 1594. It was still there at the time of the 1850s map. Apart from the prison, the main feature of Brasside today is a quarter of a mile wide pond frequented by ducks, geese and grebes.

The main pond at Brasside is immediately south of the prison with a slightly smaller, adjoining pond. A third pond lies north of the prison west of Brasside village close to the Finchale road. Brasside village overlooks the prison and is separated from Newton Hall estate by the London

to Edinburgh railway. The railway crosses a bridge over a road that links the two communities.

Like Newton Hall estate the history of Brasside village is quite recent. Durham Rural District Council built the first street here called Finchale Avenue in 1928, to re-house residents from an earlier, rather isolated village that was also called Brasside.

The older Brasside village was situated on Frankland Lane, (south of the ponds) and was a coal mining community that sprung up in the 1840s to serve the Earl of Durham's Frankland and Brasside Collieries. Employment could also be found in this locality at some neighbouring sandstone quarries.

Frankland Prison (NE)

The two collieries closed before the end of the nineteenth century but were seemingly reworked in the 1920s and 1930s. By this time most Brasside residents were working at one of two brick and tile works also called Brasside Brickworks and Frankland Brickworks. Both works came into being in the second half of the nineteenth century and were established because of the extensive clay deposits that could be used in making bricks. It was the excavation of clay by these works that resulted in the clay pits that later became the Brasside Ponds that we know today. However the oldest of the clay pits was filled in for the foundations of Frankland prison. The Brasside brick and tile works were the first to open but closed in the early twentieth century. The nearby Frankland works were still operating in the 1950s.

Old Brasside consisted of colliery streets called Long Row, Short Row and Office Street with around 40 households in total. Only two buildings now remain. One is the village's former 1920s community hall that is now inhabited by the owner of some dog kennels that stand close by. The other may have belonged to the brickwork's manager.

A school converted from two houses opened in Long Row alongside Frankland Lane in 1886 and a brick church opened nearby around 1904. This was dedicated to St. Chad, because Durham University students from St. Chad's theological college were involved in the services.

Both school and church were finally demolished in 1935 along with the rest of the village. Some relocated residents in the new Brasside village continued to work at Frankland brick works but employment also came for a time at two new brick works called Finchale brickworks and Newton Grange brickworks that were located near the new Brasside village.

Many wagonways and railways served the industries of the old Brasside area and some of these are now popular footpaths. However, in early Victorian times the main railway network lay to the east of the River Wear where the main north to south route was once the Leamside Railway.

Finchale Priory in the snow (NE)

From the 1840s Brasside, Frankland and Framwellgate Moor Collieries were linked to this network by a wagonway that crossed the Wear on a wooden bridge half a mile south of Finchale Priory.

Around 1857 a new railway was built through the area that was the Bishop Auckland branch of the North Eastern Railway. It crossed the river gorge by a new

viaduct linking Brasside with Belmont on the eastern bank. This impressive viaduct, though not accessible to the public, still stands today.

Framwellgate Moor's Colliery railway was linked to the viaduct by a rail spur in 1857 but Brasside and Frankland Collieries were not and when these two collieries closed later in the nineteenth century their wagonways were removed.

In the early 1870s part of the Bishop Auckland line through Durham City became the main London to Edinburgh line and superseded the earlier Leamside line to the east of the river. Although the new line initially retained its link with the Brasside viaduct the main route headed directly north to Edinburgh in a curve past Low Newton Farm on what is now the edge of Newton Hall housing etstate. This curve was straightened out slightly in the 1970s to accommodate faster trains.

From the 1940s much land around Low Newton and Brasside belonged to the War Department who built a munitions dump just to the north. Low Newton Youth remand centre opened up on another part of this land in 1965 when the idea of a new high-security prison was also discussed.

Despite local concerns, the construction of Frankland Prison commenced in 1975 next door to the remand centre and over a hundred new houses were built for prison employees at the new Brasside village. The Prison was scheduled to open in 1982, but due to a prison officers' dispute in October 1980 it was filled with prisoners under the supervision of the Army.

When the dispute ended the following January, the prisoners were removed. The army departed, enabling the final completion of Frankland Prison. It permanently re-opened in April 1982. In 1997 the neighbouring Low

Newton remand centre was designated a female prison and the prison building now dominates the area near Brasside Ponds.

Finchale Priory

Stone Age flints and finds of Roman pottery are testament to the human habitation of the Finchale area in ancient times, but the name Finchale did not come into being until Anglo-Saxon times around AD 600.

Pronounced 'finkle', it signified a river meadow inhabited by finches or perhaps a dog-leg in the river since the word 'finkle' often means dog-leg.

The first mention of Finchale was in AD 765, when a meeting was held in which the reigning king of Northumbria was forced out. Records also show that in AD 792, 798 and 810, Finchale was the site of synods, or religious meetings that discussed church matters and discipline throughout Northumbria. Such events demonstrate Finchale's early importance. All of these events took place about 200 years before the story of Durham City even begins.

However, Finchale owes its fame to St. Godric, who lived there centuries later. Born in Walpole, Norfolk, in about 1065, he worked as a pedlar for many years, but longed for adventure. Eventually he and some friends got together and built a boat to take them to sea. It gave them greater opportunities for trading their wares.

Early journeys took Godric as far north as St. Andrews, in Scotland, and from an early stage in his life, he took a keen interest in Christian pilgrimage. The Farne Islands and Lindisfarne, in Northumberland, were regular stopping points for Godric on his journeys, and he became fascinated by St. Cuthbert, the hermit who had inhabited those isles four centuries earlier.

As time passed, Godric's career became more adventurous. He sailed to Brittany, Flanders and Denmark and travelled overland to Rome and the Holy Land. Some sources said Godric was a pirate and he may well have been 'Guderic', an English pirate remembered for transporting King Baldwin of Jerusalem. However, 'pirate' could simply mean he was an independent mariner.

Shortly after Godric visited St. James the Apostle's shrine at Compostella, in Spain, he made the life-changing decision to become a hermit. In 1104, he chose Carlisle for his hermitage, perceiving it to be a remote part of Britain. However, he soon sought enlightenment elsewhere and his wandering brought him to a wild and heavily wooded site by the banks of the River Wear. This was not Finchale, but Wolsingham, in Weardale, where Godric encountered a hermit called Aelric, a former monk of Durham, with whom he became great friends.

Finchale Priory (NE)

After Aelric died in 1106, Godric received a vision from St. Cuthbert instructing him to go to Finchale. Godric did not know where Finchale was, but headed to Durham. He became a bellringer at St. Giles church, at Gilesgate, in the city, but later joined the congregation of St. Mary's Church, in the Durham Bailey, where he received an education in a boy's school. Godric was previously illiterate.

One day, according to legend, Godric was walking near Durham when he overheard shepherds discussing Finchale. He remembered the vision and enquired about Finchale's location.

Ranulf Flambard, the Bishop of Durham, granted land at Finchale to Godric and Godric initially established his hermitage at Godric's Garth a mile up-river from where Finchale Priory is now located. Godric later moved his hermitage to Finchale itself. Miracles were associated with Godric at Finchale, and he is said to have spent winter nights naked with water up to his neck in the middle of the River Wear. Acts of endurance were part of a hermit's life, but it did not seem to do Godric any harm. He passed away in 1170 at the remarkable age of 105.

Following Godric's death, Finchale became a small monastic cell inhabited by Benedictine monks from Durham Cathedral priory.

In the meantime, a man called Henry Pudsey, son of Hugh Pudsey, the powerful Bishop of Durham had invited Augustinian monks (canons) from Guisborough to establish a priory near Durham. They settled at Haswell, east of Durham, but moved to Baxter Wood, a more preferable site by the River Browney, at Crossgate Moor, west of the city.

The Benedictine monks of Durham Cathedral Priory were unhappy with Augustinians so near their monastery and when Bishop Pudsey died, they pressured Henry Pudsey into giving up the Baxter Wood land. The monks were very powerful and Pudsey was forced to ask the Augustinians to leave. As an appeasement to Henry, the Benedictines agreed to establish a Benedictine priory at Finchale.

It was granted to Henry so he could be proclaimed the founder – and find favour with God – but Pudsey agreed to return it immediately to the Cathedral priory. And so it was that Finchale Priory was established in 1196, with Thomas, the Sacrist of Durham Cathedral appointed as its first prior.

The first priory buildings at Finchale were modest, but the presence of Godric's tomb made it popular with pilgrims. Significant development took place from 1237. In the 1300s, the priory became a holiday retreat for monks from Durham Cathedral.

Details show that in 1408, there was a prior and four permanent monks at Finchale. Four visiting monks from Durham also lived at the priory, but these four visitors changed every three weeks.

Finchale has a beautiful riverside setting, but because it was always tied to the Benedictine establishment at Durham, it never grew into a wealthy monastery such as Fountains Abbey in Yorkshire. It closed in 1538 during the Dissolution of the Monasteries, in the reign of Henry VIII, and subsequently fell into ruin.

The tomb of Godric may have been robbed and desecrated at this time but was rediscovered in the 1920s and can still be seen at Finchale, within the priory. It is an empty tomb and the whereabouts of Godric's bones is unknown.

Part of Finchale's charm is that it still stands in unspoilt surroundings. The major reminder of the twentieth century is an amunition dump a quarter of a mile west and a nearby caravan site. There is a farmhouse, but no village, although plenty of people live nearby in Frankland Prison and in the Newton Hall Housing Estate. Both are only a mile away.

Frankland and Kepier Wood

Most visitors to Durham are familiar with the lovely wooded riverbanks that loop around the cathedral in the centre of the city but Kepier and Frankland Wood a mile east of the city centre are perhaps just as beautiful.

The Viaduct, Kepier Wood (MR)

Of course there is no cathedral or castle here to attract the tourists, but the sylvan banks of Kepier and Frankland slope steeply down to the rapids of the River Wear and are a popular spot for a summer stroll.

Forty or 50 years ago the whole woodland area was an unofficial playground for scores of local boys and girls who whiled away their youth splodging in the river or climbing trees, but today the woodland is quiet by comparison. But this was not just a place of play. For many local people, the woods were a place of work for miners and quarrymen.

Steep-sided rock faces that almost form caves amongst the trees at the southern end of Kepier Wood are perhaps the most obvious sign of industrial activity. They are remnants of stone quarrying that took place perhaps as late as the nineteenth century, although stone used in the building of Durham Cathedral is thought to have been quarried hereabouts many centuries ago.

Coal mining was a major activity in both woods, and traces of overgrown drift mines are almost everywhere. Drifts are particularly noticeable near river level below the point where Kepier Wood is accessed by footpath from the A690. Several footpaths cut through Kepier Wood and many served as towpaths alongside little narrow gauge rail tracks that have long since been removed.

The rail tracks were tubways that dissected the woodland at almost every point. They allowed coal to be hauled from the drifts in little wheeled tubs. On removal from the drifts, the tubs laden with coal ascended the riverbank by an incline where they were hauled by stationary engines. There seem to have been at least two such inclines in Kepier Wood, but there were others in Frankland Wood on the opposite riverbank where a separate network of drifts and tubways existed.

Occasionally remnants of rails, coal tubs or metal haulage wheels turn up in the riverbank or on the overgrown woodland floor. At one point the rusted remnants of a stationary engine associated with an incline can be seen on the fringe of Kepier Wood.

Many of the mining features in Kepier and Frankland have been identified by local historian Graham Robson of Carrville who has been able to pinpoint the site of powder sheds, a weighbridge and an overhead gantry amongst many other features.

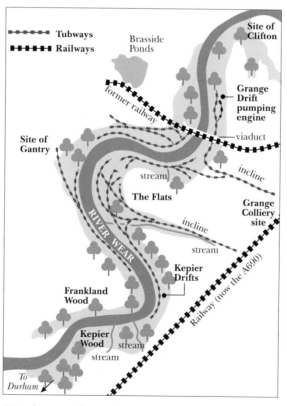

Map showing tubways of Kepier Wood and Frankland Wood (NE)

Graham has identified two sets of drift workings on the Frankland side and at least three on the Kepier side. Unfortunately the tubways are not shown on any old maps but after careful study of the ground Graham has carefully plotted the woodland tubways as shown in the accompanying map. There seems to have been an extensive network but the tub-ways on the map were not necessarily contemporary with each other.

Little is known about the history of drift mining in the woodland but at Rainton Park Wood, a riverside wood that lies just to the north of Kepier Wood, mining is thought to go back to medieval times.

Mining in Kepier Wood itself dates back to at least the early nineteenth century when it was most likely associated with Kepier Grange Colliery and Grange Colliery (later an ironworks) that stood on level land at the top of the river bank.

We know more about the twentieth century mining activity in the woods that took place mostly in the 1930s and 1940s. Roy Lambeth, a local man who played in the woods as a boy has been researching the drifts in the woodland and believes they opened in the war years because the secluded woodland hid the mines from German bombers. Interestingly German bombs are known to have fallen on the nearby ironworks, that lay just outside the wood.

In Frankland Wood, drifts were mined until around 1934 but those on the Kepier side lasted a little longer. A retired miner called John, now in his 70s who resided at nearby Brasside tells me that he remembers playing in the woods during the 1930s and firing catapults at unfortunate pit boys who worked at the entrances of the drifts and dived into the mines for cover.

When he reached the age of 14 in 1942 John himself began work in a mine operated by Frankland Coal Company near Finchale Priory but transferred to the Grange drift mine in Kepier Wood two years later. The Grange Drift seems to have been a newly opened mine in the 1940s and was operated by a Mr Holliday, who was apparently a tobacconist in Durham City. John assures me that in terms of pay Mr Holliday was one of the most generous coal owners in the Durham coalfield.

Grange drift was the most northerly drift in Kepier Wood and stood north of the now disused Brasside Belmont viaduct. The remnants of its drift mine and a brick building that was once the pumping house can still be seen. This continued to operate until the late 1960s when it pumped water from a neighbouring colliery at Rainton. There had been earlier drift workings in more southerly parts of Kepier Wood where photographic evidence of tubways from the 1930s shows a boy playing a banjo near a tubway as it ascends an incline.

Railways in the City

Durham City lay at the heart of a railway region, but railways never had such a profound effect in the city as they did in the industrial areas of the North East. However, railways brought the city closer to the outside world and today the railway sweeps above the city's skyline, providing impressive views of cathedral and castle from the station and viaduct.

Durham's present station was only one of a number serving the city and there was also more than one viaduct. Four separate stations provided services to the city at one time or another and although three of these buildings survive today, only one serves its original purpose.

Durham City's first station was in Shincliffe village at the western terminus of a line from Sunderland constructed by the Sunderland Dock Company in 1831. The line was called the Sunderland and Durham Railway and from Sunderland proceeded through Ryhope, Murton, Hetton-le-Hole, Pittington and Sherburn House.

Elvet Station

Initially, the line terminated at Sherburn House Station, near Sherburn Hospital, but it was intended to extend the line to Old Elvet. However, objections were raised about the Elvet route and the line was taken to Shincliffe instead.

Shincliffe station opened on 28 June, 1839 and the line approached the village station from the east, crossing the village's main street near the Railway Tavern which closed in the early 1990s. Shincliffe station was called Shincliffe Town Station and was the first of two stations in the village.

From Shincliffe, a colliery wagonway formed an extension of the railway that continued across the River Wear by a bridge to Houghall Colliery and then, after passing through a short tunnel, beneath some woodland, terminated at a pit near Burn Hall, Croxdale.

Near Shincliffe branches were also constructed from the railway to mines at Whitwell, Old Durham and Shincliffe's Bank Top Colliery.

The Sunderland and Durham Railway was mainly a colliery railway but also served passengers. Locomotives operated some stretches of the line, while stationary engines for hauling wagons up inclines operated other sections. In one stretch, between Murton and Hetton, carriages and wagons descended 'free fall' under the influence of gravity.

The Sunderland and Durham Railway was only a local line. The main line from London did not reach Durham City until the middle of the 1840s. It was the Sunderland-born railway entrepreneur George Hudson that built this line northwards from York, starting in 1841.

Near Durham, Hudson's line still exists. Now called the Leamside line, it lies to the east of the city. In Hudson's time it was called the Newcastle and Durham Junction Railway and became part of the North Eastern Railway in the early 1850s.

At Shincliffe Bank Top (or High Shincliffe), a railway station was built on the Leamside line in 1844. Called the Shincliffe York British Station, or Shincliffe Bank Top Station, the building still exists and after a stint as a restaurant is now a private house alongside the railway close to the road between Bowburn and High Shincliffe.

The former Shincliffe Bank Top Station (NE)

Durham Viaduct under construction in the 1850s

In the same year that this station was built, a branch line was brought into Durham that resulted in the first railway station in Durham City itself.

The new branch line was joined to the Leamside line at Belmont Junction and headed west into the city, following the course of the present A690. It terminated at Gilesgate Station (formerly Archibalds DIY store) and is now a hotel and restaurant near the Gilesgate roundabout.

Shincliffe Bank Top and Gilesgate stations were both built in stone by the architect J. T. Andrews of York, and both are rather attractive almost Georgian looking buildings. Three railway stations served Durham by 1844, with two at Shincliffe and one at Gilesgate. Gilesgate was the mainline passenger station but two new stations would soon be built in the city.

The Durham station and viaduct we know today were first built in 1857 in the western part of the city at the top of North Road. Neither station nor viaduct were initially part of the main line from London. Instead, they were merely part of a new branch line from Bishop Auckland to Durham. If you headed south on a train from Durham

station in those days your first two stops would have been Brandon and Brancepeth, rather than Darlington and York.

The railway from Durham Station followed the course of today's Brandon-Bishop Auckland footpath. Entering the city from Brandon, the railway approached the city's outskirts at Relly junction just west of Crossgate Moor. Only then did it follow the course of the present main line northward – in other words it crossed the River Browney through Crossgate Moor via Redhills cutting and then continued over the viaduct into Durham station.

Durham Station and viaduct were not intended for the main line to London. When they were opened in 1857. The engineers probably did not appreciate the significance of their work. They were nevertheless highly praised for their achievement. The viaduct crossed Durham's boggy Flass Vale and this proved a great challenge for the constructors.

North of Durham station, the Bishop Auckland line continued, following the course of the present main line north to Newton Hall. On reaching this point, unlike

The old Gilesgate Station (MR)

today, it did not continue directly north towards Newcastle but veered off east, crossing the River Wear via the Brasside-Belmont Viaduct also known as Kepier viaduct. On crossing the viaduct the line joined the Leamside route (then a main line) and it was by this course that it eventually reached Tyneside.

Dating from the 1850s, the Brasside-Belmont viaduct still exists over the steep gorge of the River Wear between Kepier and Frankland Woods. The railway across the viaduct has long since gone and the viaduct is not accessible to the public, but the impressive structure can be admired from the woodland path below. Kepier viaduct was one of two viaducts associated with the Leamside line near Durham City. A wooden viaduct also existed on the Leamside line itself, south of Sherburn, where the railway crossed a small stream. This was built in 1844, but was later converted into an embankment.

Returning to the west side of the city, the stretch of the Bishop Auckland line between Relly and Newton Hall did not become part of the present main line from London until the early 1870s. The section from Newton Hall to Newcastle (via Chester-le-Street and the Team Valley) was completed in 1868. The southern section from Relly to Tursdale (from which point it still follows the Leamside line) was completed in 1872. The completion meant that the main line from London was now entirely to the west of Durham City. The old Leamside line to the east gradually declined in importance and is now a largely disused line, awaiting revival.

Sadly, the opening of the new line resulted in the demise of the Gilesgate branch line of the Leamside railway and Gilesgate station was demoted to goods only.

However, Gilesgate was not the last passenger station built in the eastern part of the City. Elvet, first proposed as the site for a station in the 1830s finally got its chance

Durham Station was built in the 1850s and rebuilt in the 1870s (DS)

in 1893 when the old Sunderland to Durham Railway was extended there.

This had been the oldest railway line in the city area but was extended across the Wear into Elvet by means of an iron bridge near Maiden Castle. The railway terminated at the newly built Elvet Station. This station stood behind Old Elvet where the magistrates' court is sited today. Its opening led to the closure of its sister station at Shincliffe Town which had been the original terminus on a separate branch of the line.

Elvet continued to operate passenger services until 1931 and worked as a goods station until 1949. Once a year, until 1953, it transported passengers from Sunderland and east Durham to the Miners' Gala. Sadly, the building was demolished in 1963.

Durham's other two stations continued to operate throughout this period. Shincliffe Bank Top Station closed its passenger service in 1941 but continued as a goods station until 1963. Gilesgate Goods station operated until its eventual closure in 1966 when its branch line was uprooted for the construction of the A690 dual carriageway.

Today, Durham City has only one railway station. Situated alongside the viaduct and dating back to 1857 it is a humble, but rather attractive stone building on a prominent hillside. It also offers one of the most impressive views of Durham Cathedral and Castle.

Victorian illustration showing view of Durham from the railway station

Chapter Twelve
Gilesgate to Ramside

Gilesgate is one of the oldest streets in Durham and along with Claypath runs along the top of a steep ridge, bordered on two sides by the Wear valley.

Kepier lies in the valley to the north of Gilesgate while Old Durham and Elvet are situated to the south. Gilesgate is sometimes called 'Gilligat' by older residents and this appears to have been the ancient name for the street, pronounced with a soft 'g'.

Gilesgate Green 'The Duck Pond' (DS)

The lower part of Gilesgate is sometimes mistakenly thought to be Claypath but Claypath ends and Gilesgate begins at Tinklers Lane. It is rather confusing because the Claypath medical centre is really located in the lower part of Gilesgate.

For centuries lower and upper Gilesgate formed a long continuous street that ascended eastward from Durham City in a rather impressive fashion. This whole effect was destroyed in the late 1960s when the A690 dual carriageway was built. The A690 was built partly along the course of an old railway branch line into the city but unlike the railway it did not terminate at the street of Gilesgate. Instead the dual carriageway cut straight through the middle of the street and a new roundabout was built on the spot. The roundabout completely severed the link between the upper and lower parts of Gilesgate.

Several prominent buildings and a whole section of houses on both sides of the street were removed to make way for the roundabout. Fortunately surviving buildings included Hild and Bede College and the former railway station that is now a hotel. All of these buildings were far enough away from the roundabout to avoid demolition.

Gilesgate buildings destroyed to make way for the roundabout included pubs, shops, houses, tenements and a drill hall. The drill hall, built in 1902, had been the headquarters for the 8th regiment of the Durham Light Infantry and was built on the site of a soap works established by the Co-operative Society back in 1874. When the drill hall was demolished in 1966, the Durham Light Infantry crest was saved and incorporated into a new Territorial Army centre that was built to the rear.

Other buildings demolished for the roundabout included the Durham Ox pub near the Drill Hall and homes in the nearby Moody's Buildings where my mother was born.

Moody's Buildings stood near the present Claypath medical centre and was accessible from an enclosed passageway.

Station Lane, now an offshoot of the roundabout was the site of a general store called Porters Stores that was also demolished. Tithe records of the seventeenth century mention a place called 'Porters Close' hereabouts but the store is thought to be named from the Porter family, who established a business here in the 1860s.

Historic view of Gilesgate Bank looking towards Lower Gilesgate. Most of the properties between the upper and lower parts of Gilesgate were destroyed in the 1960s

In the 1960s, prior to its demolition, the store became Cowie's motorcycle shop. A grocery shop called Johnson and Cosgrove's also stood nearby. A couple of doors up bank from the grocers was the Volunteer Arms.

On the north side of Gilesgate roundabout is Station Lane leading to the neat Georgian hotel of beige coloured stone that was once the railway station of 1844.

Station Lane was in existence long before the railway but I don't know its old name. It was interlinked with Magdalene Lane (or Maudlingate) now Magdalene Street which led to the St. Mary Magdalene Chapel that now lies in ruins alongside the A690.

Another prominent building that stood in the region of the roundabout, this time on the south side was Lowe's Marble Works, which stood close to Bede College. In July 1904 its owner Councillor Charles Lowes was murdered by an apprentice called Robert John Allen. Mr Allen, the son of a Durham prison warder who was sentenced to twenty years imprisonment.

On the south side of the roundabout are the impressive dark stone buildings of St. Hild and Bede College. These once separate colleges amalgamated and became a part of Durham University in 1979.

Bede College was the older of the two. It dates from 1839 and its main building is located on Pelaw Leazes Lane (Bede Bank) which descends towards the river. A building further down the lane was a 'Model school' used by trainee teachers from the college but it closed in 1933.

St. Hild's College dates from 1845 and lies in the neighbouring St. Hild's Lane where most of the buildings are located to the rear of Gilesgate Bank and St. Giles Church. The college includes a rather impressive Victorian chapel (now the Joachim Room) attached to the main building.

Associated with the colleges are several prominent old houses. These include the impressive early eighteenth century mansion called Belvedere House on Gilesgate Bank and a neighbouring house called The Grove near St. Giles Church. The Grove was once home to the Principal of St. Hild's. Also belonging to the college are the St. Giles' Vicarage, which is a red brick building now called Charles Stranks House. It is named after a former Archdeacon of Durham. Next door to the vicarage is the Gilesgate Manor House and close to Gilesgate bank, Manor Lodge, which also belong to the college.

Heading east from the roundabout at Lower Gilesgate we begin to climb the upper part of Gilesgate called Gilesgate Bank. Here there are a number of smart looking houses along the street, some of which are of Georgian origin.

Compared to the more working class community of Gilesgate Moor at the top of the hill, the street of Gilesgate with over 200 houses seems to have been a home to middle class occupants during the nineteenth century when its residents included city aldermen and magistrates.

Nineteenth century illustration of St. Giles Church

In the 1881 census, only five properties in the street of Gilesgate were occupied by coal miners. A prominent and rather stately looking building of the twentieth century with a large L on its facade reminds us that the Marquess of Londonderry, a well-known coal owner was a major landowner hereabouts.

The oldest building in the street of Gilesgate is the medieval church of St. Giles which gives its name to the entire street. It is set back from Gilesgate and overlooks the banks of Pelaw Wood to the south where paths lead down towards the river and the site of Old Durham.

St. Giles stands close to a picturesque, village-like area of Gilesgate bank called Gilesgate Green. This green is lined with cottages and is known to locals as the 'Duck Pond'. It has been called this since at least 1584 when a local man is known to have scoured the pond there.

The actual pond on the green was filled in during the 1840s for health and safety reasons so it is perhaps remarkable that the name survives at all. Just behind the Duck Pond area we find modern housing of the 1990s called St. Giles Close at the entrance to an old lane leading to Pelaw Wood.

The old lane was once known locally as Wood and Watson's Lane from a mineral water and soft drink manufacturer of that name. Wood and Watsons were founded in 1894 and the business stood in Gilesgate on the corner near the entrance to the lane where it stood for just over a hundred years. W. H. Wood, the founder of the firm was the Mayor of Durham in 1909.

Further up the bank Gilesgate splits into two at the 'road ends' formed by the junction of Sherburn Road and Sunderland Road. Close by on the south side of the Gilesgate street stood a toll house marked on a Durham City map of 1820. Here we are at the very top of Gilesgate Bank where prominent pubs include the historic Queen's Head. To the rear of the pub stands the impressive Vane Tempest Hall. Erected in 1863 and built in the style of a mock castle it was the headquarters for the 2nd Durham Militia and served as a barracks for many years. It is now a local community venue for the people of Gilesgate and is reputed to have a ghost.

The military connection continues on the other side of Gilesgate opposite the Queen's Head in the form of a pub called the Durham Light Infantryman. Called the DLI for short, it used to be called the Bay Horse but was renamed in 1968. Just down Gilesgate bank from here is a former Methodist Chapel (now an Undertaker) and next door once stood the Canteen Inn or 'For Alls', a pub that was frequented during the nineteenth century by soldiers from the local barracks.

Up the bank from the DLI pub Gilesgate becomes Sunderland Road. Here a petrol station stands on the site of the St. Giles Gate School of 1874. The school was demolished in the late 1960s but part of the school wall remains alongside the filling station.

Opposite the school stood a nineteenth century pub called The Railway Coach, later called the Three Horse Shoes. The present Three Horse Shoes is of twentieth century origin. The first pub was probably called The Railway Coach in anticipation of the Gilesgate branch of the Leamside line terminating at this point. In the event the line was built further to the north where we now find the A690 dual carriageway.

Where Gilesgate splits into Sunderland Road and Sherburn Road there once stood in between the two a rather intriguing feature called the Maiden's Arbour. It was situated approximately where Young Street now stands. Some theories suggest it was a Roman signal station associated with neighbouring sites at Old Durham, Maiden Castle or Pelaw Wood. It is interesting to note that the name Pelaw could signify a fortified hill with a palisade.

The purpose of Maiden's Arbour is unknown, but a marble cross was located here until the 1500s and milkmaids once milked their cows here.

Kepier and Caldecotes

Most of Gilesgate's early history is focused upon St. Giles Church and the medieval hospital of Kepier. The former hospital of Kepier stands on the banks of the River Wear just north of Gilesgate and is one of the most historic buildings in Durham.

Kepier Hospital's early history is closely tied to Gilesgate and particularly to St. Giles church. It was Ranulf Flambard, a powerful Prince Bishop of Durham, that built this church in 1112 and he built a hospital alongside it. The church was probably dedicated to St. Giles because the saint was so closely associated with the poor and needy.

The hospital was burned down in the 1140s during a battle between two bishops. This incident involved a notorious usurper called William Cumin, who with the support of David, King of Scotland, falsely claimed to be the Bishop of Durham.

Kepier Hospital

Cumin had taken up residence in Durham Castle and from here he terrorised both city and county. Unfortunately in 1143, the real Bishop of Durham who was called William St. Barbara, failed to oust Cumin from the post and had to take refuge in St. Giles Church. Here the real Bishop was ambushed by Cumin's forces the following morning and the hospital was set alight. Fortunately St. Barbara made a lucky escape and Cumin was eventually ousted from the bishopric the following year.

In 1154, a new bishop called Hugh Pudsey relocated St. Giles hospital to Kepier on the banks of the River Wear just to the north of Gilesgate. St. Giles church was still linked to this hospital by the ancient street of tenements called Maudlingate, and from the 1400s a chapel dedicated to Mary Magdalene stood close by. This is the chapel that now lies in ruins alongside the A690.

Kepier Hospital belonged to the Bishops of Durham but was a monastic-type of establishment with a master and 13 brethren. Each of the brethren had a specific role in managing the hospital lands which extended as far west as Ramside, near Belmont. The hospital was a place of relief and refuge for pilgrims and for the poor but could also play host to the wealthy. It was never a leper hospital as is sometimes thought.

On one occasion King Edward I was entertained here, but a more unwelcome visitor was the Scots king, Robert the Bruce, who attacked and burned the hospital in 1306 during a Scottish raid.

In medieval times the suburbs of Gilesgate Moor or Belmont didn't exist and the whole area of open agricultural land north of Gilesgate belonged to Kepier Hospital. Before the hospital came into being in the mid 1100s the land had belonged to the manors of Caldecotes and Clifton.

Caldecotes seems to have encompassed much of the area around Gilesgate Moor, while Clifton covered the area around the present Carrville.

Caldecotes was first mentioned in the 1100s and the name meaning 'cold shelter' may refer to a derelict habitation of some kind that was perhaps Roman or Anglo-Saxon in origin. The manor was either focused upon Kepier or situated in the land near Gilesgate Moor that was later called High Grange. If Kepier (where the hospital now stands) was part of the manor it seems to have initially been a place where fish were caught as the name Kepier derives from 'Kep Weir', meaning the 'fish catching place'.

A Roman road is thought to have passed north-south through this area from Old Durham near Shincliffe towards Chester-le-Street but the course through Kepier is uncertain.

Arms of the Heath family

When Kepier Hospital acquired Caldecotes in the twelfth century some of the Caldecotes' land came to be known as High Grange or Near Grange. It later became a farm in its own right but the home farm for the area was always Kepier Farm at Kepier Hospital.

The farm buildings at High Grange included a massive medieval tithe barn that stored grain. It is interesting to note that in medieval times the word 'grange' meant 'granary'. Unfortunately High Grange farm and barn were demolished in 1960 and the High Grange housing estate at Gilesgate now stands on the farmland site. High Grange farm house stood approximately where Gilesgate Junior School is now located.

Kepier Hospital owned both High Grange and Low Grange but the hospital itself was the property of the Bishop of Durham. When Henry VIII dissolved the

monasteries and redistributed church land, Kepier was seized and passed in succession to Sir William Paget and then to a Scot called John Cockburn, the Lord of Ormiston.

In 1555 Cockburn's land, along with Old Durham near Shincliffe was sold to the Heath family and from 1568 it became the property of a Londoner called John Heath. It was unusual for a southerner acquiring northern land at this time to actually uproot from the south, but Heath came to live here and died at Kepier in 1590. He was buried in St. Giles church in Gilesgate where his effigy can still be seen.

In subsequent years Heath's Kepier lands were divided between two branches of his family, with Low Grange going to one side and High Grange to another. By the 1600s Heath's land in and around Gilesgate Moor consisted of four divisions centred upon the farms at Kepier, High Grange, Low Grange and Ramside plus a separate land holding at Old Durham.

Kepier Farm stands by the river near the Sands in Durham City and incorporates the medieval gatehouse of Kepier Hospital. A Roman road may have crossed the river near this point, perhaps where the rapids can be seen in the river. The Heaths built their manor house next door to the farm and it eventually became a pub called the White Bear Inn in the 1820s. The manor house has now largely disappeared but the decorative arches of its lower walls can still be seen.

In 1629, the Heaths sold Kepier and High Grange to a Newcastle merchant called Ralph Cole of Gateshead but Old Durham and Low Grange remained Heath property. The Heath family continued to hold these properties until 1642 when Elizabeth Heath, last of the line married John Tempest, a Durham MP. In 1819, their descendant, Frances Anne Tempest married the third Marquess of

Londonderry and as a result Low Grange and Old Durham subsequently became Marquess of Londonderry property.

Meanwhile, back in 1674, Ralph Cole sold his Kepier and High Grange properties to Sir Christopher Musgrave of Carlisle, but the part of Musgrave's newly acquired land called High Grange seems to have been sold to the Carr family of Cocken Hall near Finchale.

The old boundary between the lands of Carr and Musgrave is marked today by Kepier Crescent and a footpath called Kepier Lane that divides High Grange housing estate from the 1950s council housing estate near Gilesgate Comprehensive School (now Durham Gilesgate Sports College). Kepier Crescent was built along part of this lane.

The streets called Musgrave Gardens, built in the 1920s lie just within what was once Musgrave's land. Carr's land extended eastward from Kepier Lane as far as Carrville High Street. In later years the Carrs of Cocken and High Grange were renamed Standish-Standish. In around 1812 William Carr of Cocken inherited some Cheshire lands plus a title through his great grandmother. He became William Standish-Standish of Duxbury Hall but chose to reside at Cocken where he died in 1856.

The White Bear, was once the Heath mansion

Gilesgate Moor, New Durham and Dragonville

The lands in between the Sherburn Road and Sunderland Roads beyond Maiden's Arbour were historically common lands called Gilesgate Moor. This moor was enclosed and divided into plots in the early 1800s and housing subsequently developed here for local miners.

The early 1800s saw land enclosures in Gilesgate Moor between the two roads and the subsequent urban development of several scattered colliery terraces within the newly enclosed land. Most land north of Sunderland Road and south of Sherburn Road remained agricultural.

Sherburn Road and Sunderland Road are the eastward extension of Gilesgate and these two ancient roads effectively became focal points or front streets for several tiny pit villages. As with the front streets of other mining villages Sherburn Road and Sunderland Road became particularly well supplied with pubs as the nineteenth century progressed.

Kepier Colliery

Sunderland Road pubs included the Londonderry Arms, Traveller's Rest, Hare and Hounds and Grange Foundry Inn. Further along, right at the eastern end of the road in Alma Terrace near Carrville was the Forrester's Arms.

The Grange Foundry Inn on the Sunderland Road is still there today and is named from an iron foundry that existed a mile to the north at Belmont. Directly opposite this pub there stood yet another pub called the Gilesgate Moor Inn. It should not to be confused with the present Gilesgate Moor Hotel which is situated in Rennys Lane at the junction with Teasdale Terrace.

Prior to the development of the colliery terraces between the two roads there were a few scattered farmhouses, homes and cottages in the Gilesgate Moor area. They included a small house called Laverick Hall and the intriguingly named Surprise Cottage on the Sherburn Road. These were certainly in existence by the 1850s and although Laverick Hall has gone it is rather a pleasant surprise to discover that Surprise Cottage is still there overlooking the Sherburn Road.

Some of the terraces that developed between the two roads were named after the Marquess of Londonderry's family. Ernest Place and Adolphus Place near Dragonville were named after the Marquess's sons.

Gilesgate Moor's first actual colliery was Kepier Colliery, situated in an area known until recently as the 'duff heap'. This was the colliery pit heap located where modern housing in Mackintosh Court now stands near Musgrave Gardens. Kepier Colliery opened briefly in 1818 before reopening permanently in 1822 when Mr Dixon and Mr Thwaites owned the pit.

It wasn't the only industrial activity in the area. Next door, where a medical practice now stands there was once a site called 'Glue Garth'. Marked on maps from the 1850s it was presumably the site of a glue factory that made glue from horse's hooves.

The 3rd Marquess of Londonderry

Two separate maps dating from the 1840s that were kept in the private papers of the Marquess of Londonderry show a wagonway heading south-east from Kepier colliery to Sherburn. It crossed Sunderland Road by a level crossing near Bells Ville and cut through the area where Ernest Place was built before crossing the junction of Rennys Lane and Dragon Lane by another level crossing. The wagonway is only known from these papers and may never have been built.

Former Methodist chapel at Ernest Place (DS)

What we do know for certain is that when the branch line of the Leamside railway was extended into Gilesgate in 1844 Kepier Colliery was linked to this line by a much shorter route.

The new wagonway linked the colliery to the branch line near to where Heaviside Place and Long Acres now stand near the A690. The Kepier Colliery pit seems to have been called Engine Pit but was accompanied by another called Florence Pit from about 1872. Florence pit was probably the mine that stood to the north, close to the river but seems to have been part of Kepier Colliery. It was located on land on which Mr Thwaites was tenant. The Engine pit was on land that Thwaites shared with Dixon.

The riverside mine called Florence Pit was disused by the 1890s map when the site is shown on a map stuck in the middle of a military rifle range. Gorse bushes are all that remain to mark the pit's site.

Concrete blocks that supported the neighbouring rifle targets can still be seen alongside the river. This rifle range extended about 900 yards west to Kepier Hospital. Up on the valley slopes above the former rifle range towards the hospital can be seen the remnants of brick kilns associated with a brick works that once stood in this area.

These works existed in the mid-1800s but by 1890 only the kilns and a water-logged clay pit called Harper's Pond (named after a local farmer) remained. The pond had been drained by the late 1960s.

Much of the valley land around Kepier is now a training ground for the electricity board but plans are being considered to construct a northern relief road through this unspoilt valley. It is proposed that this road would link the A690 to Aykley Heads via the Crook Hall area and is likely to become the subject of a heated environmental campaign.

In addition to the Kepier brick works another Victorian brick works stood near Sunderland Road in Gilesgate Moor where a street of the 1920s called the Moorlands now stands. Like the Kepier works this particular industrial concern had closed by the 1890s.

The eastern suburb of Durham called Gilesgate Moor shares many similarities with Framwellgate Moor to the north of the city. For a start both have similar names that ultimately derive from ancient Durham streets, both encompassed open moorland until enclosure in the early nineteenth century, and most importantly, both owed their population growth to mining settlements of the early 1800s.

The big difference was that whilst Framwellgate Moor formed a mining village clustered along a Front Street serving a single colliery, Gilesgate Moor was a dispersed scattering of separate terraces that served several local collieries. Historians of the 1800s seem to have considered Gilesgate Moor terraces like Ernest Place, Teasdale Terrace and Marshall Terrace as almost being tiny little mining villages in their own right. In fact many had their own chapels and pubs just like larger mining settlements.

From 1852, for example, Ernest Place had a Primitive Methodist Chapel and though this is no longer used as a chapel it can still be seen today. Here there was also a Victorian pub called the Bonny Pit Lad and another called the Grapes that stood close by in neighbouring Lodge Hill. Similarly, Teasdale Terrace was home to a Wesleyan Chapel and a pub called the Lord Seaham or the Gilesgate Moor Hotel as it is known today.

Some terraces in and around Gilesgate Moor had names that appeared to aspire to village status. Thus we have Bell's Villa where my grandmother grew up. There was also Dragon Villa and beyond Gilesgate Moor was Carr Villa, a place of much greater size. All of these places came to be spelled 'ville'.

Dragon Villa was a nineteenth century settlement, probably named from a pub. There was a Dragon Villa pub here in the nineteenth century and also at one time or another there were pubs called the George and Dragon, Victoria and The Lass o' Gowrie.

The Bay Horse at West Sherburn (DS)

Dragon Villa was a very small settlement but merged with an older farming hamlet called West Sherburn where there was a pub called the Bay Horse. This pub, thought to be 300 years old, still exists today and despite several name changes over the years (the Coal Hole and Tavern being examples) it is once again called the Bay Horse.

The Bay Horse pub lies tucked away between Dragonville Industrial Estate and the Sherburn Road just before the road crosses over the A1(M) motorway. Nearby and still standing in 2006 is the a house that was in recent times the Autumn Leaves Guest House. It was formerly the George and Dragon Inn.

A little west of Dragon Villa and adjoining Sherburn Road stood the largest mining village in Gilesgate Moor. This was New Durham village and was the home to about 700 people. It consisted of pit terraces like Love Street, Chapel Street, John Street, Cottage Street and Dike Street.

New Durham's Chapel Street was the home to a New Connexion Methodist Chapel established in 1838 but this was later relocated to a nearby site in Dragon Lane.

Whitwell House, Sherburn Road (DS)

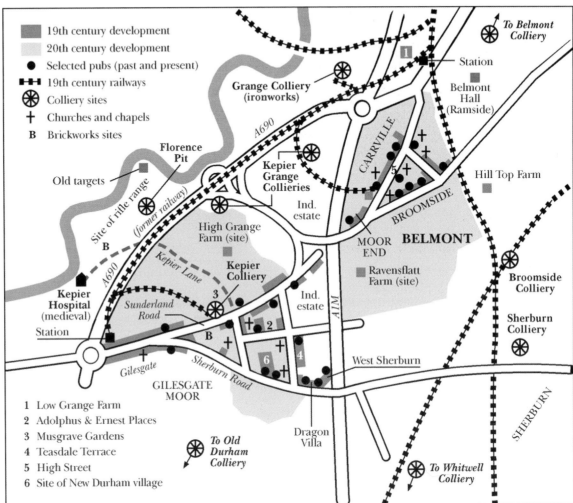

19th century development
20th century development
● Selected pubs (past and present)
⊢⊣ 19th century railways
⊛ Colliery sites
✝ Churches and chapels
B Brickworks sites

1 Low Grange Farm
2 Adolphus & Ernest Places
3 Musgrave Gardens
4 Teasdale Terrace
5 High Street
6 Site of New Durham village

Gilesgate Moor Map (NE)

The relocated chapel occupied a former military drill hall that also served as a school. Called the Old Durham or Londonderry School, after its founder Lady Londonderry its precise location was on the corner of Sherburn Road and Dragon Lane. These recently demolished buildings (called Vane Villas in their later days) were one of three nineteenth century barracks located in the Gilesgate and Gilesgate Moor area.

Love Street in New Durham was named from a local coal owner of that name but the name of New Durham itself was probably chosen because the village looked out across the countryside towards Old Durham Farm.

Most New Durham inhabitants were miners, and probably worked at several different mines. Some may also have worked at the adjoining New Durham Corn Mill. This is shown on the 1850s map and stood, not surprisingly, in Mill Lane, approximately where New Durham Working Mens' Club now stands.

By the end of the nineteenth century the collieries in Belmont and Gilesgate Moor had closed and a Durham directory of 1894 states without further comment that New Durham, Carrville and Dragonville had fallen into decay.

Most of New Durham was demolished before the end of the century and even by the time of the 1881 census we find many houses were already vacated. Demolition of the streets had certainly begun by the 1890s but remnants of Love Street survived into the 1920s. A few buildings in John Street were still standing in the mid-twentieth century.

Today the only survivors of New Durham are a couple of stone buildings facing the Sherburn Road. Here were Victorian pubs called Whitwell Inn and The Rising Sun. The Rising Sun was destroyed by fire in 1996 and subsequently demolished, but the former Whitwell Inn survives as a private house.

Whitwell Inn was named after Whitwell Colliery, that stood a mile south near Shincliffe village and it seems that most New Durham miners worked there. Whitwell Colliery opened in 1837 and was owned by Andrew White who developed New Durham Village. He is recorded as the village owner on an 1840s tithe map.

In earlier times colliery developments had been undertaken at Whitwell by Abraham Teasdale whose family were closely linked to Whitwell. The Teasdale family name is commemorated in Teasdale's Terrace, now called Teasdale Terrace at the junction of Rennys Lane and Dragon Lane.

Former Majestic Cinema, Sherburn Road (DS)

As New Durham village decayed, the Sherburn Road area of Durham experienced a huge loss of population during the late nineteenth century. However the 1930s slum clearances in Durham city centre brought new people to this part of the city. The ancient, densely populated streets of Framwellgate and Millburngate were demolished and the residents were relocated to Gilesgate Moor.

A brand new housing area called Sherburn Road Estate was specially constructed on the south side of the Sherburn Road directly opposite the site of New Durham village. In October 1934 the *Durham County Advertiser* interviewed some of the delighted residents who had relocated to the new estate. At about this time a new street called Frank Street was also built on the north side of the Sherburn road occupying the spot where New Durham village had once stood.

Many of the people who relocated to Gilesgate Moor from the Framwellgate area were Roman Catholics of Irish origin who had worshipped at St. Godric's church in Castle Chare. Since there was no Catholic church in Gilesgate Moor, services were initially held in the Crescent Cinema (later the Rex) on Sunderland Road.

Priests from St. Cuthbert's Roman Catholic church in Elvet provided the services at the Crescent Cinema until a purpose built church hall opened in Mill Lane in 1939. Services were held at Mill Lane under the jurisdiction of the Elvet church until Gilesgate Moor became a separate Roman Catholic parish in 1948. The actual Roman Catholic church next door to the church hall was not built until 1966 and is dedicated to St. Joseph.

Incidentally, the cinema on Sunderland Road was open from 1927 to 1958 and was one of two in the Gilesgate Moor area. The other was called the Majestic (1938-1961) and was situated on Sherburn Road. Both buildings can still be seen.

The Crescent Cinema was built by a local butcher called George Lamb and opened in June 1927 with a capacity of 318 seats. There was no balcony for customers who wished to pay for higher seats and the projectionist, who had to reach his projection room by a ladder, probably had the loftiest view. In 1941 the cinema came under new management and was renamed The Rex. It tended to show older films, already seen elsewhere and Westerns were especially popular. The Rex closed in January 1958 and served for a time as a Bingo hall – a fate that befell many local cinemas. The Projection House remained intact until about a decade ago but the old cinema is now a tool hire company. It still has a distinctive facade that betrays its original purpose.

The Majestic Cinema on Sherburn Road was a substantially larger cinema and is now a club and Bingo hall but served for a time as a furniture warehouse. It still retains its original name. This cinema opened on August 29, 1938. The admission prices to the Majestic at about this time were 6 pence for a seat in the stores or 9 pence if reserved. Balcony seats cost a shilling a time, or a shilling and 3 pence if reserved. The Majestic closed as a cinema on 4 December, 1961 but technically retained its licence until 1970.

The Sherburn Road Estate stands on the opposite side of the road to the old cinema and following the development of Musgrave Gardens in the 1920s it was one of the first post-colliery housing developments in the Gilesgate and Gilesgate Moor area. It signified the transition of the whole area from a pit community into a city suburb.

The next major housing development would come in the 1950s, with the opening up of a large council estate north of the Sunderland road. The war years provided a theme for the street names here and thus we have Montgomery Road, Churchill Avenue and Roosevelt Road. Other streets are named from local Victoria Cross winners like Annand, Bradford, Donnini, Heaviside, McNally, Kenny and Wakenshaw.

Despite the demolition of New Durham village and the closure of collieries around Gilesgate Moor in the late nineteenth century, some of the early mining terraces of Gilesgate Moor survive around Rennys Lane, Sunderland Road and Dragon Lane.

Some old colliery streets like Teasdale Terrace and Alma Place, (named from a Crimean War battle of 1854) now stand alongside more recent industrial and retail developments.

The development of industrial estates in and around Gilesgate Moor owes its growth to the construction of the motorway and the adjoining A690 during the late 1960s. These were also a factor in the subsequent growth of private housing estates at High Grange, Gilesgate Moor and the area south of Broomside Lane that came to be known as Belmont.

Former Rex Cinema, Sunderland Road (DS)

The Industrial estates built at Dragonville after the war and at Belmont near the border with Gilesgate Moor in the 1970s are another feature of this suburban development that continue to develop today. Most recently in the early years of the present century these estates have seen further developments on their periphery. They include several large out-of-town retail premises including a hotel, a Tesco supermarket, a restaurant and a huge five-a-side football arena.

A number of car sales outlets can be found here and there but the most recent development of all is the Durham Retail Park occupying land adjacent to Dragonville Industrial Estate. The days when Gilesgate Moor consisted of nothing more than a scattered collection of decaying pit settlements seems a long time ago.

Carrville and the Grange

In Medieval times what is now Carrville corresponded to the ancient manor of Clifton. Little is known about this manor except that it was acquired by Kepier Hospital in the 1100s. Clifton was later called Low Grange or Far Grange to distinguish it from the High Grange at Gilesgate.

Clifton may have been focused on a village called Clifton that was possibly located in an open area of land near the River Wear between Grange Wood and Black Wood. It is about half a mile north of Kepier viaduct beyond Kepier Wood. Some old mine workings can be seen at this site along with traces of a medieval ridge and furrow system. There are also feint outlines of buildings that may have belonged to a medieval village. It is an enigmatic site with a prominent cliff forming a backdrop.

The Clifton lands closely corresponded to those of Low Grange Farm but the present Low Grange Farmhouse is on the opposite side of the motorway half a mile east of this possible village. The farm has a less than idyllic setting wedged between the A1(M) motorway and A690 near the Belmont motorway interchange.

For most of the Medieval period Low Grange belonged to Kepier Hospital but after the dissolution of the monasteries in the 1500s it passed to a succession of landowners including Ralph Cole.

Cole sold his Kepier and High Grange properties to Sir Christopher Musgrave in 1674 but High Grange then seems to have been sold to Carr family of Cocken Hall.

The Carr's land extended as far east as the northern side of the old highway from Durham to Sunderland that now forms Carrville High Street. Carrville is an early nineteenth century mining village and may well be named after the Carr family. Carr could also simply refer to boggy land or moorland.

The history of Carrville, Broomside and Belmont is almost inseparable from that of Gilesgate Moor. Notably, many of the collieries that served Carrville also served the communities of Gilesgate Moor. We have already mentioned Kepier Colliery where Mackintosh Court now stands and have noted that Whitwell Colliery was served by New Durham but there were other important collieries in the area.

Collieries around Gilesgate Moor included the Marquess of Londonderry's Broomside Colliery that operated from 1829 to about 1890 and Old Durham Colliery (1848-1894) in the land south of Sherburn Road.

On the border between Gilesgate Moor and Carrville was Kepier Grange Colliery (1844-1924) where Belmont Industrial Estate now stands and further north the Grange Colliery (cl844-c1870) on a site that is now located close to the motorway. Also to the north was Belmont Colliery (c1830-1870) near Ramside Hall.

Kepier Grange Colliery was the nearest colliery to Carrville and should not be confused with Kepier Colliery in Gilesgate. It opened around 1844 and like Kepier was connected by a wagonway to the Durham branch of the Leamside line.

North Hetton Colliery Company (owned by Lambton, the Earl of Durham) was proprietor of Kepier Grange in the 1850s although the colliery was located on land belonging to Carr who was otherwise known as Standish-Standish. The colliery's wagonway terminated near a pub called

Kepier Grange Inn (now gone) that stood on the north side of Carrville High Street. The wagonway presumably supplied coal to both the village and the pub.

North of Kepier Grange Colliery and also connected to the branch line was Grange Colliery. This opened around the same time as Kepier Grange and stood on the Marquess of Londonderry's Grange or Low Grange Estate.

Workers at the Grange Iron Foundry (MR)

Grange Colliery site was located next to what is now the A690-A1(M) motorway intersection where a caravan site now stands. The colliery had closed by 1867 because it is known that the site became an iron foundry in that year.

A terrace called Wood Row was built near the colliery for the miners and was followed by Grange Row and Vane Terrace when the iron foundry opened. Vane was of course the Londonderry family name but the three streets were demolished in the late 1960s to make way for the motorway intersection that now stands on the site.

The Grange Foundry opened in 1867 and manufactured steam engines, colliery equipment, buildings, bridges and ship anchors. Employees came here from as far away as New Durham, Dragonville, Leamside and Fencehouses.

Unfortunately, like the colliery before it, the foundry fell on hard times and the business closed in 1926. Today, the major clue to its existence is an isolated row of houses called Maureen Terrace. Maureen is said to be a misspelling of marine, recalling maritime orders that were part of the business but Maureen was also the name of a member of the Londonderry family. The terrace and a nearby house, once occupied by the management were built to serve the ironworks.

The Grange Colliery and Kepier Grange Colliery reopened as small concerns in the twentieth century and in the 1920s and 30s they seem to have been linked by tubways to drift mines in neighbouring Kepier Wood. The secluded wood was probably the main source of coal and was possibly chosen because the mines were invisible to German aircraft.

During the Second World War, German aircraft bombed the Grange colliery site in an incident that apparently brought danger to Durham Cathedral.

The Kepier Grange Colliery that closed in 1890 had stood where Belmont Industrial Estate is now located but when it reopened in the twentieth century it was on a different site near the railway line that is now the A690. The new location for this colliery was approximately where the road from Belmont industrial estate now joins the A690 at a trumpet shaped junction close to a modern street called Prebends Field.

During the 1920s and 30s some Gilesgate Moor and Carrville miners are known to have found work just outside the area, as a significant number crossed the River Wear on a daily basis to work at the reopened Frankland Pit near Brasside. The Grange iron foundry constructed a bridge across the river for the miners, but this bridge has long since gone.

The nineteenth century mining activities which saw the opening of collieries like the Grange and Kepier Grange had brought about the birth of the mining village of Carrville as well as stimulating the population growth at Gilesgate Moor. It also brought about the foundation of a brand new parish called Belmont.

Carrville developed as a long terrace of miners' houses on the northern side of the main road to Sunderland and this ultimately became Carrville High Street. The first houses were concentrated on the north side of the street which was land belonging to Carr. The land on the south side of the street belonged to the Pemberton family.

As with all new pit villages, a number of pubs and chapels sprung up to serve the community and there were a fair share of Victorian pubs in Carrville High Street. These included the Grange Inn (demolished in 2006) on the corner with Bainbridge Street, but opposite was another pub called the Wild Boar. To the south along the High Street was the Grey Horse along with the Two Mile Stone Inn, Kepier Grange Inn and Sportmans Arms at Moor End at the southern extremity.

For spiritual needs, the Primitive Methodists worshipped on the north side of the High Street from 1839 but were relocated to the south side of the street in 1868. When the various strands of Methodism merged in the mid-twentieth century, the 1868 chapel remained in use and served the whole area until it was demolished and replaced by a spacious modern chapel in 2002.

Belmont and Ramside

In the 1850s Broomside, Carrville and Gilesgate Moor were brought together to form the new Church of England parish of Belmont, that was partly annexed from the earlier medieval parish of St. Giles in Durham.

Today, the A1(M) motorway separates Carrville and Broomside from Gilesgate Moor and has artificially created two quite separate suburbs of Durham City. In truth Carrville High Street and Broomside Lane were actually a continuation of Gilesgate Moor's Sunderland Road. The Sunderland Road split into these two roads at Moor End which literally marked the end of Gilesgate Moor. Moor End is now isolated on the Carrville side of the motorway.

Ramside Hall (NE)

Moor End has a rather village like appearance and is best known as the home of the Sportsman's Arms pub. Fields still separated Moor End from the houses in Carrville High Street as late as the 1950s. Since the construction of the motorway which underpasses Sunderland Road, Moor End has become separated from Gilesgate Moor and is now more closely associated with Carrville and Broomside.

The Belmont parish church of St. Mary Magdalene lies hidden amongst the trees in a triangle of land between the two roads at Moor End. It was built by a well-known Victorian architect called Butterfield in 1856 and still serves the communities on both sides of the motorway.

St. Mary Magdalene's churchyard at Broomside was the site of the first school in the area and served Carrville, Broomside and Gilesgate Moor. It opened in 1838 but became infants only after 1872, when a new, stone school was built in Broomside Lane. The church school was later demolished and replaced by a brick-built infant school in the early twentieth century. Belmont's present Junior and Comprehensive Schools of the 1960s and an Infant School of 1980 stand close to the site of the earlier establishments.

Belmont Comprehensive School (now Belmont School Community and Arts College) was built on the site of a demolished farm called Ravensflatt that was first noted in 1364. It probably belonged to John Raven who was mentioned in connection with Raven's Meadows at West Rainton in 1365. Ravensflatt land extended west into what is now Dragonville Industrial Estate.

Belmont's parish church of St. Mary Magdalen and the old churchyard school were built on land granted by the Pemberton family who owned all the land between Broomside Lane and Carrville High Street.

Further east, Broomside Lane becomes Pittington Lane and Carrville High Street becomes the A690 but the land in between the two roads was still Pemberton land. At the heart of the Pemberton land was Belmont Hall, built and named by Thomas Pemberton in 1820.

Pemberton chose the fanciful French sounding name of Belmont to suggest a place of beauty. His hall was built on the site of a farm called Ramside Grange and incorporated parts of the earlier building that had belonged to Kepier Hospital in medieval times.

After the Dissolution of the Monasteries in the 1500s Ramside Grange became the property of John Heath who granted the Ramside portion of his estate to one of his younger sons called Edward Heath.

Ramside passed in the later 1600s to the Smith and Martin families before it was bought in 1737 by the Huttons of Marske.

In 1749 Ralph Gowland purchased Ramside but sold the property twenty years later to John Pemberton of Bainbridge Holme in Sunderland. Pemberton's son, Stephen, subsequently sold Ramside to the Hopper family but the Pembertons acquired the property again in 1820.

The Pembertons also owned Hawthorn Tower near Easington and are principally famed for opening Sunderland's Monkwearmouth Colliery in the 1830s. Also called Pemberton Main colliery this was for a time the deepest colliery in the world. It was also the last colliery in the Durham coalfield to close (in 1994) and is now the site of the Sunderland Stadium of Light.

The Pemberton family, later called Stapylton Grey Pemberton left Belmont Hall in 1947 and in 1963 the hall became a hotel, reverting to its original name of Ramside.

Just north of Ramside Hall near the golf course is a site called the Rift. From the 1830s this was the location of Belmont Colliery, also known as the Furnace Pit. It was linked to a network of wagonways serving collieries at Pittington but seems to have closed in the 1870s. A short terrace of miners' houses was built alonsgide the colliery along with a pub called the Belmont Tavern. Hole 16 of Ramside Golf course now occupies the colliery site.

The mining village called Broomside developed on Pemberton's land mostly as terraced housing along the north side of Broomside Lane during the 1800s. Broomside Colliery or Lady Adelaide pit was established in 1829 on land just to the south of the Lane. Broomside Colliery initially belonged to the Marquess of Londonderry's family but later came into the ownership of the Bell family who also owned Belmont Colliery but Broomside colliery had closed by the 1890s.

Broomside's Hill Top Farm is the site of an earlier agricultural settlement that was the original Broomside. The name means broomy (or gorse covered) hill. Old Broomside was situated a little to the west of the colliery site and was first mentioned in the 1400s. It changed its name to Hill Top in the nineteenth century probably to avoid confusion with the new mining village.

There were three nineteenth century pubs in the mining village of Broomside and all were situated in Broomside Lane. One was the Masons Arms (otherwise known as the Stanley Hotel) and another was the Travellers Rest. The second of these was later relocated to a nearby site and is now an Indian restaurant. Further east beyond the junction of Broomside Lane and Bainbridge Street was yet another pub called the Londonderry Arms.

Bainbridge Street links Broomside to Carrville High Street and is named after Bainbridge Holme, a Pemberton family mansion that was swallowed up by the growth of Sunderland.

Bainbridge Street was part of Broomside rather than Carrville and became the home of the first Methodist Chapel in the area in 1835. This Wesleyan chapel was later demolished and replaced by a new one in Carrville High Street in 1881.

Although they can no longer be described as mining communities Carrville, Broomside and Belmont have successfully developed as outer suburbs of Durham City.

Broomside Colliery

During the late twentieth century housing estates have sprung up on the south side of Broomside Lane and north of Blue House Farm in Carrville High Street. The blue painted house marked on nineteenth century maps was formerly a farm but is now a shop. The housing developments and neighbouring industrial estates around Belmont were particularly encouraged by the completion of the A1(M) motorway in the early 1970s.

The Bombing Raid Mystery

In 1942, people living in Britain's historic cities lived in fear. Industrial towns had long been targets for German raids but now attention was turned to places of culture and history. Cathedral cities with dense historic cores became prime targets in the Baedeker raids. Named from a German guidebook that assigned asterisks to buildings of special interest, the Nazis used their British volume as a guide for the revenge attacks that followed the bombing of the German City of Lubeck in March 1942. Lubeck is a Baltic port where shipyards and industry stood close to an historic centre where many buildings were destroyed.

Baedeker raids began on 23 April in the cathedral city of Exeter and continued until 27 June when Norwich was the target. The other affected cities were Canterbury, Bath and York. Cathedrals in these cities suffered damage but not one was destroyed. Damage was mostly to houses and surrounding buildings. Was the sparing of the cathedrals a miracle or a policy of deliberate avoidance?

Only Coventry Cathedral had been destroyed in a raid in 1940 but this was not a Baedeker raid. On April 28, 1942 York was bombed and the BBC reported York Minster's narrow escape. The Lord Mayor of York was infuriated by the report and complained to the Ministry of Information. News items were censored during the war and raids were usually reported in vague terms. A raid on Sunderland might for example be reported in *The*

Durham from the air (NE)

Northern Echo simply as a raid on a North East town, with no mention of its name. Detailed information about raids was of value to German intelligence. To the Lord Mayor of York, the BBC report seemed like an invitation for the Germans to try again.

The mayor's complaint appears in *The Northern Echo* on the morning of Friday 1 May, 1942. Residents in Durham reading that morning's paper must have shown great interest. Only hours earlier, during the darkness of that May morning the bombers had seemingly set their

sights on Durham. Thirty-eight German bombers visited the region during those early hours, hitting Sunderland, Newcastle, South Shields and Jarrow, the industrial towns that bore the brunt of raids across the region. But bombs also fell within miles of Durham City, a small and vulnerable place to aircraft passing overhead. Around 2.55am Bombs fell at Beamish village to the north west, causing damage. Here one timed device exploded later in the day, killing eight people.

The closest bombs to Durham City came at 3.10am when four fell in and around the disused Grange Colliery site (the former ironworks) at Carrville to the east of the city. One fell on a road near Wood Row terrace where the motorway intersection now stands, one fell in the works yard, another near a mineshaft and one on a railway. Close by the Brasside-Belmont viaduct remained standing but perhaps this was the target the Germans had in mind.

At the same time, less than a mile to the north, two bombs fell either side of a loop of the River Wear at Finchale Priory. Germans could well have mistaken the priory ruins for Durham Cathedral.

Meanwhile ten miles to the north west planes bombarded an area around a prominent but unpopulated meander of the River Derwent at Lockhaugh near Whickham. Here the only feature of significance was another viaduct. By the time the bombers departed from the North East, 36 people had been killed across the region. Ten enemy aircraft were shot down either over the region or as they returned to their base in France. It was a major loss for the enemy.

Some believe Durham cathedral, the city and its viaduct were targets that night and that the enemy aircraft had lost their way. But it was a bright moonlit night, how could bombers have missed such a prominent landmark? Many Durham residents insist St. Cuthbert intervened from his resting-place in the cathedral and summoned up a sudden mist to foil the approaching aircraft.

This miraculous event is not easily confirmed and some doubt it actually happened. One problem is that even if it did, censorship would ensure it was not reported, particularly in view of the complaint from York. The first locally published account of the incident appeared on 11 May, 1945 in an article by Alan Maitland, an 18-year-old journalist on the *Durham County Advertiser*. He was inspired by a paragraph he had read in a national magazine called *The Leader* that briefly mentioned the mist.

An embarrassed Maitland later claimed he embroidered the story and concluded that he helped create a modern myth. However Maitland admitted that the author of the original magazine article was not known. The newspaper's readers confirmed that a mist did engulf the cathedral that night but Maitland himself was not convinced. He drew attention to the remarks of George Greenwell, Durham's chief air raid warden on the night in question.

Greenwell called the story a pretty tale for the guidebook, claiming bombers had flown over Durham's skies many times during the war and St. Cuthbert had often remained indifferent to their passage. Nevertheless, Greenwell claimed the mist was a regular natural occurrence and admitted that on this particular night a mist covered the cathedral. However he insisted that the upper part of the tower remained exposed.

Despite his doubts Greenwell mentioned two unusual events that occurred that night. One was the appearance of some extra firemen and the other was the placing of a large hose from the river directed to Palace Green. Nevertheless, Greenwell writing in 1945 stated sceptically that, 'If the German intention had been to bomb Durham, a vagary of weather would not have prevented it. They would have come back again in better conditions'. But they never did and at the end of June 1942, the Baedeker raids were over.

Index

The Durham Villages
by David Simpson
ISBN 978 1 901888 51 5
Price: £12.95

The Durham Villages is based on the 'Durham Memories' column that appears in *The Northern Echo* and features the history of more than 70 villages and hamlets within a five to six mile radius of Durham City. It includes all the villages within the present administrative district of Durham City as well as Sacriston, Edmondsley, Plawsworth, Lanchester and all the villages in the Browney valley. Some of the places covered are mining villages whose histories are limited to the nineteenth century whilst others have much longer histories. However, it is indisputable that all lie in beautiful countryside that is intersected by the charming valleys of the Browney and Deerness in the west and enriched by the rolling scenery of the limestone hills in the east.

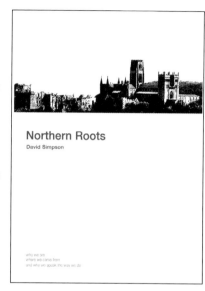

Northern Roots: who we are, where we come from and why we speak the way we do   *by David Simpson*

ISBN 1 901888 35 5   Price: £7.95

Northerners speak with distinct local dialects and have their very own sense of history. In the guise of Yorkshiremen, Cumbrians, Geordies, Scousers, Lancastrians or Northumbrians, all have contributed to the rich culture of Britain.

But who are these Northerners and where did they come from?
What clues exist in history to the ancient and more recent origins of Northerners and their speech? This book traces the languages and origins of various people who have settled in the North over two thousand years to give it the distinct character it has today.

North East England: places, history, people and legends   *by David Simpson*

ISBN 1 901888 37 1   Price: £8.95

Stretching from the River Tees to the River Tweed the North East of England was the ancient heartland of the Kingdom of Northumbria. It was the birthplace of the railways, the 'borderland zone' of the Scottish raids and the quiet retreat of the ancient Celtic saints. It is a region steeped in history and a home to wonderful sites like Durham Cathedral, Hadrian's Wall and the bustling Quayside of Newcastle upon Tyne. Travelling across the region from Durham to Teesside to England's northernmost county of Northumberland, this book explores the places, history, people and legends of this remarkable northern region.

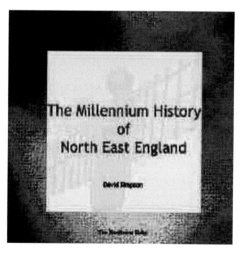

Millennium History of North East England   *by David Simpson*

ISBN 09536984 3 2   Price: £7.50

North East England has a strong sense of identity that sets it apart from other areas of England. The roots of this identity lie in two thousand years of distinct history that have made the region what it is today. From the Roman frontier zone of Hadrian's Wall, to the powerful Christian Kingdom of Northumbria, through the gloomy days of Border warfare up to the great age of coal mining and railways, each era has played its part. This unique, 336 page, beautifully illustrated hardback book explores the events, people and places that have shaped the region's history over the last two thousand years.